Deregulation
of Network
Industries

Deregulation of Network Industries

What's Next?

Sam Peltzman
Clifford Winston
editors

AEI-BROOKINGS JOINT CENTER
FOR REGULATORY STUDIES
Washington, D.C.

Deregulation of Network Industries: What's Next? may be ordered from:
Brookings Institution Press
1775 Massachusetts Avenue, N.W.
Washington, D.C. 20036
Tel.: 1-800-275-1447 or (202) 797-6258
Fax: (202) 797-6004
www.brookings.edu

Library of Congress Cataloging-in-Publication data
Deregulation of network industries : what's next? / Sam Peltzman,
Clifford Winston, editors.
p.   cm.
Includes bibliographical references and index.
ISBN 0-8157-7004-9 (cloth)
ISBN 0-8157-7003-0 (alk. paper)
1. Public utilities—Deregulation—United States. 2. Airlines—
Deregulation—United States. 3. Railroads—Deregulation—
United States. 4. Telecommunication—Deregulation—United States.
5. Electric utilities—Deregulation—United States. 6. Deregulation—
United States. 7. Industrial policy—United States. 8. Business networks—
Government policy—United States. I. Peltzman, Sam. II. Winston, Clifford, 1952–
III. Title.
HD2766 .D473 2000   00-009824
388'.0973—dc21   CIP

9 8 7 6 5 4 3 2 1
The paper used in this publication meets minimum requirements of the American National Standard for Information Sciences—Permanence of Paper for Printed Library Materials: ANSI Z39.48-1992.

Typeset in Adobe Garamond

Composition by Northeastern Graphic Services
Hackensack, New Jersey

Printed by R. R. Donnelley and Sons
Harrisonburg, Virginia

Contents

Preface

When the United States began in the late 1970s to deregulate network industries—energy, transportation, and communications—the hard work appeared to be over. Once intractable political forces were overcome, and as deregulation moved forward it seemed only a matter of time before markets instead of regulators would fully determine the allocation of resources in these industries.

More than twenty years later, markets are functioning in these network industries—and so are regulators. The airline industry has been completely deregulated, but in the past few years Congress and the U.S. Department of Transportation have raised concerns about how unregulated airline competition is working, and they have signaled their intention to take corrective action if necessary. Congress, for example, has been debating proposals that would create a new commission to review airline pricing strategies, and the Transportation Department has drawn up competition guidelines that attempt to identify instances of predatory behavior and establish acceptable zones of pricing behavior. The industry has felt compelled to draw up a "passengers' bill of rights" to help fend off legislation.

Deregulation has given the railroads substantially more operating and pricing freedom, but maximum rate "guidelines" were retained for certain shipments thought to be captive to rail, such as coal and chemicals. The Surface Transportation Board was given the authority to determine the reasonableness of rates that are challenged by shippers under these guidelines. Because the board has not effectively mediated rate disputes, tensions between some shippers and railroads run strong. Widely publicized service disruptions following rail mergers have also prompted concerns about the appropriate direction of regulatory policy in the rail industry. Congress and the Transportation Department are proposing policies that would increase governmental scrutiny of and control over rail operations and rates. The Surface Transportation Board has recently imposed a moratorium on further rail mergers.

Unregulated competition has evolved much more slowly in telecommunications than in transportation. A moderate degree of competition exists in long-distance services, but there still are restrictions on entry, especially by the regional Bell operating companies. Long-distance carriers are equally frustrated about the slow progress toward competition in local markets. Congress sought to stimulate competition in local and long-distance services though the passage of the 1996 Telecommunications Act. The 1996 law invites the Federal Communications Commission to advance the public interest by "forbearing" from regulating new services when appropriate, but it also increases the scope of FCC and state regulations and tries to establish precise conditions under which new entry would be permissible. Since the law was passed there has been much argument before regulatory agencies about its implementation, but little entry by the regional Bell operating companies into long-distance markets or by the long-distance carriers into local markets.

Based on a variety of performance indexes, the regulated electric power sector has performed fairly well over time. Electricity has been supplied with high levels of reliability, investment in new capacity has been readily financed to keep up with demand, and system losses are as low as or lower than those in other developed countries. Nonetheless, a few pioneering states, as opposed to the federal government, are embarking on major changes that would affect regulation in this sector. In just the past few years, California, Illinois, and some states in the Northeast have initiated fundamental reforms that govern access to and the operation of electric transmission networks that can support competing generators of electricity. The emerging evidence on electricity market performance is leading regulators throughout the country to consider the desirability of moving to a less regulated electric power sector.

Although the airline, railroad, telecommunications, and electric power industries are at very different stages in adjusting to regulatory reform, each industry faces the same critical public policy question. Are policymakers taking appropriate steps to stimulate competition, or are they turning back the clock by slowing the process of deregulation? This volume addresses that issue and identifies the next steps that policymakers should take to enhance public welfare in the provision of airline, railroad, telecommunications, and electricity services. A concluding chapter identifies how interest groups continue to exert influence on regulatory agencies and Congress and potentially undermine deregulation.

The papers included here were initially presented in December 1999 at a conference sponsored and organized by the American Enterprise Institute–Brookings Institution Joint Center for Regulatory Studies, directed by Robert W. Hahn and Robert E. Litan. Funding for the Center is provided by foundations and corporate contributions. Additional funding for this project was provided by US Airways, CSX Railroad, Unicom Corporation, and the Edison Mission Energy Corporation. Martha V. Gottron edited the manuscript and Jennifer Eichberger verified its factual content.

The views expressed in this book are those of the authors and should not be ascribed to those persons or organizations whose assistance is acknowledged or to the trustees, officers, or other staff members of the American Enterprise Institute or the Brookings Institution.

Sam Peltzman
Clifford Winston

Deregulation of Network Industries

STEVEN A. MORRISON
CLIFFORD WINSTON

1 | The Remaining Role for Government Policy in the Deregulated Airline Industry

When it comes to a public policy, success can be in the eye of the beholder. Economists tend to think that a public policy has been successful if its benefits exceed its costs. By that standard no one can argue with Washington's decision in 1978 to allow airlines to set their own fares and decide which markets to serve. As shown in figure 1-1, travelers' fares in this deregulated environment were immediately lower, on average, than they would have been had they continued to be regulated. As the airline industry adjusted to deregulation, the benefits from lower fares fluctuated, but since 1994 air travelers have enjoyed stable fare reductions of roughly 27 percent. And these gains have been widely shared. Based on the data used to construct figure 1-1, during 1998, 80 percent of passengers, accounting for 85 percent of passenger miles, paid fares that were lower than our estimate of regulated fares.

Deregulation has also affected service. We have found in previous research that travelers have gained substantially from the increase in flight frequency facilitated by the acceleration of hub-and-spoke operations.[1]

The authors are grateful to Dennis Carlton, Andrew Joskow, Richard Johnson, Sam Peltzman, Larry Phillips, and conference participants for helpful comments.

1. Morrison and Winston (1995) provide a detailed discussion of the findings reported in this paragraph.

Figure 1-1. *Percentage Reduction in Fares Relative to Regulated Fares,*
1978–98

Percent

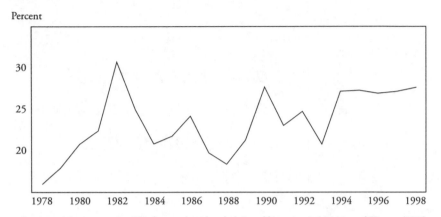

Sources and data construction: This figure updates the calculation of fare savings in Morrison and Winston (1995). The source of the fare data was the U.S. Department of Transportation's Ticket Origin-Destination Survey (Data Bank 1A), a 10 percent sample of airline tickets. Although deregulation formally started in 1978:4, the Civil Aeronautics Board began relaxing its regulations as early as 1976. Fares were not included in Data Bank 1A until 1978:4, however. To be reasonably sure that the tickets for a particular journey reflect travel from one origin to one destination, only tickets with one (directional) destination were used. Round trips had to return to the initial point of departure (with no ground segments, that is, no open-jaw tickets). Only one-way tickets with two or fewer coupons (that is, flight segments) and round-trip tickets with two or fewer coupons on the outbound and return legs were used. Because of possible coding errors in the data carriers submit to the Department of Transportation, the U.S. General Accounting Office's fare screen (GAO, 1990) was used to screen out fares that seemed too high. In order to keep frequent flier tickets, a low fare screen was not used. Taxes (percentage ticket tax, segment tax, and Passenger Facility Charges) were subtracted from the reported fare to obtain fare charged by the carrier. Our estimate of regulated fares was based on the Standard Industry Fare Level (SIFL), which was the basis for setting fares during the last few years of airline regulation. The Transportation Department continues to update the SIFL every six months based on changes in cost per available seat mile. Because it is likely that deregulation has led to productivity increases that lowered the SIFL relative to what it would have been, we used the estimates of the productivity increases caused by deregulation calculated by Caves and others (1987). In particular, we used their midpoint figure and thus increased the SIFL by 1.2 percent for each year from 1976 to 1983, when their study ended. Because productivity increases likely continued, this estimate is conservative. From 1978 to 1986 the percentage of passenger miles that fell below the fare screen was fairly constant, averaging 2.6 percent of all passenger miles. This figure increased dramatically in 1987 (and has averaged 8.2 percent since then). Beginning in 1987, calculated yield was increased by the difference between the percentage of passenger miles in that year falling below the fare screen and 2.6 percent.

Because deregulation freed airlines to serve all markets, travelers have also gained from having to make fewer connections that require changing airlines. These gains have been partially offset by more crowded flights, travel restrictions that are inconvenient for business travelers (especially the required Saturday night stay), a few more connections, and slightly longer flight times because of congestion. Accounting for fare and service quality changes, the annual net benefits to travelers from airline deregulation currently exceed $20 billion.[2]

2. Morrison and Winston (1999, p. 486).

Despite these benefits, dissatisfied fliers and policymakers insist that government must intervene to correct what they claim are significant flaws in unregulated airline competition. These flaws include predatory strategies by large established carriers to drive smaller low-fare entrants out of the industry; poor treatment of passengers, ranging from stranding them on runways for several hours to charging inequitable fares; and blatant attempts by large carriers to build dominant airport hubs and monopolize gates to develop market power.

As a result, the U.S. Department of Transportation (DOT) has drawn up competition guidelines that attempt to identify instances of predatory behavior and establish acceptable zones of pricing behavior. The U.S. Department of Justice has brought an antitrust suit against American Airlines for engaging in predatory pricing and may bring suits against other carriers. National lawmakers have proposed legislation that would create a new commission to review airline pricing strategies. Both Justice and DOT have indicated that they intend to take a tougher stance on proposed airline mergers. Congressional debates calling for a "passengers' bill of rights" spurred the airline industry to draw up and publicize its own bill of rights—and to provide large political contributions—to fend off actual legislation. Congress has also been debating a flurry of proposals to change how airport gates and slots (a system that limits takeoffs and landings at Chicago O'Hare, New York LaGuardia and John F. Kennedy, and Washington Reagan National airports) are distributed among carriers and to require carrier-dominated hubs to file plans explaining how they will open up airports to competition. Many defenders of deregulation interpret this activity as an attempt to re-regulate the airline industry; policymakers respond that they simply wish to recapture the spirit of deregulation by promoting competition.

As air carriers adjust to various economic cycles and contingencies that dramatically affect their financial performance (fuel prices, gross domestic product, aircraft replacement, and so on) and continue to adjust to competition in a deregulated market, they are likely to draw the ire of a vocal minority of travelers and each other for the foreseeable future. But the federal government's proposed fixes, notwithstanding their economic (or political) intentions, may be missing the big picture.[3] After more than twenty years of airline deregulation, it is time to start thinking about a

3. As recently as 1993, the National Commission to Ensure a Strong Competitive Airline Industry, proposed by the White House and authorized by Congress, was investigating why the airline industry was losing so much money and considering what could be done to turn the industry around. In the end, no action was taken, and the industry achieved record profitability a few years later.

long-run *policy* equilibrium. In other words, what remaining steps, if any, should policymakers take to enhance competition in the deregulated environment so that carriers can be free of periodic government interventions and can focus entirely on becoming as efficient as possible?

In this chapter we explore alleged imperfections in air transportation, including the formation of hubs, predatory pricing, mergers, customer practices, slot controls, and the availability of gates. We survey each issue and offer preliminary evidence on how travelers' welfare may be affected. We then pull the threads of our analysis together in a single model and determine which imperfections warrant corrective policy. We find policymakers' current preoccupation with carriers' behavior—hub formation, pricing strategies, mergers, and service—largely unwarranted. The industry's primary inefficiencies stem from government management of airport and airspace capacity, which limits competition and compromises service. Government, however, has been reluctant to improve airport capacity and slow to improve air traffic control. If the public is to enjoy the full benefits of airline deregulation, airports and air traffic control may need to be privatized.

Hubs

Hub-and-spoke systems were designed to decrease carrier costs (relative to point-to-point service) by centralizing maintenance and allowing the use of larger planes that are filled closer to capacity because people can be gathered from many places, sorted out at the hub with timely connecting flights, and sent on to many other places. By offering more connections between cities, the systems also increased flight frequencies for travelers. At a typical hub, more than half the passengers boarding planes are in midroute rather than beginning a trip. Because connections between different carriers have all but disappeared, hub airports tend to be dominated by one or two airlines. Policymakers worry that this airport dominance raises fares paid by travelers who begin or end their trips at a hub.

A carrier that has a large share of departures at an airport generally offers more convenient service than other carriers serving the airport. Thus, in theory, a dominant carrier could raise its fares without losing much traffic unless its competitors could provide a comparable level of service.[4]

4. As indicated by the so called S-curve, a carrier's market share rises more than proportionately with the number of its flights.

If a dominant carrier did raise its fares, other carriers could match them. In any case, the elevation in the fare that travelers pay on a route connected to a hub, as compared with the fare on comparable routes not connected to a dominant hub, is called the *hub premium*. An appropriately calculated hub premium reflects a market imperfection because it is created by an entry barrier that requires other carriers to enter hub airports at a large scale to provide a level of service that would discourage the dominant carrier from raising its fares. (A "pure" hub premium is not related to an airport's physical capacity, which may constrain other carriers from offering more, or any, flights. This problem is discussed later.)

Measuring hub premiums is controversial because it is not clear what influences should be held constant to ensure a fair comparison between fares on hub routes and fares on other routes. In a 1990 study, the U.S. General Accounting Office (GAO) made the first estimate of a hub premium without holding any variables constant by comparing yields (average fare per mile) for trips originating at fifteen hub airports dominated by one or two carriers with yields at a control group of thirty-eight unconcentrated airports.[5] But by merely comparing yields, the GAO in effect assumed that the trips taken from the two groups of airports were identical. Accounting for route distance, number of plane changes, traffic mix, carrier identity, and frequent flier tickets results in a more appropriate comparison and lowers the GAO estimate of the hub premium significantly.[6]

Here we take a different approach. Policymakers who are concerned that travelers on hub routes may be paying higher fares than those on other routes seem to take little comfort in explanations of fare differences that focus on nonmarket power factors, such as traffic mix, carrier identity, and plane changes. Thus we calculated a hub premium for 1998 that controlled only for distance, an essential determinant of fares, and included frequent flier tickets. And because Southwest Airlines substantially lowers fares in the markets it serves and has achieved a national presence, we also identified whether airports served by Southwest are included in the control group of airports.

Applying GAO's definition of a concentrated hub airport to data on 1998 enplanements results in twelve concentrated airports.[7] Our control

5. GAO (1990).

6. Morrison and Winston (1995).

7. An airport was considered concentrated if it was one of the seventy-five busiest airports in the country based on enplanements and if one carrier accounted for 60 percent or more of passenger enplanements or if two carriers accounted for 85 percent or more of passenger enplanements. Following

group was the nation's unconcentrated airports, with a subgroup that included airports not served by Southwest. All trips from the unconcentrated airports were used to calculate the yield for distance bands of 100 miles.[8] We then calculated what the fare for each trip from the concentrated airports would be if its price were based on the yield for a comparable trip from the unconcentrated control group. The fare premium was the percentage by which actual revenue at the concentrated airports exceeded the revenue that would have been collected had airlines used the same pricing scheme at concentrated and unconcentrated airports.[9]

We found that fares in 1998 for trips at the twelve concentrated airports were 23.1 percent higher than fares for trips at the control group of airports.[10] But if the control group included only unconcentrated airports not served by Southwest Airlines, then fares at concentrated airports were 5.8 percent *lower* than those at the control group.[11]

How then should the hub premium be interpreted? Does it reflect the harmful exercise of market power? Or does it reflect higher fares that carriers charge in *any* market when they do not have to compete against Southwest? In our view, both forces are at work, an observation that should give one pause before proceeding with sharp policy conclusions.

Asking how competition at hubs has changed over time can shed more light on this issue. Relative to all unconcentrated airports, the hub premium

---

the GAO, we excluded airports that were located outside of the forty-eight contiguous states and airports that served metropolitan areas that were served by more than one airport. This procedure identified the following twelve airports: Atlanta, Charlotte, Cincinnati, Denver, Detroit, Memphis, Miami, Minneapolis, Philadelphia, Pittsburgh, St. Louis, and Salt Lake City. These calculations used the U.S. Department of Transportation's Airport Activity Statistics data (Form 41, Schedule T-3, Data Bank 22, hereinafter Form 41 data) for the fourth quarter of 1998.

8. The fare data were from the U.S Department of Transportation's Data Bank 1A (hereinafter Data Bank 1A).

9. The distance of each route in the analysis was multiplied by the yield for the appropriate mileage block to obtain comparison fares.

10. Because we are not controlling for traffic mix, carrier identity, and plane changes, this estimate of the hub premium is upwardly biased. But when informed, for example, that hub routes have a higher share of business travelers than nonhub routes, which elevates fares paid on hub routes, members of Congress respond that their (business) constituents are nonetheless paying higher fares and that should not be ignored.

11. Southwest does serve three of the concentrated airports. If these three airports are excluded from the analysis, then fares at the remaining nine concentrated airports are still *lower*, by 1.2 percent, than fares at the control group of unconcentrated airports. The nature of the results does not change if routes involving slot-controlled airports are eliminated from the analysis. Fares are 29.1 percent higher at the twelve concentrated airports than at all other airports, 1.4 percent lower when compared with airports that Southwest does not serve, and 3.7 percent higher when concentrated airports not served by Southwest are compared with all other airports not served by Southwest.

has hovered around 20 percent for the past five years. But it has declined relative to unconcentrated airports not served by Southwest since deregulation began. This reflects Southwest's steady growth and growing impact on fares.

Recently, market shares at hubs have been changing. From 1991 to 1998, the leading carrier's share of enplanements at six of the twelve hubs declined, its share at three increased, and its share at the three others remained constant.[12] Enplanement shares of other low-fare carriers, in addition to Southwest, have grown at concentrated hubs (a recent example is Frontier's expanded operations at Denver's airport).

Measurements of hub premiums are controversial. But even if a hub premium elevates fares on some routes, the number of these routes may fall as Southwest and other low-fare carriers expand their operations. Policymakers, however, have become concerned that large carriers have and will continue to defend routes connected to their hubs by predation.

Predatory Behavior

Critics have been accusing airlines of predatory practices for more than a decade.[13] But no carrier has ever been found guilty of predation. Defining predatory behavior, let alone measuring it, has proved an unresolved problem for courts, regulatory agencies, and academics.

Nonetheless, in response to an effective campaign by lobbyists for new airlines, business travelers, and small cities, the Transportation Department issued the following statement in the spring of 1998:

> In recent years, when small, new-entrant carriers have instituted new low-fare service in major carriers' local hub markets, the major carriers have increasingly responded with strategies of price reductions and capacity increases designed not to maximize their own profits but rather to deprive the new entrants of vital traffic and revenues.[14]

This was not empty rhetoric. The department announced that it would bring proceedings against a major carrier in one or more of the following

---

12. Michael Miller, "Airlines Lose Share at Major Airports since 1991," *Aviation Daily*, April 1, 1999.

13. For example, Gulf Air, based in Hyannis, Massachusetts, filed suit in a federal district court in March 1987 charging Texas Air and its affiliates with predatory business practices.

14. U.S. Department of Transportation, Office of the Secretary, Docket No. OST-98-3713, Notice 98-16. For a discussion of the lobbying efforts that preceded the department's policy statement, see Louis Jacobson, "Unexpected Turbulence," *National Journal*, June 27, 1998, pp. 1504–8.

situations if the major carrier's local revenue was lower than a "reasonable alternative response":

—The major airline adds seating capacity and sells too many seats at very low fares.
—The major airline carries more local passengers at the new entrant's low fares than the new entrant carries.
—The major airline carries more local passengers at the new entrant's low fares than the total seat capacity of the new entrant.

These competition guidelines put large carriers on notice, and small carriers did not hesitate to remind their bigger competitors that the environment had changed. For example, Vanguard Airlines publicly denounced United's plan to add capacity and lower fares in the Des Moines–Chicago market even before Vanguard announced plans to enter this market.

The guidelines, and a subsequent predatory pricing case brought by the U.S. Department of Justice against American Airlines, have attracted criticisms by antitrust experts, some of whom were serving as consultants to airlines. Janusz Ordover and Robert Willig, for example, pointed out several problems with trying to implement DOT's guidelines and argued that a major airline could be guilty of predatory behavior even if its prices exceeded its costs.[15] Many critics concluded that the guidelines could force major carriers to reduce or even eliminate service on a route where a major carrier and a small carrier could operate in the absence of the guidelines. The department's preoccupation with carriers' capacity increases was troubling because large fare cuts would generate additional trips, either by people currently traveling or by people induced by lower fares to initiate travel, thus justifying additional flights.

The basis for the guidelines has also been faulted on empirical grounds. Dennis Carlton and Gustavo Bamberger provide circumstantial evidence suggesting that large carriers are very unlikely to have engaged in predatory practices to drive small carriers out of their markets or to deter such carriers from entering them.[16] For example, the survival rates of major carriers and nonmajor carriers following entry of a major carrier are similar, especially at hub endpoints; large fare or capacity changes by major carriers in response to entry by nonmajors are unusual, even on a subset of routes;

15. Verified statement of Ordover and Willig (1998).
16. Carlton and Bamberger (1998).

and large fare increases by a major carrier following a carrier's exit are also unusual. In previous research, we found that Southwest Airlines, a carrier generally not thought to engage in predatory behavior, has been much more successful than other carriers at discouraging competitors from entering its routes and encouraging competitors to exit them.[17]

Regardless of their size, the life of new entrants to the airline industry has always been perilous. Out of fifty-eight carriers that started operations between 1978 and 1990, only one carrier (America West) is still operating. Nonetheless, new carriers continue to enter the industry. Vanguard, ProAir, Spirit, ATA, Frontier, Legend, Access Air, and Sun Country are among the most recent start-ups, while JetBlue Airways began service on the East Coast in February 2000. These carriers appear undaunted by their larger competitors. ProAir, Spirit, and Sun Country are taking on Northwest on various routes, Frontier is competing with United, and JetBlue is not avoiding major carriers because its operations are based out of Kennedy airport. If, as is generally thought, successful predation secures freedom from new entry, major carriers engaging in predation have been singularly unrewarded by it.

Mergers

During the regulated era, airlines' merger requests were almost always denied except when the merger was designed to keep one of the carriers from going bankrupt.[18] Since deregulation, antitrust authorities have blocked few mergers. But the Justice and Transportation departments expressed strong concerns when United and Delta, American and US Airways, and Continental and Northwest proposed alliances a few years ago. Those alliances have not materialized, but they might be resurrected.[19] In addition, other major carriers might propose mergers, and some new entrants might be absorbed in a future wave of airline consolidations.

17. Morrison and Winston (1995).

18. We are grateful to Tara Watson for her assistance with this section.

19. The United and Delta alliance collapsed when the pilots' union did not get a seat on the board; the Department of Justice has filed a suit challenging Northwest's acquisition of the controlling block of Continental's voting stock and is continuing to review the two airlines' code-share agreement; and the American and US Airways alliance has, thus far, amounted only to consolidating frequent flier miles and airport lounges. Continental has recently expressed an interest in buying back its stock from Northwest. If this purchase materializes, the Justice Department may withdraw its objection to this alliance.

If hubs are thought to be the root (or route) of current airline mischief, mergers may be the seeds because they can make it much easier for carriers to develop dominant hubs. But mergers can also enable carriers to develop more efficient networks and use their capital and labor more efficiently. Thus the social desirability of an airline merger rests on the trade-off between efficiency gains (including improved service) and potentially higher fares.

Because there is no way of knowing how carriers' networks and pricing strategies would have evolved in the absence of a merger, measuring this trade-off is difficult. We have provided suggestive evidence about the effects of potential mergers by estimating how fares respond when an acquired carrier is eliminated from the market and other carriers (including the acquiring carrier) enter the routes it once served.[20] In most cases we found that fares fell below premerger levels, but it is possible that fares might have been dramatically affected by other influences had two carriers not merged. For example, intense competitive interactions might have touched off fare wars that led to steep fare declines.[21] It is also not clear what the merged carriers' network will look like when it reaches equilibrium. For example, USAir eventually dropped all the routes it acquired from PSA (Pacific Southwest) in their 1987 merger, and American Airlines eventually dropped all the routes it acquired from Air California in their 1987 merger.

Given the inherent difficulty in isolating the effects of an airline merger, we instead suggest how mergers might affect travelers' welfare by investigating why carriers merge in the first place. The academic literature offers three broad explanations: operational and financial motives, anticompetitive motives, and industrywide forces. To determine the extent to which each explains merger activity in the airline industry, we identify all possible merger pairs for each year from 1978 to 1995 among the fifty-six major and national carriers operating at some time during that period.[22] The dependent variable in our analysis takes a value of

20. Morrison and Winston (1995). Retrospective studies of actual mergers include Werden, Joskow, and Johnson (1991); Kim and Singal (1993); and Morrison (1996).

21. For evidence of how carriers' competitive interactions spur fare wars, see Morrison and Winston (1996).

22. Carriers were included in the data set and considered potential merger partners only in years when their revenues exceeded $100 million (that is, when they were a major or national carrier), when they filed data with the Department of Transportation, and when they were not a wholly owned subsidiary of another carrier.

Table 1-1. *Actual and Attempted Airline Mergers, 1978–1995*

Year	Actual	Year	Attempted
1979	North Central, Southern	1979	National, Eastern
	Pan Am, National		Texas International, National
1980	Republic, Hughes Airwest		Continental, Western
1981	Continental, Texas International	1981	Continental, Western
1985	People Express, Frontier	1982	Western, Air Florida
	Southwest, Muse	1985	Continental, Frontier
1986	Continental, Eastern		TWA, Continental
	Continental, People Express	1987	Pan Am, Braniff
	Northwest, Republic	1990	American, Air Wisconsin
	TWA, Ozark	1991	Northwest, Midway
	Delta, Western		Delta, Pan Am
1987	American, Air Cal		Northwest, Trump Shuttle
	USAir, Pacific Southwest		
	USAir, Piedmont		
1992	USAir, Trump Shuttle		
	United, Air Wisconsin		

Source: The list of mergers was constructed from periodical searches on Lexus, the *New York Times*, the *Wall Street Journal, Aviation Week and Space Technology*, and the *Merger Yearbook*. The initiation date of the merger is used to determine the year of the merger. Merger filings are submitted confidentially to the Federal Trade Commission and the U.S. Department of Justice and are not publicly disclosed. Justice verified, however, that this list of actual and proposed mergers was complete.

one for each actual and attempted merger among the set of all possible mergers (table 1-1), zero otherwise.[23] Although carriers have pursued mergers since airlines were deregulated, most activity occurred in the 1985–87 merger wave. Other U.S. industries also tend to experience merger waves.

Operational and Financial Motives

Carriers are likely to be favorably inclined toward a merger if it will allow them to exploit economies of scale, density, or scope. They may be disinclined toward merger if their labor and capital are incompatible. Financially distressed carriers may see a merger as a way to avoid bank-

23. Although actual and attempted mergers are initially filed under confidential conditions, all the attempted airline mergers have apparently been reported in the popular press (see table 1-1).

ruptcy, or they may become a takeover target because they are perceived to be poorly managed.

ECONOMIES.   Carriers consider consolidating their operations to achieve higher load factors (the percentage of seats filled with paying passengers), use larger planes that cost less per seat-mile than smaller planes, increase aircraft utilization and customer service because they can provide more frequent flights, and make more efficient use of ground personnel and equipment.[24] These economies can arise when carriers achieve greater route densities.[25] We constructed the combined route density for each possible pair of carriers relative to their individual densities.[26] A merger is more likely when the combined route density exceeds the individual densities. Carriers could also benefit from economies of scope that arise from serving a greater number of domestic and foreign cities. Using DOT's Data Bank 1A, we constructed the number of domestic and foreign routes that each possible pair of carriers could serve relative to the number they served individually. The likelihood of a merger should increase as carriers' combined route coverage exceeds their individual coverage.

COMPATIBILITY.   The business world acknowledges that corporate cultures exist and can influence whether two firms will be able to merge their operations successfully. For example, merger discussions between United and US Airways broke down in 1995 because the employee-owners of United feared that the carriers' corporate cultures would clash. It is also important for air carriers to have compatible fleets so that they can economize on maintenance, repair, and pilot training costs and to have labor forces that are receptive to a merger. Fallick and Hassett, for example, point out that unionism can influence merger activity.[27]

Although we were unable to quantify corporate cultures explicitly, we constructed the percentage of aircraft types that each possible pair of carriers had in common and created a dummy variable that indicated

24. Hurdle and others (1989).
25. Caves, Christensen, and Tretheway (1984).
26. Each route segment served by the potential merger partners was identified using Data Bank 1A. The annual traffic density for each carrier was calculated based on the passengers carried and the quarters during each year that a carrier served a route. The density for each potential merger was calculated by summing the passengers for each of the potential merger partners for each route segment that they both serve.
27. Fallick and Hassett (1996).

whether a carrier's pilots, mechanics, and flight attendants were represented by a union.[28] Carriers are more likely to merge if they have a greater percentage of aircraft types in common. In the airline industry, merging unionized labor forces can create special problems such as reconciling the seniority lists of two unions' pilots, an issue recently confronted by American Airlines and Reno Air. Thus, we would expect mergers to be less likely if carriers' labor forces are unionized.

FINANCIAL DISTRESS. Empirical evidence suggests that failing firms are seen as takeover targets by efficiently run firms or that they encourage a merger to avoid bankruptcy.[29] Mergers may also provide distressed firms with a palatable way to restructure their debt and regain financial health.[30] Although it is difficult to distinguish between these explanations empirically, they suggest that the relative financial strength of a pair of carriers may influence whether they merge. We use assets and cash flow as financial measures and expect that a carrier with relatively small assets or a relatively small (or negative) cash flow will tend to encourage a merger.[31]

Anticompetitive Motives

Firms generally find it difficult to achieve market power in the long run—however long that is—but mergers may enable firms to raise prices in the short run without attracting entry. Knapp, for example, finds that rival airlines experience 3 percent to 6 percent positive abnormal returns immediately after they announce a merger.[32] We use a fare equation to predict how prices would change following a merger between each possible

28. Annual fleet data, including owned and leased aircraft, for each carrier in our sample were obtained from Back Associates of Reston, Virginia. The number of aircraft of all types that both potential merger partners operated was divided by the sum of the two carriers' individual fleet sizes. The union status of pilots, mechanics, and flight attendants for each carrier from 1978 to 1995 was determined from a large number of sources including the National Mediation Board, *Airline Pilot* magazine, Regional Airline Association, Bureau of National Affairs, individual carriers, and the unions themselves.

29. DeBondt and Thompson (1992) and Matsusaka (1993) provide evidence that poorly run firms are takeover targets. Shrieves and Stevens (1979) argue that some failing firms find the cost of merging less than the cost of bankruptcy.

30. Clark and Ofek (1994).

31. These data are from the DOT's Form 41 data compiled by Data Base Products in Dallas (www.airlinedata.com [April 11, 2000]).

32. Knapp (1990).

pair of carriers.[33] Higher predicted prices should increase the likelihood of a merger.

Airlines compete on many dimensions including price, service, and promotions such as frequent flier programs. As noted, carriers have developed competitive relations with each other that sometimes lead to fare wars and intense service and promotional competition. Carriers may therefore pursue mergers to end all aspects of competition with their fiercest rivals. We capture this possibility by calculating the percentage of commonly served routes where a fare war broke out between each possible pair of carriers.[34] The likelihood of a merger should increase as this percentage rises.

Industrywide Forces

Forces may act on an entire industry to promote merger activity, which may help explain why mergers often occur in waves. The cost of financing a merger is obviously an important consideration. We capture this cost by using the maturity yields for each carrier's bonds from *Moody's Bond Records*. Lower bond rates should increase the likelihood of a merger.

Changes in macroeconomic growth may also influence merger activity.[35] Managers may seek immediate increases in capacity through a merger to take advantage of expected improvements in economic growth or pursue a path of slow internal expansion during expected downturns. We capture this possibility with a variable that compares predicted gross domestic product (GDP) with actual GDP.[36] Mergers are more likely to occur when the economy exceeds expected levels of output.

33. We estimated a conventional log-linear fare regression for each quarter from 1978:4 to 1995:4 using data from the 1,000 most heavily traveled routes. Average fares were specified as a function of distance, the product of the populations of the end-point metropolitan areas, the number of effective competitors serving the route (expressed as an inverted Herfindahl index), the number of effective competitors at the airport on the route that is most concentrated, four dummy variables for each of the slot controlled airports (Chicago O'Hare, New York Kennedy and LaGuardia, and Washington Reagan National), and a constant. The estimated fare was calculated before and after all potential mergers, with appropriate adjustments to the airport and route competition variables. Fares before and after the merger were multiplied by each route's passengers and summed to obtain total carrier revenue before and after a merger. The resulting variable was the percentage that the merged carrier's revenue would exceed the sum of the individual carriers' revenue.

34. This variable was calculated from Data Bank 1A, using fare wars that were identified in Morrison and Winston (1996).

35. Melicher, Ledolter, and D'Antonio (1983).

36. Because airlines must make capacity decisions (years) in advance of aircraft delivery, a given year's GDP was predicted two years in advance assuming that the percentage annual growth rate in GDP during the previous eight years would continue for the next two years. This procedure was previously used in Morrison and Winston (1995).

Estimation Results

A binary logit model was used to estimate the effect of operational and financial motives, anticompetitive motives, and industrywide forces on the probability that a pair of carriers attempted to merge or actually merged in a given year during 1978–95. The sample consists of 4,136 possible carrier pairs.

The estimation results, presented in table 1-2, lend qualitative support for all the potential influences on merger activity.[37] Operational and financial variables have plausible signs and, in general, are statistically reliable. Carriers are more likely to seek a merger if it increases their traffic density and expands their international markets and if they have common aircraft types, while they are less likely to seek a merger if their pilots, mechanics, and flight attendants are represented by unions. In addition, the smaller the minimum of the two carriers' cash flow and assets, the more likely the carriers will seek a merger.[38] This finding suggests that airline mergers are motivated by financial distress.[39]

Anticompetitive motives cannot be dismissed because carriers are attracted to mergers that are expected, within limits, to raise their prices and

37. We also estimated a model that attempted to explain actual mergers only and found that this model did not lead to conclusions that differed from the one based on actual and attempted mergers. We specified (in different models) individual carrier dummies, carrier pair dummies, and major and national size classification dummies to capture unmeasured fixed effects, such as corporate culture, but these variables were insignificant. We also attempted to capture unobserved temporal effects with time dummies that characterized possible merger waves in the airline industry, but these too were insignificant.

38. We considered other operational and financial variables and alternative ways to specify the variables we included in the final specification. Carriers' combined route density could be compared with the average, minimum, or maximum of the individual carriers' densities. We obtained the best statistical fit by comparing the combined route density with the maximum density of the two potential partners. (We also estimated models that compared the carriers' combined load factors with their individual load factors, but that variable was insignificant.) Similarly, we obtained the best statistical fit by comparing combined foreign routes with the maximum of the foreign routes served by the two potential partners. (Including domestic routes did not improve the model.) We also found that the effect of common aircraft types was strongest with an initial overlap, roughly 25 percent, of the carriers' fleets, and that unionism had its greatest and most reliable effect when the entire labor force of both prospective partners was unionized. Finally, we obtained the best statistical fits when the minimum cash flow and assets of the two potential partners was specified. The maximum cash flow was found to be statistically insignificant, which contrasts with the view that airline mergers are more likely to occur when an acquirer has excess liquidity. Using a return on assets, based on operating profits, also did not lead to improvements.

39. It could be argued that assets are a measure of size rather than financial distress. (Cash flow is likely to be a questionable measure of size because large carriers had negative cash flow in a number of cases.) But we obtained the best fits using the *minimum* assets of the potential partners. It would be expected that combined assets would have outperformed minimum assets if carriers' motivation for merging was to increase their size, as measured by assets.

Table 1-2. *Probability of an Actual or Attempted Merger by a Pair of Carriers in a Given Year*

Independent variable	Parameter estimate (Standard error)
Constant	−7.1669
	(1.1677)
Operational and financial variables	
Combined route density relative to the maximum route density of the potential merger partners	0.8281
	(0.4181)
Combined foreign routes served relative to the maximum foreign routes by the potential merger partners	2.7806
	(0.6476)
Percentage of aircraft types potential merger partners have in common (defined for 25 percent and above, 0 otherwise)	0.8289
	(0.7711)
Unionized labor force dummy (1 if the pilots, mechanics, and flight attendants have union representation in both potential merger partners, 0 otherwise)	−0.5551
	(0.2535)
Minimum assets of the potential merger partners	−1.11E-09
	(3.80E-10)
Minimum cash flow of the potential merger partners	−1.79E-09
	(7.25E-10)
Anticompetitive variables	
Predicted revenue increase from a merger based on the preceding year's competitive conditions (defined for increases between 1 and 5 percent, 0 otherwise)	67.1908
	(19.6633)
Percentage of routes jointly served by potential merger partners that experienced a fare war in the preceding year	5.335
	(1.9258)
Industrywide variables	
Interest rate (defined as the minimum bond rate for two national potential merger partners, 0 otherwise)	−0.203
	(0.0991)
Interest rate (defined as the minimum bond rate for two major potential merger partners or the bond rate for the only major carrier in a merger pair, 0 otherwise)	−0.1463
	(0.0792)
Predicted GDP relative to actual GDP in the preceding year	−0.111
	(0.0575)
Number of observations	4,136
Log-likelihood at zero	−2,866.85
Log-likelihood at convergence	−139.58

Source: Authors' calculations. See text for explanation.

that eliminate competition with a fierce rival.[40] And the economy matters. Mergers are more likely when interest rates fall, especially when the potential merger involves two national carriers, and when GDP is better than predicted.[41]

Our findings appear to defy any sharp conclusions because they support many explanations of airline mergers. But sharp conclusions do emerge from the quantitative importance of these explanations. Table 1-3 presents the share of merger activity attributable to each variable in the model.[42] Operational and financial motives account for 72 percent of merger activity during the 1978–95 period, industrywide forces 22 percent, and anticompetitive motives just 6 percent. Greater international coverage, financial distress, and lower financing costs are the leading explanations for mergers since deregulation and during the most recent year in our sample. Mergers are an attractive way for carriers to expand service on international routes and overcome regulatory impediments to entry. This motivation for merger could be reduced if international airline markets are deregulated. Being able to raise prices or stifle competition does not play a large role in carriers' merger decisions.[43] Based on carriers' motivations, one would expect that past and future airline mergers have not reduced (and will not reduce) travelers' welfare.

40. The effect of predicted prices, and hence revenue, was greatest between a range from 1 percent to 5 percent. We speculate that a predicted price increase greater than 5 percent might attract the attention of the antitrust authorities; thus it weakened the effect of this variable on the likelihood of an actual or attempted merger. We explored other anticompetitive motives for a carrier to merge such as to eliminate competition with carriers where it had extensive multimarket contact or to raise substantially the concentration levels in its markets, as measured by the (inverse) Herfindahl index, but these variables were insignificant.

41. Using economywide paper rates, Treasury-bill rates, and the like produced less satisfactory results than using bond rates for individual carriers. Carriers' stock prices are also likely to affect the cost of a merger. But these prices may be too volatile during a given year to use here. In addition, the information contained in stock prices is likely to be reflected in the carriers' financial characteristics—assets and cash flow—which are included in the model. Other potential industrywide influences were considered. The tax code was more favorable to merger activity between 1981 and 1986 than in later years because the 1986 tax reform act eliminated important tax motivations for mergers. We specified a (favorable) tax code dummy for 1981–86, but it was statistically insignificant. Airline mergers could also be affected by the extent of merger and acquisition activity in the country, but this was not supported empirically.

42. The fraction of merger activity attributable to a particular variable equaled the fraction that the absolute value of the variable and its coefficient contributed to the systematic part of the regression (excluding the constant), weighting each observation by the combined assets of the potential merger partners and enumerating through the sample.

43. We also calculated the elasticities for all the determinants of airline mergers and found that the elasticities for the anticompetitive variables were very small. Carlton and Perloff (1994) conclude that the increased value of a consolidated firm in U.S. industry is not typically due to the creation of market power.

Table 1-3. *Portion of Merger Activity Attributable to Variables in the Model, Selected Years*

Percent

Variable	1978–95	1995
Operational and financial considerations		
Route density	3.4	2.8
Foreign routes	36.9	33.7
Aircraft types	2.7	1.8
Unions	3.5	1.7
Assets	21.5	28.1
Cash flow	3.6	3.7
Anticompetitive influences		
Price (revenue) increases	4.8	6.2
Common routes with fare wars	1.3	1.6
Industrywide variables		
Interest rates (2 national carriers)	1.0	0.3
Interest rates (1 or more major carriers)	17.3	16.2
Predicted GDP	3.9	3.8

Source: Authors' calculations.

Service and Perceived Pricing Inequities

Recent congressional hearings have featured angry citizens testifying about unexplained delays, lost luggage, sudden cancellations, rude employees, and other service complaints. Senators John McCain and Ron Wyden rounded up broad support for a so-called passengers' bill of rights that, among other things, required airlines to tell passengers when their flights are overbooked and whether they are offered the cheapest fares, and to give prior notice and honest explanations for delays and cancellations. Although the bill was shelved for the time being, the industry has pledged to respond to these matters and "put customers first" by implementing a "customer service commitment." Senator Wyden, among others, has expressed his doubts about the industry's sincerity.

Dissatisfaction with airline service has probably been intensified by perceptions that airline pricing is increasingly unfair. For example, it is not unusual for travelers who fly at the last minute to pay fares that are three times higher than their seatmates' fares. Fare dispersion has grown since deregulation (figure 1-2), but it has not increased during the past decade.

Figure 1-2. *Fare Dispersion in U.S. Domestic Markets, 1978–98*

Gini coefficient

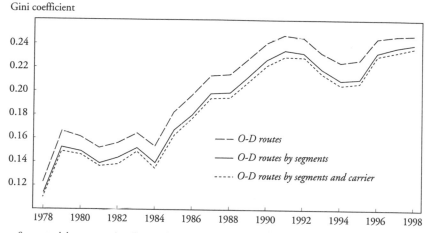

Sources and data construction: Data are from Data Bank 1A. Fare dispersion is measured at the route level using the Gini coefficient. Multiplying the Gini coefficient by two gives the expected difference in fares for two randomly drawn tickets as a percentage of the average price. Dispersion was measured using three different categories: the origin-destination route level (O-D routes) includes all carriers and both direct and connecting flights; the O-D routes by segments category separates direct and connecting routes; and the O-D routes by segments and carriers classification treats each direct and connecting flight by each carrier separately. As shown in the figure, the spread of fares increases as the category under consideration is broadened.

Moreover, variations in fares often reflect cost-based differences, which arise, for example, because business travelers place a much higher value than pleasure travelers on the convenience of booking a seat at the last minute. Airlines therefore carry a larger inventory of seats for business travelers relative to their expected demand than they do for pleasure travelers. The cost of these extra seats is reflected in the higher unrestricted fares business travelers pay. Some additional price variation is attributable to the proliferation of so-called niche carriers such as ProAir and Vanguard, which stimulate a greater range of fare offerings by all carriers. To be sure, some fare dispersion also reflects carriers' ability to align fares with passengers' willingness to pay (price discrimination). Although this practice may be perceived by some travelers and policymakers as unfair, carriers are increasingly using it on the Internet to set discount prices to fill seats that would otherwise be empty.[44]

44. Yield management systems are becoming more sophisticated and facilitating carriers' ability to price discriminate. But there is no evidence that such systems have enabled carriers to raise average fares. Airlines were prevented by a 1994 Justice Department consent decree from announcing the ending dates of their fare promotions. Morrison and Winston (1996) suggest, however, that this decree has had no effect on fares.

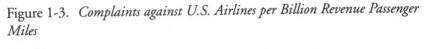

Figure 1-3. *Complaints against U.S. Airlines per Billion Revenue Passenger Miles*

Complaints

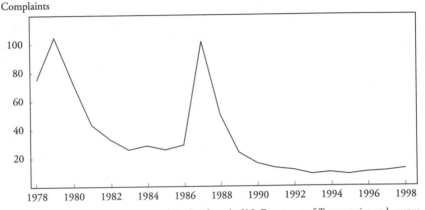

Sources: Authors' calculations using complaint data from the U.S. Department of Transportation and revenue passenger mile data from the Air Transport Association, Washington, D.C.

What about airline service? Has it seriously deteriorated in the past several years, and are carriers to blame? Policymakers and the popular press cite the recent increase in customer complaints to the Transportation Department as evidence that airline service is at an all-time low. But figure 1-3, which controls for the growth in air travel, presents a different and more accurate characterization. Complaints per billion passenger miles increased immediately after deregulation and then decreased until the industry completed its merger wave. After peaking in 1987, passenger-mile-adjusted complaints declined sharply until 1990 and have remained fairly constant since then.[45] What has changed during this decade is that the percentage of seats filled by paying passengers (average load factor) has risen from 62 percent to 71 percent.

We assessed the role that crowded planes have on passenger complaints by estimating the relationship from 1978 to 1998 between complaints per billion revenue passenger miles and average load factor, a time trend, and a constant. All coefficients were statistically significant at the 1 percent

45. Recently released figures from Bridge News Service (3/7/00) show that airlines' on-time performance, rate of luggage claims, and rate of involuntary denied boardings improved from 1998 to 1999. At the same time, the Transportation Department has released passenger complaints in 1999, which are nearly double passenger complaints in 1998. This sharp increase, however, is largely attributable to the proliferation of websites that have made it much easier to complain.

level.[46] The time trend revealed an annual decline of 7.2 complaints per billion passenger miles, all else constant. Countering this was an increase of 6.4 complaints per billion passenger miles for each percentage point increase in the average load factor. Thus, complaints are not only close to historic lows on a passenger mile basis, but the current dissatisfaction with air service appears to be largely attributable to pressures on carrier capacity—a problem that does not call for government intervention.

What about specific complaints like overbooking, delays, and cancelled or limited service? In 1998 only 1.1 million out of 514 million passengers, 0.2 percent, were denied boarding because of overbooking, including 45,000 who were bumped involuntarily.[47] Delays have recently increased, but the Federal Aviation Administration has assumed much of the blame by admitting that it uses airspace inefficiently, responds slowly and clumsily to bad weather, and suffers from procedures that vary from one region to another.[48]

Travelers to and from smaller airports bemoan inconvenient service, but carriers are making efforts, or can be induced, to improve matters. For example, a new generation of fifty-seat regional jets has spurred new service to roughly 160 smaller communities.[49] Regional jet service is expected to grow because many travelers dislike turbo-props, which are used in small markets, and are willing to drive several hours to avoid flying in them. The only thing likely to inhibit carriers from expanding this service is union clauses that currently cap the number of regional jets most carriers can use. In addition, America West has agreed to serve Eugene, Oregon, ProAir has agreed to serve Detroit, and United has agreed to serve Des Moines, sometimes at reduced fares, in return for guaranteed patronage. Forged by business leaders of their respective communities, these agreements are being seen by business groups in other cities as an appealing strategy to obtain more convenient air service and make their city more attractive to businesses. Contractual relationships between communities and carriers have far more potential to improve air service than complaints to DOT, passenger bills of rights, and airline industry pledges.

46. We corrected for serial correlation of the residuals.

47. *Aviation Daily*, March 19, 1999.

48. "A Jam at 32,000 Feet," *Economist*, February 5, 2000, p. 57.

49. This figure is based on data from the *Official Airline Guide* reported in *Proposition RJ: An Alliance to Enhance Airline Competition*, published by GKMG Consulting Services, Inc., Washington, D.C., May 1999.

Airport Access

Entry barriers are thought to exist at dominated hub airports because new entrants are at a competitive disadvantage unless they offer many flights. Nonetheless, new entrants are not prevented from serving these airports. New entrants *are*, however, prevented from serving airports if they cannot get takeoff and landing slots or gates.

Since 1969 there have been limits—called slots—on the number of takeoffs and landings per hour at LaGuardia, Kennedy, National, and O'Hare. Slot controls were initially designed during regulation to reduce congestion, but in a deregulated environment they also reduce competition and raise fares.[50] Competition is also reduced at LaGuardia and National by perimeter rules that prohibit carriers from offering flights that exceed 1,500 miles and 1,250 miles, respectively.[51]

During the 1950s and 1960s, airlines agreed to pay off billions of dollars in airport revenue bonds for expansion projects. The quid pro quo was exclusive-use gate leases, which during regulation were innocuous because carriers were prevented from entering other routes. But in the deregulated airline industry, exclusive-use leases have effectively given carriers a long-term lock on gates and veto power over new facilities for would-be competitors.[52]

Table 1-4 shows data on 1998 airport gate availability for forty-one large and midsize U.S. airports. Airport gates are classified as either exclusive use (leased exclusively to one airline), preferential use (the airport operator may assign the gate temporarily to another carrier when it is not being used by the lessee), or common use (the airport authority makes all gate assignments). Gates available for use by new entrants consist of common use gates, preferential use gates that an airport authority makes available, and exclusive use gates that incumbent carriers make available.

50. Morrison and Winston (1997).

51. The Wright Amendment, a provision contained in Section 29 of the *International Air Transportation Competition Act of 1979*, also reduces competition and raises fares by allowing airlines that use Love Field in Dallas to offer flights only to other cities in Texas and to Alabama, Arkansas, Kansas, Louisiana, Mississippi, New Mexico, and Oklahoma.

52. Many of the contracts between airport authorities and airlines contain "majority in interest" clauses, which give the airlines signing the contract the right to approve certain capital expenditures, including spending on terminals and gates.

Table 1-4. *Gate Usage at Selected Airports in 1998*

Airport	Exclusive use	Preferential use	Common use	Available for use by others	Total
Atlanta	137	0	32	32	169
Austin	0	25	0	5	25
Baltimore-Washington	0	66	9	15	75
Boston	68	0	17	17	85
Charlotte	44	0	15	18	59
Chicago Midway	26	0	4	9	30
Chicago O'Hare	147	0	22	22	169
Cincinnati	63	56	0	8	119
Cleveland	43	0	1	1	44
Dallas Love	16	0	1	2	17
Dallas–Ft. Worth	112	0	8	12	120
Denver	0	64	26	27	90
Detroit Metro	68	23	6	10	97
Fort Lauderdale	20	3	16	16	39
Honolulu	0	0	42	42	42
Houston Bush	74	0	14	23	88
Houston Hobby	0	28	0	10	28
Kansas City	0	40	13	13	53
Las Vegas	0	87	8	37	95
Los Angeles	73	0	55	62	128
Memphis	66	0	2	13	68
Miami	0	0	113	113	113
Minneapolis–St. Paul	13	57	0	8	70
New York Kennedy	112	0	28	62	140
New York LaGuardia	60	0	12	17	72
Newark	76	0	15	15	91
Oakland	0	20	2	2	22
Orlando	72	3	6	6	81
Philadelphia	51	5	7	12	63
Phoenix	92	0	5	16	97

(continued)

Table 1-4. *(continued)*

Airport	Exclusive use	Preferential use	Common use	Available for use by others	Total
Pittsburgh	60	9	6	15	75
Portland	0	38	16	16	54
St. Louis	12	76	0	3	88
Salt Lake City	67	2	1	1	70
San Diego	0	31	19	19	50
San Francisco	64	4	10	23	78
San Jose	12	18	1	1	31
Seattle	63	0	17	17	80
Tampa	16	23	13	13	52
Washington Dulles	0	74	8	8	82
Washington Reagan National	0	44	0	2	44

Source: Air Transport Association, airport survey.

The table suggests that new entrants could find it difficult to find any available gates at several airports in the country.[53]

Notwithstanding the contractual arrangement that exists between the airport and the tenant airlines, the airport has a legal obligation to provide *reasonable* access to the facility. Policymakers, however, have yet to define precisely what reasonable access means.

Another problem facing nonincumbent carriers, especially at airports where most gates are exclusively leased, is that they must often sublet gates from incumbent carriers at nonpreferred times and at a higher cost than the incumbent pays. Spirit Airlines, for example, has been unable to acquire or sublease gates from any of the entrenched carriers at Detroit Metro Airport. Thus, it rents their spare gates at more than twice the cost of owning two gates with jetways. The airport's suggestion, that Spirit build a multimillion dollar pier of six or eight gates, would clearly exceed Spirit's financial reach.[54]

53. Long-term leases on exclusive-use gates have been criticized for several years by the Transportation Department, GAO, and others as potential barriers to entry. The FAA/OST Task Force (1999) provides a full discussion of the issue.

54. Bruce Ingersoll, "Flexible Flyer: Gateless in Detroit," *Wall Street Journal*, July 12, 1999, p. A1.

Policies and institutional arrangements that effectively constrain airport capacity may have been innocuous when they were begun under regulation, but in today's deregulated environment they are restricting competition. Policymakers in Washington appear to recognize this problem and are debating proposals that would expand or even eliminate slots, end perimeter rules and Dallas Love Field restrictions, and give airports more funds so they can allocate or build gates for new entrants without having to get incumbent carriers' approval. Improving the allocation and efficiency of airport capacity would benefit travelers—but, as we discuss later, that benefit may be realized only through privatization.

Policy-Related Influences on Fares

The theme that has emerged from our discussion is that policymakers have focused on issues in air transportation that do not appear to require corrective action, while paying insufficient attention to issues that do. We explore this theme more systematically by estimating regressions that measure the impact of policy variables and background variables, which reflect cost and demand influences, on fare changes since airlines were deregulated in 1978 and on fare levels during the most recent quarter, 1998:4, for which data are currently available.[55] Our data set is constructed from the 1,000 most heavily traveled routes in 1998:4 that were also served in 1978:4.[56] The dependent variable in our first model is

55. Fare equations have been used to analyze a variety of policy-related issues in air transportation. They are interpreted as reduced form models that treat competition and background variables as exogenous. We have not found in previous work that findings are materially affected when competitors are treated as endogenous. Morrison and Winston (1995) discuss this issue and provide a summary of studies.

56. The source of the fare data was Data Bank 1A. Although deregulation formally started in 1978:4, the Civil Aeronautics Board began to relax its regulations as early as 1976. But fares were not included in Data Bank 1A until 1978:4. To be reasonably certain that the tickets for a particular journey reflect travel from one origin to one destination, only tickets with one (directional) destination were used. Round trips had to return to the initial point of departure (with no ground segments, that is, open-jaw tickets). Only one-way tickets with two or fewer coupons (flight segments) and round-trip tickets with two or fewer coupons on the outbound and return legs were used. Because of possible coding errors in the data that carriers submit to DOT, the fare screen contained in the General Accounting Office (1990) was used to eliminate fares that seemed unreasonably high. In order to keep frequent flier tickets, we did not use a low fare screen. Taxes (including the percentage-based ticket tax, segment tax, and Passenger Facility Charges) were subtracted from the reported fare to obtain fares charged by a carrier.

the percentage change in real average fares on each route during this period.[57]

Background Variables

We control for route density, an influence on costs, by specifying dummy variables that characterized all the airport hub classifications contained in the data.[58] Under regulation short-haul fares were set below costs, and long-haul fares were set above costs; we include route distance to capture this effect on fare changes since deregulation. Demand effects are captured by the product of per capita income in the routes' origin and destination metropolitan areas. Trip and traveler characteristics also affect fares. The percentage of travelers who change airlines when making a connection en route is included because these interline trips are more expensive than trips taken on one airline. Business travelers pay higher fares than other travelers do because they require seats, which raise carriers' costs, in case they travel at the last minute and because they tend to have smaller demand elasticities than other travelers. Thus we include the percentage of air travelers who are flying on business between the states where the origin and destination airports are located.[59]

Policy Variables

Travelers' fares are greatly affected by competition on airline routes. Our specification distinguishes among pre-deregulation carriers (such as American, United, Delta, and so on), Southwest Airlines, and low-fare

57. The use of real fares is a simple approach to isolate the change in fares since deregulation. A more rigorous approach would be to construct a counterfactual measure of how fares today differ from what they would have been had regulation continued. We constructed such a measure by adjusting the Standard Industry Fare Level (SIFL) as explained in the notes to figure 1-1. For each route, the resulting dependent variable was the percentage by which actual average fares on the route differ from the adjusted SIFL fares. But this approach did not lead to any fundamental changes in our conclusions; thus our analysis uses real fares.

58. Airports accounting for 1 percent or more of passenger enplanements were classified as large hubs; those enplaning 0.25 percent or more but less than 1 percent were classified as medium hubs; those enplaning 0.05 percent or more but less than 0.25 percent were classified as small hubs; and those enplaning less than 0.05 percent were classified as nonhubs. These classifications were determined based on Form 41 data for 1998. The Federal Aviation Administration aggregates airport level data into metropolitan area data; thus its definition of a hub class differs from the one used here. Finally, because the route density dummy variables cover all possible route combinations in the data, a separate constant term was not included.

59. This variable was calculated from data on trip purpose for air travelers contained in the U.S. Department of Transportation's *1995 American Travel Survey*.

carriers besides Southwest because these carriers may have different effects on a route's fares.[60] We also include the potential and adjacent competition supplied by Southwest and other low-fare carriers. Potential competition is defined as the number of airports on a given route served by a carrier that does not serve the route; adjacent competition is assumed to exist when a carrier serves origin and destination airports that are within fifty miles of the origin and destination airports that make up a given route. For example, Southwest does not serve the Washington D.C. Dulles–San Francisco route, but it supplies adjacent competition on the Baltimore-Washington (BWI airport)–Oakland route.

Next we turn to measures of (possible) imperfections in the air transportation market affecting fares that could be addressed by public policy. We capture the effect of airport dominance on fares by identifying whether the origin or destination airport on a given route is among the seventy-five busiest in the country and is served by a major carrier that accounts for 70 percent or more of passenger enplanements at that airport.[61] Although economists do not agree on how one should measure predatory behavior, the Transportation Department has advanced a policy based on its view that predatory behavior has occurred in the airline industry. We define a dummy variable for those routes where, according to the department's guidelines, predatory behavior is likely to have taken place during 1998:4 and routes where predatory behavior is likely to have taken place but ceased by 1998:4.[62] Airline mergers also may have affected fares. We identify those routes that were affected by three controversial mergers, two of which,

60. A carrier had to have at least a 10 percent share of passengers on a route to be counted as serving that route. The low-fare carriers identified by the Transportation Department that were operating during 1998, other than Southwest, were AirTran, American Trans Air, Frontier, Kiwi, ProAir, Reno, Spirit, Tower Air, Vanguard, and Western Pacific.

61. The Transportation Department classifies a major carrier as having annual operating revenue of at least $1 billion. The variable was calculated from enplanement data in Form 41 for 1998:4. Our findings were not sensitive to plausible alternative assumptions regarding a carrier's share of passenger enplanements or whether we considered somewhat more or fewer than the seventy-five busiest airports.

62. These data were obtained from the U.S. Department of Transportation. Starting with 2,793 domestic markets that were served by low-fare carriers between January 1994 and September 1998, DOT determined when the low-fare carrier entered each of these markets and used the dominant carrier's passenger and revenue data for the two quarters preceding entry as a benchmark. If, after low-fare entry, the dominant carrier's passengers increased 10 percent or more and its revenue declined 10 percent or more, then the route was subject to further investigation. In particular, DOT determined whether the dominant carrier sold substantially more tickets at low fares after low-fare entry; whether the dominant carrier sold more seats at low fares than the low-fare carrier's total seats; and whether the dominant carrier's revenue declined. If these three criteria were met for more than one quarter, then the dominant carrier was deemed likely to have violated the department's predation guidelines. The

Northwest-Republic and TWA-Ozark, were opposed by the Justice Department.[63] Mergers are an extreme form of collusion. Implicit collusion may develop if carriers compete on many of the same routes. We therefore specify a variable to control for multimarket contact.[64]

Estimation Results

Table 1-5 presents the estimated parameters for our model of fare changes since deregulation. Background variables have plausible and statistically reliable effects. As traffic densities and distances increase, the percentage reduction in average fares since deregulation increases. As the shares of business travelers, travelers making interline connections, and travelers traveling to or from metropolitan statistical areas with greater incomes increase, average fares since deregulation increase.[65]

Whether it actually serves a route, could potentially serve a route, or serves an adjacent route, Southwest Airlines causes average fares to fall. Indeed, Southwest's ability to lower fares since deregulation as a potential competitor exceeds pre-deregulation and other low-fare carriers' ability to lower fares as actual competitors. It has been claimed that Southwest's presence on a route has the harmful effect of driving carriers out of nearby airports and causing fares to rise on routes that Southwest does not serve.[66] In contrast, we find that Southwest has a positive effect on travelers as an adjacent competitor.

Fares increase as one carrier increasingly dominates an airport, but previous (controversial) mergers and alleged predatory behavior have either

---

department strongly suspects predatory behavior has taken place on a total of twenty routes, including six where it was ongoing in 1998:4.

63. A route is considered to have been affected by a merger if it was one of the 1,000 most heavily traveled routes in 1993 and if it was served by both of the merging carriers (each with at least 10 percent of the route's passengers) four quarters before the merger. This variable was calculated from Data Bank 1A using routes contained in Morrison (1996).

64. The variable was specified as the maximum multimarket contact between two carriers serving a given route. Multimarket contact is measured as the percentage of a carrier's systemwide revenue in 1998:4 earned on routes served by the other carrier. As before, a carrier had to have at least a 10 percent share of a route's passengers to be considered as serving the route.

65. In addition to these background variables, we also estimated models that included the populations of the origin and destination metropolitan statistical areas, the percentage of travelers making connections (as opposed to flying nonstop), and regional dummies, but these variables were statistically insignificant.

66. Perry Flint, "Deregulation: Trouble in the Heartland," *Air Transport World,* July 1998, pp. 48–54. This alleged effect could also arise if Southwest attracted price sensitive traffic to its routes and left the higher paying traffic behind.

Table 1-5. *Parameter Estimates for Percentage Change in Real Average Air Fares from 1978:4 to 1998:4 for the 1,000 Most Heavily Traveled Routes in 1998:4 That Were Served in Both Periods*

Independent variable	Coefficient (Standard error)
Background variables	
Large hub–large hub (dummy)	−0.153055
	(0.093356)
Large hub–medium hub (dummy)	−0.189352
	(0.091596)
Large hub–small hub (dummy)	−0.230926
	(0.087826)
Large hub–nonhub (dummy)	−0.403426
	(0.114783)
Medium hub–medium hub (dummy)	−0.231509
	(0.09679)
Medium hub–small hub (dummy)	−0.362965
	(0.086959)
Small hub–small hub (dummy)	−0.48192
	(0.069473)
Distance	−0.000217
	(1.69E-05)
Percentage of air travelers between the origin and destination states whose trip purpose is business	0.335052 (0.047527)
Percentage of travelers on route making interline connections	2.733743
	(0.555588)
Product of per capita personal income of the origin and destination metropolitan statistical areas (divided by 1,000,000)	0.000187 (6.83E-05)
Policy variables	
Difference in the number of pre-deregulation carriers on route in 1978:4 and 1998:4	−0.019658 (0.006369)
Southwest Airlines serves route in 1998:4 (1 if Southwest serves the route, 0 otherwise)[a]	−0.30908 (0.02911)
Number of low-fare carriers on route in 1998:4[a]	−0.06772 (0.057301)
Number of airports on route served by Southwest Airlines in 1998:4 (for routes Southwest does not serve)[a]	−0.075801 (0.02699)
Number of airports on route served by low-fare carriers in 1998:4 (for routes low-fare carriers do not serve)[a]	−0.004464 (0.050084)

(continued)

Table 1-5. *(continued)*

Independent variable	Coefficient (Standard error)
Southwest serves an adjacent route in 1998:4 (1 if Southwest serves an adjacent route, 0 otherwise; for routes Southwest does not serve)[a]	−0.069815 0.015327
A low-fare carrier serves an adjacent route in 1998:4 (1 if a low-fare carrier serves an adjacent route, 0 otherwise; for routes a low-fare carrier does not serve)[a]	−0.060954 (0.019607)
Origin or destination airport is one of the 75 busiest and a major carrier accounts for 70 percent or more of passenger enplanements in 1998:4 (1 if the airport satisfies these conditions, 0 otherwise)	0.173061 (0.042458)
Route affected by the merger of Northwest Airlines and Republic Airlines (1 if the route is affected, 0 otherwise)	−0.008894 (0.046121)
Route affected by the merger of Trans World Airlines and Ozark Airlines (1 if the route is affected, 0 otherwise)	−0.061603 (0.039019)
Route affected by the merger of USAir and Piedmont Airlines (1 if the route is affected, 0 otherwise)	−0.01433 (0.041341)
Predatory behavior occurred on route in 1998:4 (1 if behavior occurred, 0 otherwise)	−0.182514 (0.078634)
Predatory behavior occurred on route before 1998:4 and is over by 1998:4 (1 if behavior occurred and is over, 0 otherwise)	−0.020559 (0.05105)
Percentage of systemwide revenue in 1998:4 earned on routes with another carrier (defined for two carriers on route with the greatest multimarket contact)	−0.144946 (0.043393)

Summary statistics

Number of observations	1,000
R^2	0.561

Source: Parameter estimates are authors' calculations, based on data cited and explained in text. Standard errors are heteroskedastic consistent.

a. These variables were not specified as differences because there were no such carriers operating in 1978:4. Southwest began service in 1971 as a Texas intrastate carrier, but did not file Data Bank 1A data until 1979:4.

lowered fares or had a statistically insignificant effect. Note that even when an alleged instance of predatory behavior has ended, average fares on a route do not rise.[67] To be sure, a carrier may gain from driving out a

67. The predatory dummies capture differences in carrier interactions across routes (in this case the occurrence of predatory behavior) that could influence fares. Thus, although predatory behavior is allegedly directed toward low-fare carriers, it is appropriate to control for these carriers in the model.

competitor even if fares do not subsequently rise. (This issue is discussed later.) Finally, multimarket contact lowers fares. Our previous work found that multimarket contact led to higher fares during the late 1980s, but when the industry's fortunes declined in the early 1990s, carrier rivalry intensified and multimarket contact led to fare wars and lower fares. Apparently, this effect has persisted into the late 1990s.[68]

The quantitative implications of these findings verify Southwest Airlines' large impact on fares but do not reveal any significant costs to travelers that should be addressed by public policy.[69] We estimate that actual, potential, and adjacent competition from Southwest accounts for $9.7 billion of the annual fare savings from the change in real fares since deregulation—nearly 40 percent of the total.[70] In contrast, pre-deregulation carriers account for $0.4 billion in annual savings and the other low-fare carriers account for $1.5 billion in annual savings. Concentrated hub airports are the only policy-related variable in the model that raises travelers' fares, but this cost amounts to less than $0.6 billion annually (roughly 2 percent of the benefits from the change in fares since deregulation).[71] Although fares are elevated on routes connected to dominant hub airports, the extent of this problem appears to be limited to a small share of travelers.

We corroborate and extend our analysis by estimating a cross-section regression to explain average fares on the 1,000 most heavily traveled routes in 1998:4. In this model, we account for the effect of slot restrictions and the availability of gates on fares. The rest of the specification parallels the one we used to explain fare changes with a few exceptions: average fare, route distance, and the product of per capita incomes of the origin and destination metropolitan areas are expressed in logarithms, and the

68. Morrison and Winston (1995).

69. The estimated fare equation was used in a simulation to estimate each variable's impact on the change in airfares from 1978:4 to 1998:4. The simulation used all 18,855 routes that were served in both periods, not just the 1,000 most heavily traveled routes used in estimation. Population estimates were obtained by inflating the results by forty to account for the use of quarterly data and a 10 percent sample. These estimates, which assume a vertical demand curve, are the amounts that travelers in 1998 would have saved if those same trips were taken at 1978 real fares.

70. Morrison and Winston (1995) estimated a model using 1988–92 data that took account of Southwest's effect on fares as an actual competitor but not its effect as a potential or adjacent competitor. Assuming Southwest exited the industry and taking account of the entry by existing carriers induced by Southwest's exit, they found that fares would rise $4 billion annually. Because Southwest's output in revenue passenger miles has increased between 1992 and 1998 by a factor of 2.3, this estimate is consistent with the finding reported here.

71. Note that this estimate does not isolate Southwest's effect on the hub premium.

number of pre-deregulation carriers serving the route in 1998:4 is used instead of the change in these carriers since 1978:4.

The parameter estimates presented in table 1-6 are consistent with the central findings from the previous model. In particular, Southwest's presence on a route as an actual, potential, or adjacent competitor substantially lowers fares; mergers and alleged predatory behavior have not elevated fares; and fares are higher as a carrier dominates an airport.[72] We also find that fares increase as the percentage of gates not available for use by other carriers increases and that slot controls at New York LaGuardia and Chicago O'Hare airports raise fares. Fares at New York's Kennedy Airport appear to be lower because it is slot controlled, but this finding could be attributable to other factors.[73] The effect of slot controls at Washington National is statistically insignificant, possibly because of competition provided by nearby Washington Dulles and Baltimore-Washington airports.

The quantitative implications of these findings indicate that airport access is an important area of concern for policymakers, but that hub dominance is even less of an issue than suggested by the previous model. Fares are $3.8 billion higher annually because of the limited availability of gates at many major and midsize airports. This cost reflects the competitive disadvantages that new entrants face when they are unable to acquire gates or can acquire them only at nonpreferred times and locations or at excessive cost.[74] In addition, fares on routes involving either LaGuardia or O'Hare or both are nearly $0.6 billion higher than fares on comparable routes. Based on the cross-sectional model that controls for airport access, the cost of hub dominance is roughly $0.4 billion.

---

72. It has been argued that predatory behavior consists of reduced prices *and* increased capacity. We tested for the effect of predatory behavior on capacity by estimating a cross-sectional regression nearly identical to the one reported above but specifying the dependent variable as the logarithm of the number of seats flown on a given route during 1998:4. (Data for seats were from the U.S. Department of Transportation, T-100 Domestic Segment Data, Data Bank 28DS.) The model was estimated for the 1,000 most heavily traveled route segments. We found that both predation dummies had statistically insignificant effects on capacity.

73. Kennedy is slot constrained primarily because of international traffic, which has different peaks than domestic traffic. Thus, slots at Kennedy are not binding for domestic traffic during much of the day. In addition, because this airport is less convenient than Newark or LaGuardia for many New York–area travelers, Kennedy attracts low-fare carriers that cater to passengers who are less time sensitive but more price sensitive than passengers who prefer the other two airports.

74. Private entrepreneurs are not precluded by airport authorities from building gates and leasing or selling them to new entrants. But they are subject to an airport authority's determination of what constitutes a fair and reasonable charge for the use of a gate. This has apparently dissuaded private entities from building gates at airports where new entrants face difficulties in acquiring them.

Table 1-6. *Parameter Estimates for Logarithm of Average Air Fares in 1998:4 for the 1,000 Most Heavily Traveled Routes in 1998:4 That Were Also Served in 1978:4*

Independent variable	Coefficient (Standard error)
Background variables	
Large hub–large hub (dummy)	0.340119
	(0.08947)
Large hub–medium hub (dummy)	0.327449
	(0.089075)
Large hub–small hub (dummy)	0.259725
	(0.090196)
Large hub–nonhub (dummy)	0.029607
	(0.110695)
Medium hub–medium hub (dummy)	0.330008
	(0.092015)
Medium hub–small hub (dummy)	0.188202
	(0.107098)
Small hub–small hub (dummy)	−0.011712
	(0.161308)
Distance (logarithm)	0.394735
	(0.014623)
Percentage of air travelers between the origin and destination states whose trip purpose is business	0.5214 (0.048047)
Percentage of travelers on route making interline connections	2.941546
	(0.462054)
Product of per capita personal income of the origin and destination metropolitan statistical areas (logarithm)	0.276419 (0.020409)
Policy variables	
Number of pre-deregulation carriers on route in 1998:4	−0.030252
	(0.011548)
Southwest Airlines serves route in 1998:4 (1 if Southwest serves the route, 0 otherwise)	−0.396296 (0.025627)
Number of low-fare carriers on route in 1998:4	−0.055901
	(0.055276)
Number of airports on route served by Southwest Airlines in 1998:4 (for routes Southwest does not serve)	−0.080498 (0.021709)
Number of airports on route served by low-fare carriers in 1998:4 (for routes low-fare carriers do not serve)	0.03383 (0.043456)
Southwest serves an adjacent route in 1998:4 (1 if Southwest serves an adjacent route, 0 otherwise; for routes Southwest does not serve)	−0.09546 (0.017996)

(continued)

Table 1-6. *(continued)*

Independent variable	Coefficient (Standard error)
A low-fare carrier serves an adjacent route in 1998:4 (1 if a low-fare carrier serves an adjacent route, 0 otherwise, for routes a low-fare carrier does not serve)	−0.098792 (0.019879)
Origin or destination airport is one of the 75 busiest and a major carrier accounts for 70 percent or more of passenger enplanements in 1998:4 (1 if the airport satisfies these conditions, 0 otherwise)	0.164219 (0.030281)
Route affected by the merger of Northwest Airlines and Republic Airlines (1 if the route is affected, 0 otherwise)	−0.028539 (0.040903)
Route affected by the merger of Trans World Airlines and Ozark Airlines (1 if the route is affected, 0 otherwise)	−0.060025 (0.054329)
Route affected by the merger of USAir and Piedmont Airlines (1 if the route is affected, 0 otherwise)	−0.013538 (0.04853)
Predatory behavior occurred on route in 1998:4 (1 if behavior occured, 0 otherwise)	−0.113532 (0.094748)
Predatory behavior occurred on route before 1998:4 and is over by 1998:4 (1 if behavior occurred and is over, 0 otherwise)	−0.019321 (0.058238)
Percentage of systemwide revenue in 1998:4 earned on routes with another carrier (defined for two carriers on route with the greatest multimarket contact)	−0.235652 (0.058137)
Percentage of gates not available for use by others (maximum value for origin and destination airports)[a]	0.122963 (0.047356)
Washington Reagan National Airport (1 if National is origin or destination airport, 0 otherwise)	−0.034707 (0.040086)
New York Kennedy Airport (1 if Kennedy is origin or destination airport, 0 otherwise)	−0.120177 (0.055873)
New York LaGuardia Airport (1 if LaGuardia is origin or destination airport, 0 otherwise)	0.054177 (0.026637)
Chicago O'Hare Airport (1 if O'Hare is origin or destination airport, 0 otherwise)	0.11793 (0.032446)
Summary statistics	
Number of observations	1,000
R^2	0.740

Source: Parameter estimates are authors' calculations, based on data cited and explained in text. Standard errors are heteroskedastic consistent.

a. The percentage of gates not available for use by others is the number of exclusive and preferential use gates that are not available for reassignment divided by the total number of gates. The percentage of gates not available was set to zero for airports other than the forty-one in table 1-4.

Policy Implications

Ask people who study airlines what policymakers in Washington could do to improve travelers' welfare, and most would recommend promoting deregulation of *international* air travel.[75] We support that policy and cabotage (allowing foreign carriers to serve U.S. routes), but we also recommend improving domestic carriers' access to domestic airports. In our view, policymakers' preoccupation with hubs, predation, and mergers does not point the way to other policies that would substantially benefit domestic travelers. Concerns about poor service are more germane, but proposed solutions miss the point!

Fares on routes connected to dominant hubs may or may not be higher than fares on comparable routes, depending on how one controls for the influence of Southwest. In any case, the cost from any fare increase is small and clearly outweighed by the benefits of hubs, which include greater flight frequency and agglomeration economies in areas surrounding the airport.[76]

Even if one accepts the Transportation Department's definition of predatory behavior, predation has not hurt travelers. One possible response is that carriers engage in predation on routes where fares are higher than on comparable routes, so that they do not have to raise fares after driving out a competitor to benefit from this strategy. We tested for this possibility by estimating a cross-sectional fare regression using data from 1994:4, before alleged predatory behavior began. The regression was identical to the one in table 1-6 except that we included a variable that indicated whether, at some later time, a given route was identified by the Transportation Department as one marked by predatory behavior. The coefficient of this variable was 0.123 and statistically significant, indicating that fares were elevated by roughly 12 percent on these routes, all else constant.[77] But based on the estimates in table 1-5, alleged predatory behavior more than eliminates this premium, and although fares return to their original level after predation ends, the gain to carriers from elevated fares on these routes amounts to only $20 million annually. It seems unlikely that carriers would

75. Morrison and Winston (1995) estimate that international airline deregulation would lower fares by 30 percent, with greater reductions in more heavily regulated Asian-U.S. markets than in European-U.S. markets.

76. Button and Stough (1998).

77. Only a small amount of this premium is related to the hub premium. The correlation of the hub variable and this predation variable is 0.13.

be willing to absorb losses in the short run with no certainty of the "quiet life" in the long run for such a small payoff.

Air carriers have not been motivated to merge for anticompetitive reasons. Moreover, some major mergers during the 1980s, which some policymakers thought would raise fares, have not done so. According to our model of merger behavior, even the proposed alliances between United and Delta, American and US Airways, and Northwest and Continental were not strongly motivated by anticompetitive effects. We are not suggesting that the airline industry should be exempted from the antitrust laws, only that the antitrust authorities have appropriately refrained from trying to shape airline competition and that travelers will be well served if they continue this policy.[78]

Air carriers have long been fodder for stand-up comedians, but some recent episodes of poor service have enraged travelers and policymakers. These service deficiencies stem primarily from carriers' nightmarish recollections of how much money they lost when they expanded their capacity too rapidly in the late 1980s. In response to the recent surge in demand, they have acquired aircraft slowly and cautiously. The result has been higher load factors and shorter tempers. As carriers continue to learn how to adjust their capacity to changes in the business cycle, it is also likely that they will smooth service disruptions that arise from strong changes in demand.

What can be done now to improve service? The same thing that can be done to lower fares—improve the efficiency of airport capacity and air traffic control. The unavailability of gates at several large and midsize airports has raised fares and significantly lowered travelers' welfare. Travelers are also hurt when carriers are delayed from taking off and landing because of runway congestion.[79] Slots, which were intended to address this problem, have reduced competition and raised fares at two major airports, LaGuardia and O'Hare. Air traffic control has been criticized for delays in introducing Global Positioning System (GPS) technology that could expand runway and airspace capacity by enabling carriers to choose speedier flight paths and to take off and land more quickly.

---

78. There is also no reason why the airline industry should continue to be scrutinized by the Justice and Transportation departments. Notwithstanding historical arrangements, the airline industry is no longer a regulated industry. Accordingly, it should be subject to antitrust enforcement by the Justice Department like other industries.

79. Morrison and Winston (1989) estimate that the annual costs from failing to charge congestion-based takeoff and landing fees exceeds $5 billion.

Efficient economic solutions are easy to express: airports should make gates available to all carriers at user fees priced at marginal cost, airports should set efficient (marginal cost) takeoff and landing congestion tolls, and air traffic control should modernize its equipment and operations and charge carriers for the marginal cost of their services. Entrenched interests, however, would have something to say about these solutions. Incumbent carriers would strongly oppose reforms to make gates available to other carriers, owners of corporate jets and small planes would continue to oppose efficient congestion tolls, and, based on its record to date, Congress would resist efforts to free air traffic control from bureaucratic constraints that impede its technological efficiency.

To be sure, some airport operators are talking about shortening lease terms for gates and forcing incumbent carriers to share gates that are not intensively used, and the federal government has explored airport congestion pricing schemes and proposed spinning off air traffic control from the Federal Aviation Administration and making it an independent government corporation that would set its own fees and control its revenues. But these incremental steps have not and, in our view, will not lead to effective change.[80]

What will? Serious consideration should be given to privatizing airports and air traffic control. Calls for privatization are growing within the United States, while other countries are moving their airports and air traffic control away from government management.[81] Canada recently privatized its air traffic control system and thereby lowered the cost of flying, upgraded the system's technology, and increased the number of flights that each employee handles. The board of directors of the new company, Nav Canada, is drawn from commercial carriers, general aviation, and labor and has sought to be responsive to the system's users.[82] Nav Canada could serve as a model for the United States.

---

80. To cite a related example of how politics can block even marginal improvements, consider Senator McCain's effort to expand flights beyond the 1,250-mile limit at National Airport. After gaining approval in the Senate, the proposal for additional flights was torpedoed by a House committee because the Senate would not approve legislation to ensure that all airline and airport fees and taxes are spent solely on financing aviation programs. Congress eventually passed an aviation reauthorization bill that allowed for roughly five departure and five arrival slots at Reagan National to be used for flights that exceed the 1,250-mile perimeter rule.

81. Indianapolis's airport is privately managed, Stewart Airport in Newburgh, New York, is being privatized, and New York City Mayor Rudolph Giuliani has issued a request for private operators who might want to manage, operate, and develop Kennedy and LaGuardia airports.

82. Matthew L. Wald, "Canada's Private Control Towers: Sale of Air Traffic System Has Led to Technical Advances," *New York Times*, October 23, 1999, p. C1.

A full treatment of airport privatization is beyond the scope of this paper, but the basic ideas can be sketched. Airports owned by separate companies would be forced to compete for traffic and free to develop their retail sector. Airports that would not be subject to competitive pressures from other airports should perhaps be owned and managed by their users, in the spirit of Nav Canada, to prevent them from setting monopoly takeoff and landing fees. In the longer run, airport competition could be enhanced if military airfields were converted to civil use. For example, Bergstrom Air Force Base (Austin, Texas), England AFB (Alexandria, Louisiana), Pease AFB (Portsmouth, New Hampshire), and Norton AFB (San Bernardino, California) are now operated as civil airports, and airfields such as Homestead AFB (Miami, Florida), El Toro Marine Station (Orange County, California), and Blackstone Army Air Field (Blackstone, Virginia) are potential candidates for conversion. In addition, terminals should probably be owned by separate companies to promote competitive access to gates. By making more efficient use of existing airport and airspace capacity and by taking full advantage of technology to expand capacity, private airports and air traffic control could facilitate more competition that would generate lower fares and better service.

In 1989 we wrote a paper arguing that the success of airline deregulation could be compromised if deregulation was not in accord with other public policies that affected the air transportation system.[83] It is gratifying that deregulation has continued to produce large benefits to travelers despite airport and air traffic control policies that promote inefficiencies. And it is gratifying that airlines continue to find ways to become more efficient.[84] But it is also disconcerting that deregulation's success has, in effect, enabled policymakers to continue to be more responsive to vested interests instead of improving the system by privatizing airports and air traffic control. When air transportation's efficiency becomes significantly compromised by its infrastructure, policymakers will find it in their interest to turn to the private sector.

---

83. Morrison and Winston (1989).

84. Most recently, carriers, such as United, have used futures markets to lock in long-term prices and blunt the impact of recent jumps in jet fuel prices. It is somewhat puzzling that carriers have not been able to reduce wages significantly, especially for pilots, since deregulation. Nonunion carriers could put pressure on wages, but such carriers have not had much of a presence in the airline industry.

References

Button, Kenneth, and Roger Stough. 1998. "The Benefits of Being a Hub Airport City." Working paper. George Mason University, Institute of Public Policy (November).

Carlton, Dennis W., and Gustavo E. Bamberger. 1998. Statement of September 24 before the Department of Transportation, Office of the Secretary, Washington, D.C.

Carlton, Dennis W., and Jeffrey M. Perloff. 1994. *Modern Industrial Organization,* 2d ed. Harper Collins.

Caves, Douglas W., Laurits R. Christensen, and Michael W. Tretheway. 1984. "Economies of Density versus Economies of Scale: Why Trunk and Local Service Airline Costs Differ." *Rand Journal of Economics* 15 (Winter): 471–89.

Caves, Douglas W., and others. 1987. "An Assessment of the Efficiency Effects of U.S. Airline Deregulation via an International Comparison." In *Public Regulation: New Perspectives on Institutions and Policies,* edited by Elizabeth E. Bailey. MIT Press.

Clark, Kent, and Eli Ofek. 1994. "Mergers as a Means of Restructuring Distressed Firms: An Empirical Investigation." *Journal of Financial and Quantitative Analysis* 29 (December): 541–65.

DeBondt, Werner F. M., and Howard E. Thompson. 1992. "Is Economic Efficiency the Driving Force behind Mergers?" *Managerial and Decision Economics* 13 (January-February): 31–44.

Fallick, Bruce C., and Kevin A. Hassett. 1996. "Unionization and Acquisitions." *Journal of Business* 69 (January): 51–73.

FAA/OST Task Force. 1999. *Airport Business Practices and Their Impact on Airline Competition.* U.S. Department of Transportation.

General Accounting Office. 1990. *Airline Competition: Higher Fares and Reduced Competition at Concentrated Airports.* GAO/RCED 90–102 (July).

Hurdle, Gloria J., and others. 1989. "Concentration, Potential Entry, and Performance in the Airline Industry." *Journal of Industrial Economics* 38 (December): 119–39.

Kim, E. Han, and Vijay Singal. 1993. "Mergers and Market Power: Evidence from the Airline Industry." *American Economic Review* 83 (June): 549–69.

Knapp, William. 1990. "Event Analysis of Air Carrier Mergers and Acquisitions." *Review of Economics and Statistics* 72 (November): 703–07.

Matsusaka, John G. 1993. "Target Profits and Managerial Discipline during the Conglomerate Merger Wave." *Journal of Industrial Economics* 41 (June): 179–89.

Melicher, Ronald W., Johannes Ledolter, and Louis J. D'Antonio. 1983. "A Time Series Analysis of Aggregate Merger Activity." *Review of Economics and Statistics* 65 (August): 423–30.

Morrison, Steven A. 1996. "Airline Mergers: A Longer View." *Journal of Transport Economics and Policy* 30 (September): 237–50.

Morrison, Steven A., and Clifford Winston. 1989. "Enhancing the Performance of the Deregulated Air Transportation System." *Brookings Papers on Economic Activity: Microeconomics:* 61–112.

———. 1995. *The Evolution of the Airline Industry.* Brookings.

———. 1996. "Causes and Consequences of Airline Fare Wars." *Brookings Papers on Economic Activity: Microeconomics:* 85–123.

————. 1997. "The Fare Skies: Air Transportation and Middle America." *Brookings Review* 15 (Fall): 42–45.

————. 1999. "Regulatory Reform of U.S. Intercity Transportation." In *Essays in Transportation Economics and Policy,* edited by José Gómez-Ibáñez, William B. Tye, and Clifford Winston. Brookings.

Ordover, Janusz A., and Robert D. Willig. 1998. Statement of July 23, attached as Appendix A of Comments by the Air Transport Association before the U.S. Department of Transportation.

Shrieves, Ronald E., and Donald L. Stevens. 1979. "Bankruptcy Avoidance as a Motive for Merger." *Journal of Financial and Quantitative Analysis* 14 (September): 501–15.

Werden, Gregory J., Andrew S. Joskow, and Richard L. Johnson. 1991. "The Effects of Mergers on Price and Output: Two Case Studies from the Airline Industry." *Managerial and Decision Economics* 12 (October): 341–52.

CURTIS GRIMM
CLIFFORD WINSTON

2 Competition in the Deregulated Railroad Industry: Sources, Effects, and Policy Issues

The railroad industry is perhaps the only U.S. industry that has been, or ever will be, deregulated be-
cause of its poor financial performance under regulation. At the end of
World War II, rail's share of the U.S. intercity surface freight market,
measured by ton-miles, stood at 65 percent. By the 1970s its market share
had declined to only 35 percent.[1] During this period a large fraction of the
nation's rail service was provided at an economic loss, with returns on
investment for most major railroads falling below the returns of other U.S.
nonfinancial corporations.[2]

In 1970 the nation's largest railroad, Penn Central, declared bankruptcy along with half a dozen other northeastern railroads. Following
Penn Central's collapse, several midwestern railroads, including the Rock
Island and Pacific, the Chicago, and the Milwaukee Road, fell into bankruptcy. Penn Central was effectively bailed out by the creation of Conrail,
a "public corporation," but one bailout was enough for policymakers.
Heeding arguments that regulation was inhibiting rail profitability and

The authors are grateful to Ronald Braeutigam, John Meyer, Sam Peltzman, and conference
participants for helpful comments and to Alise Upitis and Ming Zhou for research assistance.
1. Gallamore (1999, p. 493).
2. Keeler (1983).

that the industry needed much greater pricing and operating freedom to avoid more bankruptcies, Congress took steps to deregulate the railroads.[3] Partial deregulation began under the Railroad Revitalization and Regulatory Reform (4R) Act of 1976. The 1980 Staggers Act formally deregulated the industry.

By enabling railroads to improve their productivity and financial performance, deregulation was expected to get the industry back on its feet, but observers were less certain what its effects would be on shippers. Richard Levin's simulations suggested that rail's financial viability could be improved only at the expense of shippers' welfare.[4] But retaining extensive restrictions on rates seemed to defeat deregulation's goal of giving railroads more operating and pricing freedom, so policymakers compromised. The Staggers Act allowed railroads to negotiate individual and confidential contract rates with shippers for any commodity, a significant change from previous practice. Railroads were given new ratemaking freedom for "exempt" commodities, giving them flexibility to adjust their rates downward to compete more effectively with trucks for commodities such as produce and TOFC (commodities shipped in trailers that are put on flatcars). Rate flexibility for other traffic was also significantly increased.

But maximum rate "guidelines" were retained for certain shipments thought to be captive to rail, such as coal and chemicals. Although the guidelines were clear in one respect—shippers had to show that a rate exceeded 180 percent of variable costs to challenge a rate successfully—they were vague in other respects. Specifically, shippers also had to show that the railroad in question has no *effective* competition and that the rate was *unreasonable*. Notwithstanding these guidelines, policymakers were generally counting on the market, instead of regulation, to determine rates.

Policymakers' faith in the market has, for the most part, been rewarded. Nonetheless, tensions between some shippers and railroads run strong. Several policy proposals currently under debate seek to address perceived deficiencies in rail freight competition, but they are not based on credible evidence about competition in the industry—for that matter, neither are perspectives supporting the status quo.

3. Although many industry analysts reached this conclusion, it did not receive wide attention among policymakers until publication in November 1973 of the Task Force on Railroad Productivity, *Improving Railroad Productivity: Final Report*, Washington, D.C. (John R. Meyer was chairman of the task force, which made its report to the National Commission on Productivity and the Council of Economic Advisers.)

4. Levin (1981).

We seek to remedy this situation by first placing the captive shipper issue in the context of the rail industry's transformation since deregulation. We then develop a theoretical overview of how competition actually works in the railroad industry and use this framework to quantify the effects of rail and intermodal competition on rates and service quality. We then estimate the extent to which captive shippers pay higher rates and suffer degradations in service.

We find that increased rail and intermodal competition lowers shippers' rates in several ways, but it generally does not improve service times. Captive shippers do pay higher rates. The aggregate annual transfer to railroads is roughly $1.3 billion, but the associated deadweight loss is very small. Economic efficiency grounds thus offer little justification for proposals aimed at increasing rail competition. But we also conclude that the Surface Transportation Board (STB) cannot be counted on to mediate effectively the ongoing dispute between shippers and railroads. We recommend that rail rates be completely deregulated, that shippers and railroads be encouraged to agree to terms governing access that would resolve their differences, and that authority for approving railroad mergers be transferred to the U.S. Department of Justice to make it possible to eliminate the STB.

Rail Freight Deregulation and Captive Shippers

By increasing operating freedom and stimulating competition, deregulation spurred the railroad industry to transform itself by achieving a much better match between its huge physical plants and work forces on the one hand and available traffic on the other.[5] The industry abandoned roughly one-third of its track and reduced crew sizes; used contracts to align cars and equipment with shippers' demand and to reduce its vulnerability to problems caused by overcapacity; and expanded the use of intermodal operations, double-stack rail cars, and computer systems to provide faster, more reliable service. Real operating costs per ton-mile have fallen steadily, and, as of 1998, were 60 percent lower than when deregulation began (figure 2-1). Some of the cost decline can be attributed to the long-run trend in rail's traffic mix to include a greater proportion of low-cost bulk traffic, but deregulation's contribution is substantial.

5. Detailed summaries of the effects of deregulation on rail operations, productivity, and rates can be found in Gallamore (1999), Grimm and Windle (1998), and Morrison and Winston (1999).

Figure 2-1. *Railroad Operating Costs per Revenue Ton-Mile, 1980–98*

1998 dollars

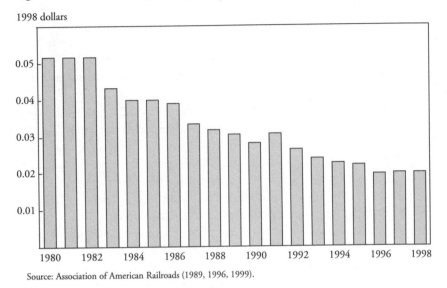

Source: Association of American Railroads (1989, 1996, 1999).

Cost reductions and productivity improvements stemmed the long-run erosion in market share. And rail traffic grew. After reaching a postwar low in the mid-1980s, originating rail carloads have grown from 19.5 million in 1985 to 25.7 million in 1998.[6] All of these factors have boosted profitability. During 1971–80, the industry's return on equity averaged less than 3 percent; during the 1990s the industry's return on equity has averaged 10.7 percent a year.[7]

But deregulation was not just a boon for the rail industry. Shippers benefited too. Based on the first decade of deregulation, one study found that the annual benefits to shippers from lower rates and improvements in service time and reliability amounted to at least $12 billion (1999 dollars).[8] And, as shown in table 2-1, shippers have generally continued to benefit from lower rail rates.[9] A major factor in deregulation's success has been the widespread use of contract rates.

6. Association of American Railroads (1999, p. 24).
7. General Accounting Office (1999a, pp. 40–41).
8. Winston and others (1990).
9. The figures in the table should be qualified because they are not counterfactual estimates that control for other influences on rail rates over time, such as increasing use by shippers of their own railcars.

Table 2-1. *Average Annual Change in Real Rail Rates for Selected Commodities, 1982–96*

Category	Average annual percentage change in rail rates	
	1982–89	*1990–96*
All commodities	−4.6	−4.1
Farm products	−6.7	−1.1
Metallic ores	−5.2	−5.2
Coal	−3.3	−7.9
Food and kindred products	−6.9	−3.7
Lumber and wood	−6.2	−4.0
Chemicals	−3.9	−2.4
Petroleum and coal products	−5.6	−3.0
Stone, clay, glass, and concrete	−5.5	−0.5
Transportation equipment	−2.4	−2.5
Intermodal	−5.8	−2.9

Source: General Accounting Office, (1999a, p. 48).

Despite this rare "win-win" outcome for consumers and industry, a recent railroad merger wave, dissatisfaction with government administration of maximum rate guidelines under the Staggers Act, and developments in deregulation of railroads abroad and in other U.S. network industries have triggered a debate about the appropriate direction of rail regulatory policy.

Like many deregulated industries, the rail industry has responded to its economic freedoms by consolidating operations through mergers, which have occurred in waves.[10] In the early 1980s, for example, Chessie System and Seaboard Coast Line formed CSX; Norfolk and Western and Southern Railroad formed Norfolk Southern; Missouri Pacific and Western Pacific became part of Union Pacific; and the St. Louis–San Francisco Railroad along with Colorado Southern and Fort Worth–Denver formed part of Burlington Northern. Generally, mergers have led to small cost reductions and some service improvements, although they may have reduced competition in some markets.[11]

The merger wave that began in the mid-1990s raised another problem. The Burlington Northern–Santa Fe and Union Pacific–Southern Pacific

10. Chaplin and Schmidt (1999) report that in the first six years following deregulation, the number of Class I rail carriers, the largest railroads in the country, dropped from thirty-six to sixteen.

11. Chaplin and Schmidt (1999); Berndt and others (1993).

mergers left only two major railroads in the western United States, while Conrail's recent absorption by Norfolk Southern and CSX left only two major railroads in the East. Moreover, Union Pacific's mismanagement of its merger with Southern Pacific and a surge in traffic led to widely publicized service disruptions. Some shippers also experienced poor service in the aftermath of the Conrail acquisition. The costly delays crystallized the problems that could arise when shippers must depend on only one railroad—a growing possibility as the industry consolidates. (Indeed, just as this paper was being completed, Burlington Northern and Canadian National Railway have proposed a merger, which, if approved, could touch off another round of mergers.)

The so-called captive shipper issue is not limited to service disruptions following mergers. Shippers, and various organizations that represent them, complain that rail rates are not always reasonable and that the Surface Transportation Board's rate complaint process is time-consuming, costly, and complex.[12] Because few shippers file complaints, which can cost from $500,000 to $3 million, few rates are found to be unreasonable. Nonetheless, the industry earns roughly 30 percent of its revenue under conditions that, if challenged, would require the board to determine in a rate case whether a railroad is market dominant.[13]

Policymakers in other network industries, such as telecommunications and electricity, and in railroad industries abroad are attempting to stimulate competition to address concerns that are similar to those of captive shippers. For example, the Telecommunications Act of 1996 requires incumbent local exchange carriers to enter into interconnection agreements with competitors to address structural monopoly at the loop level. Other countries are taking steps to separate ownership of the track from provision of service to

12. General Accounting Office (1999b). The Surface Transportation Board is the successor to the Interstate Commerce Commission and has the authority to determine the reasonableness of challenged rates in the absence of competition. After a shipper files a complaint, the board assesses whether the railroad has "market dominance." By statute, a railroad does not have market dominance if its revenue is no greater than 180 percent of its variable costs for transporting a shipper's commodities. If the railroad's percentage exceeds the statutory level, the board next determines whether the shipper has a competitive alternative in the form of access to other railroads or other forms of transportation, such as trucks or barges. Until January 1999, the board also considered two other forms of competition: the ability to ship from or to alternative locations (geographic competition) and the ability to substitute other products effectively for the one the railroad ships (product competition). If the board finds that a railroad dominates the shipper's market, then it proceeds with further assessments to determine whether the actual rate the railroad charges is reasonable. Under its standard guidelines, shippers are required to demonstrate how much an optimally efficient railroad would need to charge.

13. General Accounting Office (1999a, p. 62).

allow competitive private sector rail service to develop. These actions are prompting calls for domestic policymakers to take more forceful measures to ameliorate concerns about competition in the U.S. railroad industry.

A range of policy proposals are currently under debate. One proposal would radically restructure the industry, unbundling the rail system into primary terminals, secondary terminals, long-haul railroads, and collection-distribution railroads. Terminals would serve as interchange points for two or more railroads and would have a significant collection and distribution function. Current terminal owners, in most cases Class I railroads, would be forced to spin off these assets and allow independent operations to form but would continue to haul freight between primary terminals.[14]

Other proposals are less radical. One put forth by the Department of Transportation would give the Justice Department primary authority for approving rail mergers and would authorize the STB to approve more reciprocal switching where added competition would benefit the public interest. Another, the Railroad Shipper Protection Act, would require rail carriers, upon shipper request, to establish a rate between any two points on the carrier's system where traffic originates, terminates, or may be interchanged. The shipper would then be allowed to challenge the rate under maximum rate guidelines.[15]

In response, the railroads argue that although their financial situation has dramatically improved since deregulation, they do not come close to earning monopoly profits. According to the STB, railroads' return on investment still falls short of their cost of capital—a difference defined by the board as the degree of revenue inadequacy (table 2-2).[16] The railroads trumpet the gains from deregulation and the disappointing international experience with forced access as support for the status quo.[17] They claim

14. According to the Association of American Railroads (1999, p. 3), Class 1 railroads had operating revenue in 1998 of $259.4 million or more; Class II had revenues of $20.8 million to $259.4 million; and Class III had revenues of less than $20.8 million. Class 1 railroads accounted for only 2 percent of the number of railroads in the country but for 91 percent of the industry's freight revenue.

15. This proposal would overturn the STB's so-called "bottleneck decision" and allow shippers to obtain competitive rail service over major parts of their routes even if only one carrier provided service over short "bottleneck" portions of the routes.

16. Rail's large sunk costs complicate attempts to estimate the industry's financial health; thus the figures in this table should be viewed with caution. In addition, because recent mergers increased railroad stock prices and carriers' market-to-book ratios, the board's determination of revenue adequacy may understate the industry's financial health.

17. Documents supporting the rail industry's position include the American Association of Railroads, "Differential Pricing: Efficient and Necessary," undated, and Mercer Management Consulting, Inc., "Assessing the Track Record of Open Access," undated.

Table 2-2. *Revenue Adequacy of Class I Railroads, 1990–97*
Percent

Year	Return on investment	Cost of capital	Degree of revenue inadequacy
1990	8.1	11.8	−3.7
1991	1.3	11.6	−10.3
1992	6.3	11.4	−5.1
1993	7.1	11.4	−4.3
1994	9.4	12.2	−2.8
1995	6.9	11.7	−4.8
1996	9.4	11.9	−2.5
1997	7.6	11.8	−4.2

Source: General Accounting Office (1999a, p. 45). Return on investment is based on the Surface Transportation Board's methodology for determining revenue adequacy. These returns may not be the same as returns on investment calculated for nonregulatory purposes.

that proposed policies to address the captive shipper issue would be counterproductive and characterize differential pricing as efficient and necessary; without it, they claim, the size and quality of the nation's rail network would have to shrink because carriers would have no plausible way to cover their fixed (and total) costs.

Sources of Railroad Competition

These conflicting policy perspectives stem from railroads' and shippers' differing views on whether the current sources of railroad competition are sufficient to enable shippers to obtain reasonable rates. Railroads compete with each other and with other transportation modes, such as trucks, barges, and pipelines. The relative costs of truck and rail in a specific market depend primarily on the commodity being shipped and the length of haul. Rail has a comparative cost advantage for long-distance movements of bulk commodities, but its slower speed puts it at a service disadvantage. Where navigable waterways exist, rail faces stiff competition from water transportation for bulk commodities. Rail competes with pipelines primarily in the transport of petroleum.

The sources of rail intramodal competition are more complex and best explained with a series of diagrams. Figure 2-2 presents three ways railroads could compete for a shipper's traffic in a given market. A shipper at industrial

Figure 2-2. *Competition Provided by Direct Railroad Service,*
Reciprocal Switching, and Terminal Switching

a. Shipper has direct service from two railroads

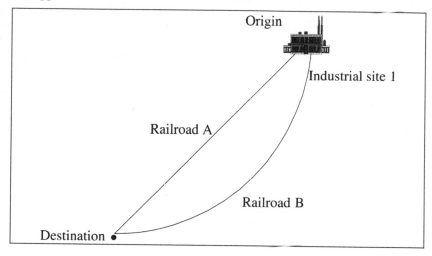

b. Shipper has competitive service from two railroads via reciprocal shipping

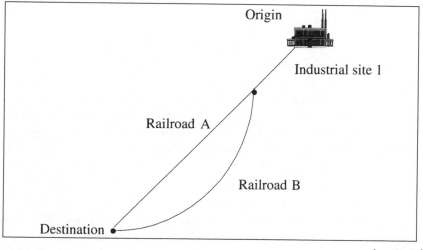

(continued)

Figure 2-2. *(continued)*

c. Shipper has competitive rail service from two railroads via a terminal switching railroad

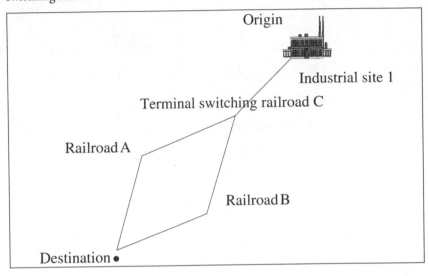

site 1 could receive *direct* service from Railroad A or Railroad B if both railroads' tracks traverse directly into the plant (figure 2-2a). Competition could also arise if the shipper can access Railroad A and B by *reciprocal switching*. In our example, the plant is served directly by Railroad A, which has a nearby junction with Railroad B (figure 2-2b). The two railroads have agreed that Railroad A will switch cars from industrial site 1 to the junction with Railroad B and enable the shipper to choose either railroad for the line-haul movement. (The agreement is reciprocal when the configuration is reversed for other shippers and Railroad B agrees to switch cars for Railroad A.) Finally, Railroad A and B could compete through a *terminal switching* railroad that they jointly own and that switches cars to its junction with either railroad (figure 2-2c). Terminal switching railroads provide a strong degree of competition between connecting Class I railroads because they operate independently of any carrier. They are found in many urban areas. The Indiana Harbor Belt Railroad Company, for example, serves South Chicago and Gary-Hammond, Indiana, and "provides fast, dependable intermediate service to and from all trunk lines operating in Chicago."[18]

18. *The Official Railway Guide* (1999, p. C116).

These forms of railroad competition are thought to be the most intense, but shippers captive to one railroad can also benefit from indirect competition supplied by a nearby carrier. Four examples are shown in figure 2-3. Industrial site 1 is now served only by Railroad B, but Railroad A is located in the vicinity. The shipper could ship its traffic to Railroad A by truck, or locate a new facility on or build a spur line to Railroad A's line (figure 2-3a).[19] All of these actions could be used as bargaining chips to obtain a lower rate from Railroad B or to get Railroad A to commit to a reduced rate. A shipper could also have captive plants located on both railroads (industrial site 2A is captive to Railroad A and industrial site 2B is captive to Railroad B), but the two plants' production levels would be determined in part by rail rates charged to each plant (figure 2-3b). This could generate competition between Railroad A and Railroad B. These carriers could also be induced to compete if two shippers (industrial sites 3 and 4) were each served by one railroad and competed in the same product market (figure 2-3c). If one carrier raised its rates, it could cause the shipper to lose sales and ship less traffic with that carrier. Finally, a shipper could be contemplating a choice between locating at industrial site 5 or 6. Railroads A and B could be induced to compete for the shipper's traffic by offering (reduced) long-term contract rates to attract the shipper to locate on its line (figure 2-3d).

Shippers could also stimulate railroad competition in some cases through product or geographic competition. For example, an industrial site served only by Railroad A in a given market may be able to use a substitute product shipped from a different origin by Railroad B, or the site could obtain the same product from an alternative origin served by Railroad B. Figure 2-4 illustrates a situation where industrial site 7 is an electric utility captive to Railroad A in the origin 1 market, but the utility can substitute coal from origin 2 and enable Railroad B to compete for a portion of the linehaul.

The Effects of Competition on Rail Rates and Service Quality

We have described how shippers that are served by just one railroad can, in theory, benefit from the alternative ways that railroads are forced

---

19. If the shipper tried to use Railroad B for the shorthaul, the STB might be needed to limit the rate charged by Railroad B.

Figure 2-3. *Competition Provided by Nearby Carriers*
a. Shipper has physical access to only one railroad but is in proximity to the other

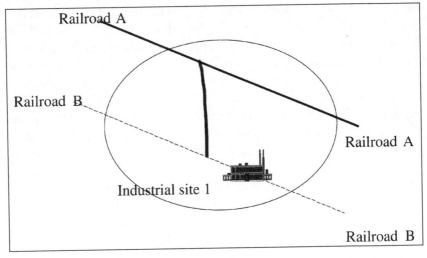

b. Shipper has captive plants on both railroads A and B

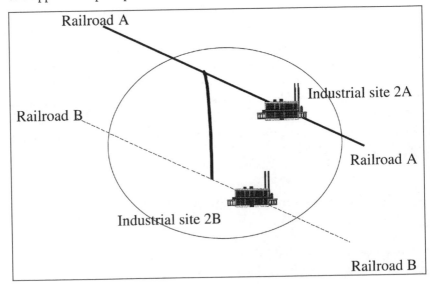

Figure 2-3. *(continued)*

c. Shippers served by different railroads competing in the same product market

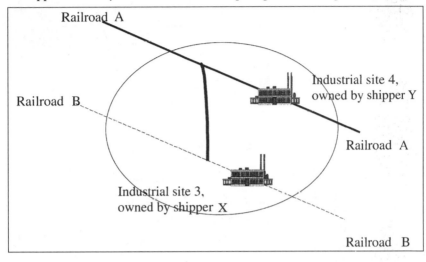

d. Shipper benefits from ex ante site location competition

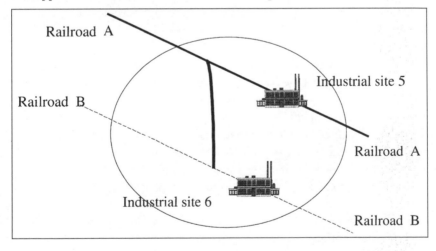

Figure 2-4. *Geographic Competition*

Receiver is served by only one railroad but can draw on alternative origins
served by alternative railroads

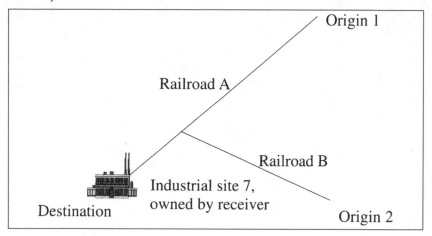

to compete. But what impact, in practice, do these competitive forces have
on rail rates? To address this question, we estimate a model that measures
the impact of railroad and intermodal competition and shipper and shipment characteristics on freight charges.[20]

The measures of competition we include are the number of railroads
serving a shipper directly, by reciprocal switching or by terminal switching. The effect of competition from railroads not serving the origin is
captured by the shipper's distance from another carrier. Geographic competition is specified as the number of different railroads from different
origins that could serve the receiver. Intermodal competition from truck
or water modes is indicated by their share of a shipper's freight.[21] It is
expected that greater rail or intermodal competition will lower freight
charges.

The characteristics of shippers that could influence freight charges
include whether their traffic is shipped under contract rates and whether

---

20. Models of the determinants of rail freight rates have been used to analyze a variety of policy-related issues in rail transportation. The model presented here draws on and extends the specification
developed in Grimm, Winston, and Evans (1992). Other studies of the impact of rail competition on
freight rates include Grimm (1985) and MacDonald (1987, 1989).

21. We specified a dummy variable for petroleum products to capture the effect of pipeline
competition, but it was insignificant.

they use their own rail cars. Relevant shipment characteristics include annual traffic volume, length of haul, and commodities that require special handling or rail cars. It is expected that shippers will pay lower freight charges if they negotiate contract rates and use their own rail cars, and pay higher charges for larger traffic volumes, longer lengths of haul, and commodities that are more costly to ship.

Policy debates and academic research on the rail industry have been hampered by a lack of publicly available data about rail shipping activity and rail competition. Accessible data, such as the Transportation Department's "waybill" sample, do not have complete and accurate information about contract rates and do not include shipper characteristics. Data on rail competition are also inadequate. Publicly available information indicates only whether a shipper is directly served by a particular railroad; other sources of rail competition cannot be determined. Thus, we conducted our own survey of rail shippers to collect information about their freight charges, shipping and shipment characteristics, and rail and intermodal competitive situations (as described above) for specific shipping corridors during 1998.[22] Shippers also reported their total freight volumes shipped and received on all corridors.

The final sample, summarized in table 2-3, consists of a range of bulk and manufactured commodities. The sample and population commodity shares and shipper and shipment characteristics are broadly consistent, indicating that the sample is representative.[23] Most rates are determined by contracts, which benefit shippers because these rates are lower than tariff rates. Contracts benefit carriers because shippers guarantee freight volumes (or lose their discount) and, in some cases, provide return loads from the destination. Moreover, contracts "lock in" a shipper's business for roughly two-and-a-half years, on average. (According to our sample, some contracts last as long as ten years.) Thus contracts force a railroad to compete fiercely for a shipper's business because years may pass before a railroad that has lost traffic contracted to another railroad can compete for the business again. Finally, 36 percent of the traffic in our sample is shipped under

22. The surveys were sent to shippers who are members of the National Industrial Traffic League, Edison Electric Institute, and Alliance for Rail Competition. We are grateful to these organizations for sending our survey to their members. Shippers provided this information for their top shipping corridors, based on carloads, in 1998. Depending on the shipper's activity, data were provided for as few as one corridor or as many as ten.

23. Our sample does not include shipments of motor vehicles and equipment and farm products, but it is not clear how this omission would affect our findings.

Table 2-3. *Summary of the Sample*

Variable	Sample	Population estimate
Percent of traffic under contract	84 percent	>70 percent[a]
Average duration of contracts	2.4 years	. . .
Average length of haul	814 miles	835 miles[b]
Traffic for which revenue divided		
by variable cost exceeds 180 percent[c]	36 percent	29–34 percent,
		during 1990–96[a]
Carloads originated by commodity[d]		
Coal	24 percent	27 percent[b]
Chemicals or allied products	9 percent	6.5 percent[b]
Food or kindred products	7 percent	5 percent[b]
Number of observations = 210		

Source: Authors' calculations.

a. Based on estimates reported in General Accounting Office (1999a).

b. Association of American Railroads (1999).

c. Estimates of variable costs for corridor movements in our sample were provided by L. E. Peabody & Associates, Alexandria, Va.

d. Other commodities included in the sample are metallic ores; nonmetalic minerals; lumber or wood products; pulp, paper, and allied products; printed matter; clay, concrete, glass, or stone products; primary metal products; waste or scrap materials; and shipping containers.

conditions that would require the STB to determine in a rate hearing whether a railroad is market dominant and whether a shipper is entitled to rate relief.

One might be concerned that 1998 was an atypical year for the rail industry because shippers were still experiencing service disruptions in the aftermath of the Union Pacific–Southern Pacific merger. We therefore test whether these disruptions have affected our findings.

Estimation Results

Our dependent variable is a shipper's annual freight charges on a given corridor.[24] It is reasonable to treat rail competition and most shipper and shipment characteristics as exogenous, but a shipper's volume of rail traffic is likely to depend on rail freight charges and therefore be endogenous.

24. We also estimated models that transformed this dependent variable into freight charges per carload, per car-mile, per ton, and per ton-mile, but these produced less precise parameter estimates and greatly reduced the regression's statistical fit.

Thus instrumental variables were used to estimate the effect of annual carloads on freight charges.[25] Parameter estimates for the complete model are presented in table 2-4.

Shipper and shipment characteristics have plausible and statistically reliable effects. Freight charges rise as shipping distances increase, but at a decreasing rate, which reflects economies from longer lengths of haul. Charges also rise for larger freight volumes but increase much less for traffic shipped under contract rates. Finally, the higher costs from specialized handling and lower shipper demand elasticities associated with transporting coal and chemicals lead to higher charges.[26]

The estimates substantiate the theoretical arguments that several forms of railroad and intermodal competition affect rail charges. An additional carrier that serves the origin either directly or by reciprocal switching lowers annual freight charges nearly $200,000, or 8 percent of average charges.[27] An additional terminal carrier lowers average charges nearly 25 percent. As suggested previously, terminal carriers are a strong source of competition because they facilitate competition among Class I carriers while maintaining independent operations.

Even if a given railroad does not serve a shipper's origin, a shipper's rates are affected by its proximity to the railroad. Our estimates indicate that a shipper located 50 miles from another railroad will pay roughly $400,000 (50 × $8,375) less in annual freight charges than a shipper

---

25. The instruments we used are a shipper's total freight volume shipped on all corridors, a shipper's total freight volume received on all corridors, and average shipment size. These variables had statistically insignificant effects on corridor-specific freight charges. Using a Hausman specification test that compared the least squares and instrumental variable parameter estimates, we rejected the exogeneity of annual carloads.

26. In addition to these shipper and shipment characteristics, we estimated models that included other commodity dummies, fixed firm effects, and regional dummies (a regional dummy was particularly specified to identify traffic originating or terminating in the Southwest to capture the effect of the Union Pacific service disruptions), but they were statistically insignificant and did not have much effect on the parameter estimates and standard errors of the shipper and shipping characteristics that were included. We also included a dummy variable that indicated whether a shipper owned its rail cars, but that too was insignificant. Rail car ownership could have an effect on shippers' freight charges for all their traffic, but apparently it does not influence charges on a specific corridor. Alternatively, this effect could be picked up by the contract rate dummy.

27. The effects of railroads serving the origin either directly or by reciprocal switching were not statistically significantly different. We also found that the number of carriers serving the destination directly or by reciprocal or terminal switching had a statistically insignificant effect on freight charges. Finally, we found that the effects of railroad or intermodal competition on freight charges were not affected by whether shippers' rates were based on contracts.

Table 2-4. *Parameter Estimates for Shipper's Annual Freight Charges on the Corridor*[a]

Independent variable	Coefficient (Standard error)
Constant	−1,964,800
	(900,518)
Length of haul (miles)	3,921.50
	(1,001.37)
Length of haul squared	−1.11
	(0.3363)
Annual carloads (defined for corridor movements not shipped under contract rates)	4,479.39
	(1,889.58)
Annual carloads (defined for corridor movements shipped under contract rates)	533.17
	(215.18)
Coal commodity dummy (1 if shipper's freight consists of coal, 0 otherwise)	3,634,890
	(1,533,340)
Chemical commodity dummy (1 if shipper's freight consists of chemicals, 0 otherwise)	807,862
	(319,839)
Number of railroads serving the origin directly or by reciprocal switching	−181,747
	(112,776)
Number of railroads serving the origin by terminal switching	−585,728
	(284,056)
Distance to nearest railroad not serving the origin (miles)	8,375.21
	(4,148.59)
Dummy variable for receivers who could be served by alternative railroads from alternative origins (1 if receiver could be served by two or more railroads, 0 otherwise)	−617,103
	(298,973)
Dummy variable for truck competition (1 if truck transports at least 20 percent of the shipper's freight in the corridor, 0 otherwise)	−450,262
	(303,912)
Dummy variable for water competition (1 if a water mode transports at least 20 percent of the shipper's freight in the corridor, 0 otherwise)	−2,035,530
	(424,209)
Summary statistics	
Number of observations	210
R^2	0.75

Source: Authors' calculations. See text for explanation. Standard errors are heteroskedastic consistent.
a. Mean of dependent variable = $2.5 million in 1998 dollars.

located 100 miles from another railroad.[28] Geographic competition also has a large impact on rates. Receivers who can be served by two or more railroads from different origins enjoy a 25 percent rate reduction from average charges. Finally, intermodal competition from truck and water modes strongly disciplines rail rates. Shippers' rail charges fall dramatically if they use water transportation for some of their traffic.[29]

Service Quality

Good service matters to shippers as much as low rates.[30] Although service quality is a somewhat amorphous concept in freight transportation, it generally includes service time and service time reliability, loss and damage, special handling and storage, and availability of railcars. Data for many of these items are difficult to obtain, but RAILINC, a company in Cary, North Carolina, provides average service times and the standard deviation of service times, a common measure of reliability.[31] We were therefore able to investigate how railroad and intermodal competition affect two of the most important aspects of service quality.

RAILINC's service times are for 6-digit Standard Place Location Codes (SPLCs), which identify the railroad stations at a corridor's origin and destination. When we tried to match our sample of 6-digit SPLCs to the SPLCs included in RAILINC's data, we lost a large fraction of observations, so we used the 4-digit, or county level, codes to obtain matches.

28. One should obviously be cautious when trying to draw conclusions from linear extrapolations using the coefficient for distance to the nearest railroad. We explored several nonlinear specifications of this variable, but they were statistically less reliable than the linear specification used here.

29. The dummy variables we use to measure intermodal competition are intended to capture the viability of alternative modes. Shippers may have the option, in theory, to use truck or water transport for their corridor traffic, but the length of haul or type of commodity may prevent shippers from actually using these modes. We obtained the best statistical fits using a 20 percent market share as an indicator that truck or water was a viable option. We obtained a far less reliable estimate for the effect of water transport on freight charges when we used a dummy variable that indicated whether a water mode was an option for any part of the movement in the corridor. We tested for and did not reject the exogeneity of the intermodal competition dummies. In addition to the instruments used previously, commodity dummies for all the commodities in the sample were included as instruments. Finally, we found that the effects of the intermodal competition dummies did not differ in accordance with the extent of rail competition in a corridor.

30. Small and Winston (1999).

31. Railroads forward a sample of their service times to RAILINC to analyze and store. We obtained from RAILINC average and standard deviations of service times in 1998 for a portion of the origins and destinations in our sample. We are grateful to RAILINC for their assistance with the data and to Burlington Northern, Union Pacific, CSX, and Norfolk Southern railroads for giving us approval to acquire these data.

We then estimated the average mean and standard deviation of service time for stations within the origin and destination counties.[32]

As with freight charges, we postulate that the average and standard deviation of service time are affected by rail and intermodal competition and shipper and shipment characteristics. The effect of rail competition on service times, however, could differ from its effect on freight charges. As suggested by Harris and Winston, an increase in rail carriers in a market could either spur carriers to provide faster, more reliable service or cause congestion and delays that reduce service time and reliability.[33] Service disruptions that could raise the average and standard deviation of service time were still being reported in the Southwest during 1998; thus, we interacted a corridor's length of haul with a dummy variable that indicated whether the traffic was originating or terminating in Arizona, New Mexico, Texas, Oklahoma, or Louisiana.

The specifications we were able to fit for the average and standard deviation of rail service time generally indicated that shippers receive better service through contracts, but that increased railroad competition actually reduces service. The parameter estimates for the average service time are presented in table 2-5.[34] As expected, a longer haul raises average service time, but this effect is greater for shippers whose traffic originates or terminates in the Southwest. Shippers who negotiate contracts receive faster service by increasing their carloads and average shipment sizes.[35] Even shippers who do not negotiate contracts receive faster service by increasing their shipment sizes because larger shipments enable a railroad to run single unit trains that are not delayed by consolidating traffic from other shippers. Average service time rises as the number of railroads serving the corridor increases and for receivers who could be served by alternative railroads from alternative origins.[36] Apparently, the delays caused either by

32. The means and standard deviations for each station within a county were weighted by carloads. The final estimates for each origin-destination pair of counties were based on at least ten separate movements. We found that results were not affected when we restricted the sample to means and standard deviations based on twenty-five separate movements. Use of the service time data reduced our original sample size from 210 to 116 observations, but there did not appear to be any systematic reason that could affect our findings why service times were not reported or sparsely available for some SPLCs.

33. Harris and Winston (1983).

34. We did not obtain any efficiency gains from jointly estimating the average service time with the standard deviation of service time to account for contemporaneously correlated errors. Maddala (1977) points out that negligible gains can occur if the source of the correlation is common omitted variables.

35. We tested for but did not reject the exogeneity of carloads in this model.

36. In this model we obtained the most reliable estimates when we specified the total number of carriers serving the corridor, not just the number serving the origin or destination.

Table 2-5. *Parameter Estimates for Average Railroad Service Time in Corridor (Days)*[a]

Independent variable	Coefficient (Standard error)
Constant	7.4781
	(0.9589)
Length of haul (measured in miles and defined if corridor origin or destination is located in Arizona, New Mexico, Texas, Oklahoma, or Louisiana)	0.00620 (0.0009)
Length of haul (measured in miles and defined if corridor origin or destination is *not* located in Arizona, New Mexico, Texas, Oklahoma, or Louisiana)	0.00425 (0.0008)
Annual carloads (defined for corridor movements shipped under contract)	−0.00013 (0.00005)
Average shipment size (measured in carloads and defined for corridor movements shipped under contract)	−0.0529 (0.0104)
Average shipment size (measured in carloads and defined for corridor movements not shipped under contract)	−0.2887 (0.1464)
Number of railroads serving the corridor	0.26053 (0.1280)
Dummy variable for receivers who could be served by alternative railroads from alternative origins (1 if receiver could be served by 2 or more railroads, 0 otherwise)	2.0827 (1.0511)
Summary statistics	
Number of observations	116
R^2	0.52

Source: Authors' calculations. See text for explanation. Standard errors are heteroskedastic consistent.
a. Mean of dependent variable = 11.5 days.

congestion enroute or by having to transfer cars to another railroad outweigh any competitive pressure to provide faster service.[37] Indeed, the

37. It is possible that our finding captured the effect of the number of routings in a market instead of the effect of rail competition. But we found that the number of routings in a market had a statistically insignificant effect on average service time and did not affect the other parameter estimates. We also investigated the effect of aggregation on our findings by estimating a model based on average service times for markets defined by six-digit SPLCs. Although this model reduced the number of observations in our sample to seventy and led to less precise parameter estimates, additional railroad competition still increased average service times. Finally, the service time data used here are based on railroad movements, not

problems of traffic interchange between railroads have attracted the attention of the popular press.[38]

The parameter estimates for the standard deviation of service time (table 2-6) are broadly consistent with those for average service time. Shipments destined to or from the Southwest experience greater unreliability as their distance grows. (Distance had a statistically insignificant effect on the reliability of shipments in other parts of the country.) Shippers who negotiate contracts receive more reliable service by increasing their carloads and average shipment sizes, but additional rail competition, specifically at the destination, reduces reliability. Although intermodal competition does not affect the average service time, shippers who use water transportation tend to get more reliable rail service.

Captive Shippers

Various forms of rail and intermodal competition help shippers lower their freight charges. But what about shippers that have very limited competitive options? Do these so-called captive shippers pay inflated rates and receive inferior service? Are these costs eroding the benefits to shippers, in general, from deregulation, thereby motivating policymakers to take corrective action?

Although there is no agreed-upon definition, it is reasonable, based on our analysis, to characterize a captive shipper as one that

— is served by only one railroad, with the only alternative railroad more than 50 miles away,
— is unable to use water transportation and does not use truck, and
— has no alternative locations that competing railroads could use to serve the receiver.

---

intermodal movements involving truck and rail. It is possible that the effect of railroad competition on service time could be different for intermodal rail traffic; thus, we estimated a model using average service times based on this traffic, but it fit our data, which were generated for rail traffic, very poorly.

38. Don Phillips, "Alliance to Forge U.S.-Canada Rail System," *Washington Post*, December 21, 1999, p. A1, points out that "one of the dumbfounding long-term problems with railroading is that companies can't seem to hand off a rail car from one railroad to another without delaying it 24 hours or more." An editorial in the *Journal of Commerce* of September 28, 1999, states that "poor coordination is still a major reason for poor customer service. . . . Railroads have been trying to enhance computer links to improve inter-line management, but that process has been slow and is only now moving forward effectively." Presumably, if railroad coordination were improved, the negative effects of additional competitors on service could be reduced or eliminated.

Table 2-6. *Parameter Estimates for Standard Deviation*
of Railroad Service Time in Corridor (Days)[a]

Independent variable	Coefficient (Standard error)
Constant	3.7320
	(0.3461)
Length of haul (measured in miles and defined if corridor origin or destination is located in Arizona, New Mexico, Texas, Oklahoma, or Louisiana)	0.00114
	(0.00036)
Annual carloads (defined for corridor movements shipped under contract)	−0.000036
	(0.00002)
Average shipment size (measured in carloads and defined for corridor movements shipped under contract)	−0.0154
	(0.0043)
Number of railroads serving the destination	0.1859
	(0.0988)
Dummy variable for water competition (1 if a water mode transports at least 20 percent of the shipper's freight in the corridor, 0 otherwise)	−2.6752
	(0.4687)
Summary statistics	
Number of observations	116
R^2	0.24

Source: Authors' calculations. See text for explanation. Standard errors are heteroskedastic consistent.
a. Mean of dependent variable = 4.2 days.

Given this definition, we constructed a dummy variable equal to one for corridor traffic that is shipped under captive conditions, zero otherwise.[39] As shown in table 2-7, roughly 20 percent of the traffic in our sample is captive, which is a plausible estimate.[40] In addition, most of it is shipped under contract. The bulk of the captive traffic is coal, nonmetallic minerals, or chemicals, originating in mountain or southeastern states and generally shipped less than 1,000 miles. Of course, a lot of coal, for example, is not

39. To be sure, a shipper who is served by only one railroad may be captive even if another carrier is closer than 50 miles away. Conversely, a shipper may not be currently using truck, but could, in theory. Any measurement error that arises here is unlikely to be systematic.

40. Recall, 36 percent of the traffic in our sample was shipped under conditions—namely, the ratio of revenue to variable cost exceeded 180 percent—that would require the STB in a rate hearing to investigate whether a railroad was market dominant. As noted, the board would then investigate the shipper's other railroad and modal options before rendering a decision on market dominance. It is plausible that if 36 percent of the traffic warranted an investigation of market dominance, then somewhat more than half, say, 20 percent, would, in fact, be captive.

Table 2-7. *Summary Statistics for Captive Shippers,*
Based on Freight Revenue

Item	Percent
Captive traffic	19.6
Captive traffic shipped under contract	94
Captive traffic by origin	
Captive traffic originating in mountain states	44
(Colorado, Montana, Wyoming)	
Captive traffic originating in southeastern states	39
(Florida, Kentucky, West Virginia)	
Captive traffic by destination	
Captive traffic terminating in mountain states	28
(Colorado, Idaho)	
Captive traffic terminating in the midwest	28
(Iowa, Michigan, Wisconsin)	
Captive traffic by commodity	
Coal	44
Nonmetallic minerals	22
Chemicals or allied products	11
Captive traffic by length of haul	
Less than 200 miles	44
Between 200 and 1,000 miles	39

Source: Authors' calculations. See text for explanation.

captive and is shipped long distances. (The average length of haul for non-captive coal shippers in our sample is 781 miles.) Finally, more than half of the captive traffic terminates in mountain or midwestern states.

One may wonder why some shippers are captive. Is the industry's consolidation since deregulation to blame? The answer to that is difficult to determine, given that several conditions characterize captivity, but mergers are unlikely to be a major explanation because most mergers have been end to end, rather than parallel, and therefore have not eliminated a direct competitor.[41]

41. In addition, conditions have often been attached to mergers that would eliminate a competitor that gives an alternative railroad access to potentially captive shippers. At the same time, shippers served by a railroad that merged with a partner nearby have generally not received competitive relief through any conditions; thus, mergers such as Union Pacific–Southern Pacific have potentially created more captive shippers.

The captive shipper dummy controls for the difference in competitive conditions facing captive and noncaptive shippers. We estimate the extent to which captive shippers pay higher rates than noncaptive shippers by replacing the railroad and intermodal competition variables in our model of freight charges with this dummy. We also specify the dependent variable as the logarithm of freight charges to facilitate interpretation of the results. Shipper and shipment characteristics are specified as before. As in the model for freight charges, these variables have plausible effects. The estimate of the captive shipper dummy is 0.19 and statistically significant, which means that, all else constant, captive shippers pay freight charges that are 20.9 percent higher than those paid by noncaptive shippers.[42]

We investigated whether captive shippers receive worse service than noncaptive shippers by replacing the competition variables in the average and standard deviation of service time models with the captive shipper dummy. In contrast to our finding for freight charges, the parameter estimate for the dummy is statistically insignificant in both models, which indicates that captive traffic does not experience greater unreliability or take longer to get to its destination than noncaptive traffic.[43]

The annual aggregate loss to captive shippers from elevated rates is $1.32 billion in 1998 dollars. (The estimate is obtained by multiplying the elevation in rates, 20.9 percent, by industry freight revenues in 1998, $32.25 billion, and multiplying this by 19.6 percent to account for the share of traffic that is captive.)[44] The annual deadweight loss associated with this transfer from captive shippers to railroads is only about $60 million, which is consistent with the view that exchange governed by contracts is generally efficient.[45]

---

42. Given that the dependent variable is the logarithm of freight charges, the percentage effect of the captive shipper dummy is $100 \times [\exp(0.19) - 1]$.

43. Although our service times were corridor specific, not shipper specific, shippers that are defined as captive within a given corridor would not likely receive substantially different service.

44. Revenue figures come from Association of American Railroads (1999).

45. A partial equilibrium approximation for the deadweight loss associated with the transfer is $\frac{1}{2} TR \cdot \varepsilon \cdot r^2$, where TR is captive shipper revenue, $6.32 billion, ε is the demand elasticity for rail, and r^2 is the markup squared, 0.04. Winston and others (1990, p. 24) estimate that rail's demand elasticity for coal movements is -0.33, and Friedlaender and Spady (1981, p. 55) estimate that rail's demand elasticity for mineral and chemical movements ranges from -0.37 to -0.59. Given that coal, minerals, and chemicals represent the bulk of the commodities that are captive, a reasonable estimate of rail's demand elasticity is -0.5. Substituting these figures into the welfare loss approximation yields $63 million. Of course, the deadweight loss would be larger if we used the markup over marginal cost as a benchmark instead of the markup over noncaptive shippers' rates. Winston and others (1990) estimate that shippers would gain several billion dollars if rail rates were equal to marginal cost. On the other hand, marginal cost prices would move the rail industry substantially (some might say hopelessly) further from revenue adequacy.

Such a small deadweight loss indicates there is little justification on economic efficiency grounds for proposals to address the captive shipper issue. Deregulation's annual benefits to shippers, in general, are largely intact because the loss to captive shippers amounts to roughly 10 percent of these benefits. The theory of railroad competition described earlier appears to explain why the loss is small. In particular, alternative sources of competition in freight markets limit the share of traffic that is truly captive, and even shippers who are captive in a particular market may have some leverage in rate negotiations through plant location competition and product competition (for example, where a coal company that faces exorbitant rail rates may lose business to natural gas companies and to coal companies in different parts of the country that pay lower rail rates, the railroad that carries that coal will also lose business, which may encourage it to lower its own rates).

As in most policy debates, distributional issues are at the heart of whether federal implementation of the Staggers Act has struck the proper balance between achieving financial health for railroads and protecting and promoting competitive options for shippers. Given the size of the transfer from captive shippers to railroads, the industry overstates the financial harm that would result from efforts to reverse the transfer through increased intramodal competition.[46] Although captive shippers have not advanced an estimate of their aggregate loss, the magnitude of our estimate explains why they press for greater competition.

A Course of Action

Railroad deregulation has generally been very good for both railroads and shippers, but it has been marred by an ongoing dispute between captive shippers that claim they pay excessive charges to monopoly railroads and railroads that counter that they do not earn competitive profits, let alone monopoly profits. Our estimates indicate that the deadweight loss from captive shippers' higher rates is small. But given that so few rates are successfully challenged, it would be difficult to claim that the Surface Transportation Board is preserving efficiency. From a distributional per-

46. In a response to the administration's proposed legislation reauthorizing the STB, Edward R. Hamburger, the president and chief executive officer of the Association of American Railroads, stated on October 19, 1999, that his organization estimated that the industry could lose as much as $2.4 billion a year if mandatory reciprocal switching (a policy designed to compensate captive shippers) were implemented. Our findings suggest that an appropriate transfer would be half that amount.

spective the STB does not appear to be protecting shippers' interests because captive shippers clearly pay higher rates than noncaptive shippers and the expected value of a rate complaint is probably negative.[47]

One may be tempted to confine the policy implications of our findings to either supporting the status quo, on efficiency grounds, or supporting measures within the STB-Staggers framework to increase rail competition, on distributional grounds. Policymakers, however, could do a better job of resolving distributional disputes, while also promoting efficiency, by setting their sights beyond these options and eliminating the STB, completely deregulating rail rates, and instituting market-based mechanisms to address the captive shipper issue.

Neither shippers nor railroads are likely to rush to embrace our proposal. Shippers, despite their perceptions of the board, will be apprehensive about additional rate increases with no recourse for complaints, and railroads will be reluctant to agree to even modest increases in competition. But there are reasons why our approach would serve both of their interests.

Deregulation has largely succeeded because railroads and shippers have, for the most part, achieved a contract equilibrium.[48] We recommend that policymakers pass legislation to prod shippers and railroads to extend their contractual equilibrium by negotiating an end to the STB and residual rate regulation. Elimination of the board would allow railroads to reduce administrative and lobbying costs and perhaps raise rates in some markets. In turn, the industry could offer shippers some recourse for reducing rates, such as identifying specific competitive situations where carriers would be given access to other carriers' track. By doing so, railroads would no longer be vulnerable to antitrust action in their monopoly markets in a post-STB world. And, although the board or Congress has yet to institute policies that have hurt the rail industry, the captive shipper issue could lead to new regulations that undermine industry performance. Eliminating the STB and resolving the captive shipper issue would substantially lessen this possibility.

Freed from the board's oversight, limited as it may be, railroads could focus completely on improving the efficiency of their operations, and shippers would not be frustrated by an agency that seems oblivious to their

47. In our sample, average annual freight charges to noncaptive shippers in a corridor are roughly $2.3 million. Thus the average annual rate increase to captive shippers in a corridor for a comparable volume of freight approaches $500,000. As noted earlier, the cost of a rate complaint runs from $500,000 to $3 million. Even if one accounts for the ongoing benefits of a successful challenge, the low likelihood of success probably yields a negative expected value from pursuing a complaint.

48. Meyer and Tye (1988).

concerns. Moreover, shippers and railroads could extend the benefits they have already achieved through contractual negotiations by achieving additional logistics efficiencies as partners, instead of quibbling over the distribution of an ever-shrinking pie as adversaries. Acrimonious relations between shippers and railroads have greatly inhibited the type of mutually beneficial just-in-time inventory collaborations that routinely occur between shippers and trucking firms.

There are precedents for shippers and rail carriers resolving competitive disputes. In recent mergers, railroads have identified and reached agreement with captive shippers that gave those shippers access to an alternative carrier. In western mergers access was provided by trackage rights; in the East a new terminal switching railroad provided formerly captive Conrail customers with competitive service between Norfolk Southern and CSX.

Obtaining STB approval of their proposed mergers gave railroads the incentive to identify and solve captive shipper problems. We have identified additional incentives that railroads have to solve this problem in general. And the current industry structure, with two dominant railroads in both the East and West, is conducive to a voluntary, reciprocal provision of competitive options to captive shippers.

It would be much easier to sunset the STB if a chair were appointed who was committed to eliminating the agency (much like Alfred Kahn's appointment as chair of the Civil Aeronautics Board and Darius Gaskins' appointment as chair of the Interstate Commerce Commission paved the way for elimination of these agencies.) We suggest that the new chair's first step should be to transfer the board's responsibility for evaluating mergers to the Justice Department, which would give railroads yet another important reason to be open to negotiating with shippers to resolve their differences.[49]

Many industry observers believe that the "final frontier" of the U.S. railroad industry is for the two remaining railroads in the East and West to form two transcontinental railroads. (The recently proposed merger of Burlington Northern and Canadian National Railways suggests this frontier may be closer than previously thought.)[50] Our findings suggest that

49. The Department of Justice has performed detailed competitive analyses and provided them to the STB as a party in every major rail merger case. But the STB has frequently rejected the department's analysis, particularly with regard to the effects of horizontal mergers.

50. In March 2000 the STB announced a freeze on all railroad mergers for fifteen months. Surface Transportation Board, "Public Views on Major Rail Consolidations: Decision," Docket EP-582-0 (March 17, 2000). As this book went to press, Burlington Northern was contesting this moratorium in court.

transcontinental railroads could enhance service but also impair competition in certain markets. The Justice Department would require concerns about competition to be addressed before approving such a major restructuring.

Railroads could be in a position to appease Justice if they first engaged in negotiations with captive shippers to establish a mechanism by which shippers' concerns about competitive options are addressed in the market, not by residual rate regulation. (Such a mechanism would lead to the end of the STB.) The same mechanism would then be used to respond to concerns about possible anticompetitive effects of the transcontinental mergers.

We do not envision that an erosion of the rate differential between captive and noncaptive shippers would mean the end of differential pricing in the rail industry. But the main differential would be across commodities, especially where there are differences in intermodal competition, instead of across geographical locations. (Recall, shippers pay higher rates, other things constant, for coal and chemical movements.) Such a rate structure would substantially lessen the chronic tension between rail's financial performance and captive shippers.

Concluding Comments

There is no question that the railroad industry has made great strides since the Staggers Act to become more efficient and innovative and to pass on some of these gains to shippers. But railroads still have a way to go to improve service times and reliability, to be more responsive to shippers, and to develop and achieve logistical efficiencies. Residual STB policies have fostered a lingering regulatory mentality in railroad management that has lessened attention to these matters, and railroads continue to have an incentive to keep from becoming too profitable for fear of triggering maximum rate cases or regulatory initiatives that mandate additional competition. Indeed, the industry still expends a great deal of corporate resources and energy trying to immunize itself from the board and Congress.

The railroads cannot simply hope that captive shippers' demands for competitive relief will eventually abate. To the contrary, as competitive access increasingly takes hold in other network industries, legislative initiatives to provide access in rail are more likely. Shippers and railroads should be encouraged to find a permanent solution to the captive shipper issue as a prelude to total rail deregulation.

References

Association of American Railroads. Selected Years. *Railroad Facts.* Washington, D.C.

Berndt, Ernst, and others. 1993. "Mergers, Deregulation, and Cost Savings in the U.S. Rail Industry." *Journal of Productivity Analysis* 4: 127–44.

Chaplin, Alison, and Stephen Schmidt. 1999. "Do Mergers Improve Efficiency? Evidence from Deregulated Rail Freight." *Journal of Transport Economics and Policy* 33 (May): 147–62.

Friedlaender, Ann F., and Richard H. Spady. 1981. *Freight Transport Regulation: Equity, Efficiency, and Competition in the Rail and Trucking Industries.* MIT Press.

Gallamore, Robert E. 1999. "Regulation and Innovation: Lessons from the American Railroad Industry." In *Essays in Transportation Economics, and Policy: A Handbook in Honor of John R. Meyer,* edited by José Gómez-Ibáñez, William B. Tye, and Clifford Winston. Brookings.

General Accounting Office. 1999a. *Railroad Regulation: Changes in Railroad Rates and Service Quality since 1990.* GAO/RCED-99–93. April.

———. 1999b. *Railroad Regulation: Current Issues Associated with the Rate Relief Process.* GAO/RCED-99–46. February.

Grimm, Curtis M. 1985. "Horizontal Competitive Effects in Railroad Mergers." In *Research in Transportation Economics,* edited by Theodore E. Keeler. vol. 2. London: JAI.

Grimm, Curtis M., and Robert Windle. 1998. "The Rationale for Deregulation." In *Regulatory Reform and Labor Markets,* edited by James Peoples. Kluwer Press.

Grimm, Curtis M., Clifford Winston, and Carol A. Evans. 1992. "Foreclosure of Railroad Markets: A Test of Chicago Leverage Theory." *Journal of Law and Economics* 35 (October): 295–310.

Harris, Robert G., and Clifford Winston. 1983. "Potential Benefits of Rail Mergers: An Econometric Analysis of Network Effects on Service Quality." *Review of Economics and Statistics* 65 (February): 32–40.

Keeler, Theodore E. 1983. *Railroads, Freight, and Public Policy.* Brookings.

Levin, Richard C. 1981. "Railroad Rates, Profitability, and Welfare under Deregulation." *Bell Journal of Economics* 12 (Spring): 1–26.

MacDonald, James M. 1987. "Competition and Rail Rates for the Shipment of Corn, Soybeans, and Wheat." *RAND Journal of Economics* 18 (Spring):151–63.

———. 1989. "Railroad Deregulation, Innovation, and Competition: Effects of the Staggers Act on Grain Transportation." *Journal of Law and Economics* 32 (April): 63–95.

Maddala, G. S. 1977. *Econometrics.* McGraw-Hill.

Meyer, John R., and William B. Tye. 1988. "Toward Achieving Workable Competition in Industries Undergoing a Transition to Deregulation: A Contractual Equilibrium Approach." *Yale Journal on Regulation* 5 (Summer): 273–97.

Morrison, Steven A., and Clifford Winston. 1999. "Regulatory Reform of U.S. Intercity Transportation." In *Essays in Transportation Economics and Policy: A Handbook in Honor of John R. Meyer,* edited by José Gómez-Ibáñez, William B. Tye, and Clifford Winston. Brookings.

Official Railway Guide—Freight Services Edition. 1999. Hightstown, N.J.: Primedia Information Inc.

Small, Kenneth A., and Clifford Winston. 1999. "The Demand for Transportation: Models and Applications." In *Essays in Transportation Economics and Policy: A Handbook in Honor of John R. Meyer,* edited by José Gómez-Ibáñez, William B. Tye, and Clifford Winston. Brookings.

Winston, Clifford, and others. 1990. *The Economic Effects of Surface Freight Deregulation.* Brookings.

ROBERT W. CRANDALL
JERRY A. HAUSMAN

3

Competition in U.S. Telecommunications Services: Effects of the 1996 Legislation

For more than fifty years the U.S. telecommunications sector was a regulated private monopoly, dominated by AT&T. During most of that period the Federal Communications Commission (FCC) and a variety of state authorities controlled the relative prices of telephone service and restricted entry. In the 1970s the first breath of liberalization swept over the sector as the FCC began to allow limited competition in the market for interstate dedicated business connections and won a battle with state regulators to open the market for terminal equipment, such as telephone handsets, answering machines, and modems, to competition.[1] Competition in long-distance markets opened wider when MCI launched long-distance service for businesses without FCC permission.[2]

1. The states challenged the FCC's right to invalidate state tariffs that required the use of terminal equipment supplied by the telephone company; see *N. Carolina Utility Commission* v. *FCC*, 552 F.2d 1036 (4th Cir. 1977). Presumably, the state regulators saw competition in terminal equipment as a threat to their attempt to maintain high rates for company-provided business equipment in return for low local residential rates.

2. The FCC attempted to block MCI's entry when MCI launched its "Execunet" business long-distance service without FCC permission. MCI successfully fended off the FCC in court; see *MCI Telecommunications Corp.* v. *FCC*, 561 F.2d 365 (DC Cir. 1977), cert. denied, 434 U.S. 1040 (1978);

AT&T's use of its local facilities to frustrate the burgeoning competition in long-distance services and terminal equipment led to a lengthy antitrust case, which resulted in a consent decree that broke up the company in 1984 and imposed a quarantine that prevented the divorced regional Bell operating companies from offering long-distance services. Although rivalry in long-distance services grew steadily after 1984, long-distance rates remained substantially above their competitive levels. Moreover, competition in local telecommunications grew very slowly because state regulators limited entry and controlled local rates. For twelve years the AT&T trial court wrestled with several difficult issues in implementing the consent decree. At the same time the regional Bell companies chafed at their continued exclusion from long-distance services, while long-distance carriers were equally concerned about the slow progress toward competition in local markets, a problem beyond the reach of the AT&T decree. As a result, Congress was finally prodded to reform the entire telecommunications regulatory structure through passage of the 1996 Telecommunications Act. This legislation opens local telecommunications markets to competition, seeks to complete the earlier market-opening process in long-distance services (including freeing the Bell operating companies from their quarantine), and creates an economic environment intended to lead to the "deployment of advanced telecommunications and information technologies and services to all Americans."[3]

The 1996 law invites regulators to "forbear" from regulating new services whenever such forbearance is in the "public interest," but unlike earlier exercises in deregulating network industries, the law sharply increases the scope of regulation and takes an unfortunate U-turn away from the FCC's decision at the beginning of the 1990s to substitute price-cap regulation for cost-based regulation.[4] The 1996 law requires regulators to establish cost-based wholesale prices for incumbents' facilities so that entrants may lease those facilities and be relieved of the burden of building

---

and *MCI Telecommunications Corp.* v. *FCC,* 580 F.2d 590 (D.C. Cir. 1978), cert. denied, 439 U.S. 980 (1978). The FCC was left to scramble for a policy that would allow MCI and other competitive carriers to interconnect with AT&T's local companies.

3. Preamble to House Conference Report 104-458, 104 Cong., 2 sess.

4. The FCC had instituted price-cap regulation—a regulatory regime that limits the rate of annual price increases for various groups or "baskets" of services—in order to divorce rate increases from cost increases. This change was made to simplify the regulatory process and to provide greater incentives for carrier efficiency because reductions in a carrier's costs would not require a reduction in regulated rates. Favorable effects on technological progress and innovation were also an expected result of the shift to price caps.

their own facilities. Moreover, the law not only retains a system of regulatory cross-subsidies erected by the states and the FCC over several decades, popularly described as "universal service" policies, but it also extends those subsidies to new services and new recipients. Furthermore, the law requires that an explicit charge or tax be levied on telecommunications companies to fund the federal portion of these subsidies.

The intensely regulatory nature of the 1996 law reflects not the considered judgment of lawmakers seeking to expand on the earlier successes of deregulation, but rather the political compromise Congress struck between the demands of the regional Bell companies, which wanted relief from the restrictions on long-distance entry imposed on them by the AT&T decree, and the long-distance companies, which pressed Congress to facilitate their entry into the provision of local services. The compromise releases the Bell companies from the long-distance quarantine, but only after they succumb to extremely onerous new regulatory conditions that benefit new entrants into local service. Apparently, no one paused to ask if this new regulatory superstructure could possibly work in light of the previous history of regulation and deregulation, nor if such regulation could adapt to changing technology and the need to provide investment incentives to diffuse this technology. The result has been four years of protracted regulatory disputes and litigation that show little sign of abating, as well as continuing welfare losses from distorted prices.

In this paper we examine the effects of the 1996 law on competition, rates (prices), and economic welfare four years after its passage, focusing in particular on the regulatory micromanagement of competition that the law has unleashed. We show that despite the early legal and regulatory uncertainties that have plagued the implementation of the legislation, local competition has begun, albeit slowly. We also show that a simpler framework, under which local competition might have developed even more quickly and the Bell operating companies could have been allowed to enter long-distance services sooner, would have promoted competition without risking deleterious effects on investment in new services by incumbent local carriers.

The enormous welfare gains that are potentially available from the development of these new services and from the movement of the prices of traditional telecommunications services to competitive levels are being squandered in the belief that detailed regulation is the best route to competition. A much less regulatory regime stressing open entry and simplified reciprocal compensation for interconnection would have been far more effective in promoting entry and investment. For proof one need only look at wireless communications, where several large national firms are spending $12 billion a year to build competitive terrestrial networks in the wake of the Omnibus Budget Reconciliation Act of 1993, which instructed the FCC to auction off substantial electromagnetic spectrum for such use.[5] Significantly, this investment is occurring in a market in which prices are totally deregulated.[6]

Market Structure before the 1996 Reform

The United States was once the leader in opening its interstate telecommunications markets to competition. The FCC allowed limited entry into long-distance services in 1969–71, although entrants were allowed to offer only dedicated private lines to business customers. In the mid-1970s MCI audaciously entered ordinary, switched long-distance markets without FCC permission and fended off the FCC's attempts to block its entry in federal courts.

The antitrust case filed by the Justice Department against AT&T in 1974 was largely the result of disputes that arose over attempts by MCI and other entrants into long-distance service to interconnect with AT&T's local companies to complete their calls and by new sellers of equipment (handsets, answering machines, key telephones, and the like) to attach their terminal equipment to AT&T's customer lines. Had the FCC pursued a deliberate policy of allowing entry and requiring equal access for all competitors, these disputes might have been avoided and the antitrust action rendered unnecessary.[7]

The AT&T litigation resulted in a settlement in 1982 that required AT&T to divest its local operating companies into seven separate regional Bell operating companies by January 1, 1984. These companies were barred by the resulting decree from offering long-distance service outside their local areas, from manufacturing equipment, and from offering infor-

5. Cellular Telecommunications Industry Association, "Semi-Annual Wireless Industry Survey," Washington, D.C. [www.wow-com.com/wirelesssurvey (5/11/00)].

6. The rates charged for interconnecting wireless calls with the traditional wire-based network are subject to the requirements of the 1996 law, but retail prices are not regulated. Nor is there any regulatory requirement for selling services to other carriers at wholesale prices.

7. Canada pursued just such a policy in 1992–93 and has not experienced the problems that triggered the antitrust case against AT&T.

mation services. The ban on information services was overturned by an appellate court in 1991, but the other restrictions remained in place until 1996. The consent decree required the divested local Bell companies to reconfigure their network switching systems so that all long-distance carriers could be interconnected on equal terms. The result was a substantial acceleration in the rate of expansion of the long-distance entrants and a corresponding decline in AT&T's share of long-distance revenues.

Despite the apparent success of the AT&T decree in stimulating long-distance competition, the long-distance sector remained quite concentrated into the mid-1990s. The Hirschman-Herfindahl index of concentration, based on carrier revenues, declined steadily, from more than 8000 in 1984 to 2640 in 1998, but it is still far above the Department of Justice's standard of 1800 for a highly concentrated industry.[8] Long-distance rates have fallen substantially since the AT&T divestiture, but a large part of the decline is attributable not to competition but to lower costs, particularly a decline in the regulated charges paid to local companies to connect their calls. In 1998 residential customers were still paying an average of 15.3 cents a minute for interstate long-distance service even though the long-run incremental cost of the service plus local carrier access charges was no more than 6 cents a minute.[9] In short, further entry and more vigorous competition is still needed to move rates to competitive levels, but the AT&T decrees and the enforcement of the 1996 law have barred the most likely entrants—the Bell operating companies.

While the long-distance markets had at least a moderate degree of competition by 1996, competition in the local services market had only just begun. The states regulate intrastate services, including the regular flat-rate local service that most residences and small businesses use to connect to the network. Entry into local telecommunications was allowed in a limited range of services, generally to connect large businesses to (interstate) long-distance carriers, including long-distance companies. But for the most part, until 1996, state regulators discouraged or blocked entry into these local services and even into intrastate long distance so as to maintain a politically crafted pricing policy of subsidizing residential local

---

8. FCC (2000, table 11.3).

9. The average price per minute is from a large national household sample of telephone bills (Bill Harvesting dataset) surveyed by PNR and Associates of Jenkintown, Pennsylvania. In 1998 the average interstate access charges per conversation minute paid by long-distance carriers to originate and terminate calls were slightly less than 4 cents a minute (FCC, 2000) and transmission and switching costs were no more than 2 cents a minute (Crandall and Waverman, 1998).

service from charges on long-distance and business service. As late as early 1996, only six states allowed entrants to serve geographically dispersed residential and small business subscribers. By limiting entry, state regulators were able to erect a rate structure for local connections that favored residential subscribers, particularly those in rural areas or on the outskirts of urban areas. Regulators have generally required business lines, intrastate long-distance, interstate access (for long-distance carriers), and advanced services to be priced substantially above long-run incremental cost so that residential lines can be priced below long-run incremental cost, particularly in rural areas.

The regulated intrastate prices under this structure resulted in very large static economic welfare losses. In figure 3-1, we show the average 1996 U.S. flat residential rate and two alternative estimates of the average long-run incremental costs incurred by the local exchange carriers for providing local service, each arrayed by density of lines.[10] The Benchmark Cost Proxy Model (BCPM) estimate is taken from a local-carrier model proffered to the FCC; the Hybrid Cost Proxy Model (HCPM) estimate is derived from the FCC's own forward-looking cost model.[11] Clearly rates depart substantially from estimated average incremental cost, regardless of the model used to estimate costs. In most states, rates *rise* with increasing density, but the cost per line obviously declines. The resulting deficit—$5.5 billion to $16.2 billion a year—is recovered in large part from (above-cost) long-distance charges.[12] If residential rates were moved to the estimated average incremental cost per line and long-distance charges were reduced by the amount of revenues raised, annual economic welfare would improve by $2.5 billion to $7.0 billion a year.[13] These losses are only from the distortions in *residential* rates. The static welfare losses from regulated business rates may be even higher.[14] Businesses account for approximately

10. These cost models estimate the average incremental cost of providing local service in a given area, not the long-run incremental cost of adding a line in any given area.
11. We critique this model later in the paper. For the present, we simply use it to provide a lower bound on local-exchange service costs.
12. Estimate based on state-by-state modeling of rates and costs by Crandall and Waverman (2000).
13. Crandall and Waverman (2000). The potential welfare gains from full Ramsey pricing would obviously be greater.
14. Wenders and Egan (1986) estimated the total welfare loss from overpricing long-distance service to business and residential customers in 1983 at $10.7 billion a year. Perl (1985) obtained very similar results for his low-cost, high demand elasticity calculation. Since that time, the average interstate long-distance rate has fallen from about 40 cents a minute to 11 cents a minute (1998 dollars), while the cost of long-distance service has fallen from about 13 cents a minute to about 3 cents a minute

Figure 3-1. *Average U.S. Local Residential Rate Compared with Average Incremental Cost, 1998*

Dollars per month

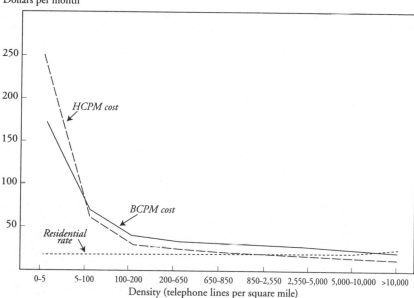

Density (telephone lines per square mile)

Source: Costs are based on the Benchmark Cost Proxy Model and the Hybrid Cost Proxy Model (see text for explanation); residential rates are from the National Association of Regulatory Utility Commissioners (1998).

60 percent of all long-distance calling and are faced with regulated prices of advanced services that are generally substantially above cost.[15]

Any estimates of the static welfare losses from mispriced telecommunications services in a regulated environment are likely to underestimate substantially the costs of regulation in this sector. Given decades of regulation, estimates of network costs are likely to be overstated because regulation, rather than competition, has driven observed network costs.[16] Moreover, given the rapid pace of technological change in telecommuni-

---

(1998 dollars) and the demand for long-distance service has expanded substantially. As a result, despite the decline in rates, the total annual welfare loss from current long-distance prices has actually *increased* from its 1983–85 level.

15. It is generally believed that the high prices for high-speed business services have attenuated the incentives for local companies to offer high-speed digital subscriber line (DSL) services for Internet connections. These DSL services must be priced to compete with cable modems, and at these prices may substitute for the much higher-priced DS1 services that many businesses use today.

16. Winston (1998).

cations, welfare losses that result from regulation-induced delays in the introduction of new technologies and services are likely to be even greater than the static welfare losses from mispricing existing services.

The electronics revolution has generated enormous opportunities for the development of new telecommunications services. Unfortunately, these services must run a regulatory gauntlet before they are introduced commercially because of regulators' desire to protect existing service providers or certain consumers from the effects of competition and the loss of universal service subsidies for traditional services. Cellular telephony, voice mail, video service delivery over telephone networks, and new satellite services have been delayed or (in the case of telephone-company delivery of video) even thwarted altogether by state and federal regulators. The FCC could have licensed cellular telephony in the early 1970s, but the first system did not begin operation until 1983 because the FCC delayed licensing the requisite frequencies. Hausman estimates that this licensing delay cost consumers $33.5 billion (in 1994 dollars) a year.[17] Using a similar methodology, Hausman estimates that regulatory delay in allowing AT&T or its regional Bell progeny to offer voice messaging services between 1981 and 1988 cost consumers $1.3 billion a year in 1994 dollars. There are no estimates of the cost of regulatory delays in offering direct broadcast satellite services, telephone-company video services, or new broadband services over local telephone company lines, but they are likely to have been substantial.

Major Provisions of the 1996 Telecommunications Act

Widespread dissatisfaction with the lack of progress toward competition and the disputes that arose from enforcing the AT&T breakup decree led Congress to pass the 1996 Telecommunications Act, which was signed into law in February 1996. The objective of this legislation is to open all telecommunications markets to competition, but the law is far from an example of deregulation. Indeed, it erects a variety of new regulatory requirements that are supposed to guide, facilitate, or otherwise stimulate competition. The most important of these provisions involves the opening of existing networks, built by "incumbent" local exchange companies (ILECs), so entrants can interconnect with them in any of a variety of

17. Hausman (1997).

ways. The incumbent companies are required to unbundle their networks into a set of components or functions and to offer them to their prospective rivals at cost-based prices.[18] In addition, entrants are to be afforded the opportunity to resell the incumbents' retail services by obtaining these services from the incumbents at their retail prices less the avoided cost of retailing the services. Finally, incumbents must exchange local traffic with entrants on equal terms.[19] All of these "interconnection" terms are to be negotiated or, failing negotiation, are to be determined in arbitrations conducted under the auspices of state regulators.[20]

The law's requirements for interconnection may be viewed as the "stick" over the heads of the incumbents, requiring them to assist in opening their erstwhile monopoly markets to competition.[21] In addition, the law provides a "carrot" for the regional Bell companies, allowing them to enter the long-distance market if they meet a detailed fourteen-point "checklist" of market-opening requirements spelled out in Section 271. (The non-Bell local companies, such as Frontier, Sprint, SNET, and GTE, are not barred from long-distance markets; hence, there is no carrot for them.) In practice, this means that each company must pass through a series of three regulatory proceedings for each state—one at the state level, one at the U.S. Department of Justice, and one at the FCC. As of this writing, only one Bell company—Bell Atlantic in New York—has been able to satisfy the three regulators along each of the prescribed dimensions. For the most part, Section 271 approval has been stalled by entrants' complaints that the Bell companies have failed to install "operating and support" systems that would allow for instantaneous transfer of customers from the Bells to the entrants at a very high transfer rate.

The 1996 law provides much more than a prescription for regulated competition in telecommunications. It makes major changes in universal service policy; mandates new subsidies for schools, libraries, and rural health facilities; substantially deregulates cable television rates; liberalizes broadcast-ownership rules; and even regulates entry into the provision of

---

18. The FCC approach to setting wholesale rates does not take account of the sunk and irreversible costs of investment in telecommunications networks. For a further discussion, see Hausman (1997, 1999b, 1999c).

19. 1996 Telecommunications Act, 100 Stat. 56, Section 251.

20. 1996 Telecommunications Act, 100 Stat. 56, Section 252.

21. This is somewhat overstated. The ILECs faced competition from urban fiber rings and wireless carriers before 1996, but they controlled virtually the entire market for local access and exchange services for residential and small-business subscribers.

alarm services. The universal service policies are to be supported by fees (taxes) levied on all telecommunications services and are to be portable so that new entrants can receive the same payments as incumbents for offer-ing services in areas where rates are below cost. In this paper, however, we focus only on the provisions directly related to opening traditional tele-communications services markets to competition.[22]

Unbundling and Wholesale Rates

Competitive telecommunications networks can survive only if they interconnect with one another. Otherwise, each subscriber would have to use separate terminal equipment for each of the competitive networks, an obvious inconvenience. No subscriber would want to have four or five separate telephone lines, handsets, and modems in his or her home or office. Interconnection can take a variety of forms, however.

The simplest form is the exchange of traffic. Indeed, national and international carriers, Internet service providers, and adjacent local tele-phone carriers already exchange traffic at a variety of switching centers with apparent ease. The cost of such exchanges for voice-grade traffic is now measured in tenths of a penny per minute although international ex-changes often are priced at 50 cents or more a minute because of a lack of competition in the telecommunications sectors of many countries.[23]

The 1996 law provides for interconnection that is far broader than the simple exchange of traffic, however. Using somewhat vague language, the law requires local telecommunications carriers to interconnect at "any technically feasible point" and to provide access to their "unbundled net-work elements"(UNEs) at just and reasonable prices "determined without reference to a rate-of-return or other rate-based proceeding." An unbun-dled network element is a network component or function that a competi-tor may lease in order to deliver its services. Indeed, under the FCC's rules, implemented in August 1996, a competitor could lease *everything* from its incumbent rival, thereby obviating the need to invest in any network facilities whatsoever.

22. For a discussion of the new subsidy programs and "universal service" policies, see Crandall and Waverman (2000). For a discussion of the increase in taxes required by these policies and the extremely large loss of economic efficiency and reduction in consumer welfare caused by the FCC's implementa-tion of them, see Hausman (1998) and Hausman and Shelanski (1999).

23. These rates are falling dramatically with the onset of liberalization in many countries and the prodding of the Federal Communications Commission.

The FCC further required that these elements be leased to entrants at "forward-looking" costs, using an approach called "total element long-run incremental cost," or TELRIC. Although these wholesale, carrier-to-carrier rates are to be part of the interconnection agreement negotiated between each entrant and each incumbent on a state-by-state basis, the rates are supposed to be guided by the FCC's forward-looking cost model or a similar model developed for each state.

These unbundling and wholesale-pricing requirements have generated enormous controversy, resulting in numerous court challenges and a recent Supreme Court decision reversing a part of the FCC's rules.[24] Specifically, the Court questioned the broad, sweeping requirement that every network element be provided to competitors.[25] The Supreme Court nonetheless upheld the FCC's right to prescribe the cost standard for pricing these network elements. The FCC's methodology was not an issue in this case, but it is being challenged in another case now before an appellate court. Therefore, the TELRIC basis for establishing wholesale prices remains in place for the present. The FCC has recently relaxed the unbundling requirements only modestly, while extending them in new directions, such as requiring incumbent companies to actually *share* customer access lines with entrants rather than simply lease them.[26]

Resale

The 1996 law requires local carriers not only to unbundle their network elements, but to allow entrants to resell their services. Such resale simply transfers the marketing and billing functions from the existing local carrier to the new (reselling) entrant. The technical details of the service are unchanged; only the identity of the seller changes. Incumbent local

24. *AT&T Corp.* v. *Iowa Utilities Board,* 119 S.Ct. 721 (1999).

25. For a consumer-welfare approach to unbundled elements, rather than the FCC's competitor welfare approach, see Hausman and Sidak (1999).

26. FCC, "Third Report and Order and Fourth Further Notice of Proposed Rulemaking, CC Docket 96-98," FCC 99-238, November 5, 1999. Specifically, the FCC removed operator and directory services from the list of unbundled elements, but it added "subloops"—or the part of the loop from the fiber/copper wire interface in digital loop carrier systems. In addition, the FCC decided not to require unbundling of new equipment required for advanced broadband services, such as digital subscriber line access multiplexers and packet switches. The FCC has recently adopted new unbundling requirements that mandate not only the unbundling of the customer line or "loop," but the *sharing* of the line between competitors and entrants. This line-sharing would allow entrants to use the upper frequencies for higher-value services, leaving the lower frequencies to incumbents for traditional voice services.

carriers must offer all of their retail services to their competitors for resale, charging them their full retail price less a discount for the "avoided costs" of marketing and billing the service. These discounts have typically been established through negotiations and arbitrations in the range of 15 to 25 percent.[27] The resale requirement has not been as controversial as the unbundling requirements because resale does not provide the entrant with as much freedom to offer a bundle of new services with the assistance of the incumbent's facilities. Substantial debates have arisen, however, over the avoided-cost discounts needed to make such resale profitable.[28]

Retail Prices

The 1996 law is noticeably silent on retail telecommunications prices, except for mandating that explicit rural subsidies be sufficient to keep local rates in high-cost rural areas at levels comparable with urban rates. State commissions still regulate incumbent carriers' intrastate services, and most of these commissions continue to administer a distorted rate structure. (Recall figure 3-1.) Intrastate long-distance rates and access charges as well as interstate access charges continue to cover the deficit between local per-line costs and local rates. Although the 1996 law prescribes cost-based *wholesale* rates, it does not require the state commissions to move retail rates toward cost. Indeed, the FCC has increased the distortions between retail rates and costs by assessing charges to fund the Internet subsidies to schools and libraries.[29]

New Services

The 1996 Act allows the FCC to forbear from regulation of advanced telecommunications services if such forbearance advances the "deployment on a reasonable and timely basis" of these new services. This provision provides the incumbent carrier with at least a theoretical possibility of building new, advanced facilities that may offer services without the burden of wholesale or retail regulation. Unfortunately, however, the FCC's

---

27. See table 3-4, below.

28. The FCC even forced SBC Communications to increase its resale discounts as a condition for approving the recent SBC acquisition of Ameritech. The increased discounts were not based on the results of any economic analysis; instead they were a required payment to allow SBC to proceed with its acquisition.

29. As expected, these increased access charges have been passed on to consumers by the long-distance carriers.

only ruling on forbearance requires that incumbents use structurally separate subsidiaries to deliver the unregulated, advanced service.[30] Moreover, it has relaxed the long-distance restrictions on Bell companies only in those cases where such restrictions are demonstrably impeding the delivery of advanced services to rural areas. Thus Bell companies cannot build advanced networks that extend beyond their regional boundaries. In addition, the FCC recently ruled that local carriers must share their access lines with competitive carriers wishing to offer only advanced, high-speed services. The result is a set of policies that continues to regulate incumbents' advanced services and the leasing of their facilities to entrants offering similar services but that leaves the entrants' services unregulated. These regulations, promulgated largely to accelerate entry, are likely to reduce the incentives for the incumbent local carriers to invest in advanced data networks that would provide faster Internet access to "all Americans" as called for by the 1996 law.

A Critique of the 1996 Act

Do the various provisions of the 1996 Telecommunications Act reflect a sound approach to market liberalization, given the U.S. experience with deregulation in numerous other sectors? From the outset, we note that the 1996 law represents a major step backward from the recent tendency of state regulators and the FCC to abandon cost-based regulation in favor of price caps.[31] Wholesale rates and universal-service subsidies are now to be determined by cost models. Furthermore, although the 1996 law opens all telecommunications markets to competition, even the once-protected local markets, it requires incumbents to cooperate in facilitating entry of potential competitors to a degree that has not been prescribed for any other recently deregulated sector of the economy.

Unbundling

The requirement that incumbents unbundle their networks and lease the pieces ("elements") to entrants is rooted in the fact that local telecom-

---

30. FCC, "First Report and Order and Further Notice of Proposed Rulemaking, CC Docket 98-147," FCC 99-48, March 31, 1999.

31. The FCC shifted from cost-based regulation to price caps in 1989 (for AT&T) and 1990 (for the local carriers' interstate rates). California was among the first states to adopt price-cap regulation for local carriers in 1989.

munications networks are expensive to build and that certain parts of them may be "essential facilities," or monopoly bottlenecks. But the unbundling provisions were enacted without any guidance from historical experience. Although it may be uneconomical for entrants to build parallel connections to subscribers' facilities, there is no empirical evidence on this matter, and there is certainly no reason to believe that *all* local network facilities are essential bottlenecks. Surely the FCC's first order, requiring the unbundling of everything, was too sweeping, but the commission has not recanted despite considerable evidence that entrants can and do build their own facilities.[32] Hausman and Sidak have proposed an economic approach to determine which local network facilities are essential bottleneck facilities.[33] They note that competitors certainly can install their own switches, interoffice transport facilities, and network intelligence.[34] Wireless and long-distance companies do so routinely; why should local wireline competitors be any different? Indeed, as we show later, there has been very little demand for even those facilities that arguably can be defined as essential facilities, namely, the copper wires extending from the incumbent's local switch to the subscriber.

A more troubling aspect of the unbundling requirements, however, is their imposition in a sector in which technology is changing extremely rapidly. Today's network is not static—it is steadily evolving into new, more advanced networks, such as those designed to deliver high-speed Internet services. If an incumbent local network operator leases part of its current network to its rivals, will it be able to adopt new technology without these rivals' (entrants') assent? Surely, one would not want these new competitors using the regulatory process simply to delay or frustrate their rivals' attempts to innovate. Furthermore, extensive unbundling at below-cost prices reduces the investment incentives for entrants and incumbents alike. Entrants are less likely to build their own facilities if their incumbent rivals' networks are available to them at even lower costs. Incumbents are less likely to invest in innovative services or facilities if their future returns are

---

32. See the "UNE Fact Report" submitted by the U.S. Telephone Association in the Matter of FCC CC Docket 96-98 (May 26, 1999), for data on the existence of competitive facilities throughout the country.

33. Hausman and Sidak (1999).

34. Indeed, mandatory unbundling in Canada extends only to the ILECs' "essential" facilities and excludes these nonessential elements that the FCC decreed must be shared. See *Local Competition* (1 May 1997), Telecom Decision 97-8, ¶ 74 (Canadian Radio-Television and Telecommunications Commission).

truncated by the prospect of having to lease such facilities to their rivals at below-cost prices. Given the uncertainty regarding technology, the current regulatory approach is likely to slow down the adoption of new technology in the wireline telephone network, in direct contradiction of the 1996 law's stated purpose of encouraging "deployment of advanced telecommunications and information technologies and services to all Americans."

The history of transportation regulation is littered with examples of such stratagems employed by carriers to block new, innovative services introduced by their competitors. Once a new local telecommunications entrant begins to offer service using its rival's local loops, switches, and network intelligence, it has every incentive to demand that these facilities not be altered. The incumbent's only recourse may be to develop *new* network facilities, separate from the existing network, and simply to allow the existing network to atrophy. Alternatively, the incumbent may choose not to invest at all.[35]

Regulating Wholesale Rates

The new law's use of cost-based regulation to determine wholesale rates is also troubling. Cost-based regulation has been in disfavor for several reasons that we need not review here. One significant problem is the difficulty that regulators have in determining the costs of providing the regulated service efficiently. How can federal or state regulators possibly know if arbitrated rates reflect the forward- or even backward-looking cost of each network element provided by an incumbent local carrier? Regulators are generally the last to know the level of costs, particularly in a dynamic industry such as telecommunications with its abundance of joint and common costs. Indeed, the FCC has spent most of the past four years building a detailed engineering model of forward-looking costs of an "optimized," but probably outdated, network to use in guiding its universal-service policy. But this model is extremely controversial and is not generally employed. As we shall see, the federal-state regulatory process has already generated wildly different rates for wholesale elements across the states.

The forward-looking approach to estimating costs, even if it could be executed with accuracy, does not take into account the sunk and irreversible

---

35. Hausman (1997) recounts how competitors to the regional Bell operating companies delayed the introduction of a new network service, voice mail, for more than ten years.

costs of network investment and therefore leads to rates for unbundled elements that are below cost, as Hausman has demonstrated in a number of papers. Instead, the FCC approach assumes, incorrectly, that all network investment costs are fixed costs, not sunk costs, an assumption that is sharply at odds with economic reality.[36] This approach gives a "free option" to the entrant—the right, but not the obligation, to purchase the use of unbundled elements—and decreases the economic incentive of existing carriers to invest in network improvements because it truncates the economic returns to new investment at the cost of the investment. In addition new entrants are discouraged from investing in their own competing local telephone facilities because the FCC's approach provides them with a subsidized price for the use of the incumbent's unbundled elements.[37]

To see how the forward-looking cost approach affects new investment by an incumbent local exchange carrier, suppose a competitor wants to lease the unbundled elements associated with this investment. The incumbent could offer the new competitor a contract for the economic life of the incumbent's investment in the leased element—say, ten years for investment in the local subscriber line, or "loop." The price of the unbundled element would be the total investment cost plus the operating costs each year for the unbundled element. If demand did not materialize or if prices fell, the new entrant would bear the economic risk of this outcome.[38] Setting wholesale rates at forward-looking cost, however, typically allows the new entrant to lease the unbundled element on a month-by-month basis. If demand does not materialize or if prices fall, the incumbent has to bear the risk for the business case of the new competitor. Thus, regulation has required the incumbent to give a free option to the new entrant to purchase the use of the unbundled elements. The monthly price of the unbundled element should be significantly higher than the price of the element based on a ten-year life because the monthly price must reflect the risk inherent in the sunk investments or, equivalently, the value of the option given to the new entrant.[39] But regulators to date have not incor-

---

36. One of the founders of the original TELRIC approach (then called TSLRIC, or Total Service Long-Run Incremental Cost) has now recognized that significant costs are omitted by this approach. See Baumol (1999).

37. This discussion is based on Hausman (1997, 1999b, 1999c).

38. The contract (or regulation) could allow the new entrant to sell the use of the unbundled element to another firm if it decided to exit the business.

39. In contracts between unregulated telecommunications companies, such as long-distance carriers, and their customers, significant discounts are given for multiyear contracts.

porated the value of the option, which arises from the sunk-cost nature of much telecommunication investment, into their price setting.

Hausman has estimated the value of the free option, which is equivalent to the subsidy given new entrants by regulators. The subsidy derives from uncertainty and the anticipated decrease in the prices of capital goods due to technological progress. The expected change in (real) prices of most telecommunications services is downward given these decreases in the price of capital goods. As a result, Hausman has calculated the required markup on the component of unbundled elements reflecting the sunk investments and uncertainty to be approximately 3.3.[40] The ratio of sunk costs to fixed and variable costs will cause the overall markup on forward-looking cost to vary, but the markup will be significant given the importance of sunk costs in most telecommunications investments.

As an example, Hausman has applied this methodology to transport facilities or "links" and to switching ports, two of the unbundled elements identified by FCC regulation. The proportion of total costs accounted for by sunk costs for the transport links is 0.59, so the markup factor for the overall investment (using a markup factor of 3.3) is approximately 2.36 times forward-looking cost. By contrast, the proportion of sunk costs for ports is about 0.10; hence, the markup factor becomes 1.23 times forward-looking cost. The markup over forward-looking cost that takes account of sunk costs and uncertainty is the value of the free option that regulators force incumbent providers to grant to new entrants—for example, 1.36 times forward-looking cost for links and 0.23 times forward-looking cost for ports.

The Impact of the 1996 Law Four Years after Its Passage

Since passage of the 1996 Telecommunications Act, competition for local residential wireline service has grown very slowly, and continued regulatory barriers preventing the regional Bell operating companies from entering long-distance markets have cost consumers a considerable amount in welfare losses. In sharp contrast, competition is robust in wireless services, where prices have been deregulated.

---

40. For a further explanation of the calculations and sensitivity analysis, see Hausman (1997, 1999b, 1999c).

Local Competition

The principal measure of success for the 1996 law must be the degree to which it opens local telecommunications markets to competition. A modicum of local telecommunications competition has existed in the United States for more than a decade. New carriers built high-capacity fiber-optic ring networks in most major business districts in the United States long before 1996. These companies, known as competitive access providers, or CAPs, generally marketed only to mid-size and large businesses because of state regulation, which typically kept residential rates below cost, thus discouraging entry.[41] After the passage of the 1996 law, a large number of other new local competitors emerged, building some facilities but relying heavily on resale of the incumbent local carriers' services. These new competitors are now known as competitive local exchange carriers, or CLECs.

By the middle of 1999 the competitive local carriers—CAPs and CLECs—had garnered about 3.4 percent of the country's local telephone access lines (table 3-1).[42] CLECs, such as e.spire, McLeod, RCN, WinStar, and Electric Lightwave, now account for an estimated 2.3 percent of the country's access lines. In addition, the older CAPs, the largest of which have been acquired by MCI/WorldCom and AT&T, and long-distance companies account for another 1.1 percent of the country's local access lines.

In the growing economy of the 1990s, this loss of lines to competitors is not even noticeable. The growth rate in access lines for the large Bell companies is the same as the overall growth rate in access lines. The incumbents have not yet suffered large losses of customers. Because the competitors have generally targeted business customers, however, their share of local telecommunications *revenues* is much greater than their share of lines. Merrill Lynch estimates that the competitors' share of local revenues grew from 2.7 percent in the fourth quarter of 1997 to 4.9 percent at the end of 1998 and to 6.3 percent in the second quarter of 1999.[43] In some large cities, such as New York, the competitors' shares are much larger, with some estimates exceeding 35 percent for medium and large business customers. Overall, however, FCC data show that local competi-

---

41. For an analysis of this competitive entry, see Hausman (1996).
42. Kastan and Reingold (1999, table 8).
43. Kastan and Reingold (1999, table 8).

Table 3-1. *Access Lines Served by Competitive Local Carriers, 1997–99*
Thousands

Company	1997:4	1999:2
Competitive local exchange carrier		
Allegiance	n.a.	122.3
CTE	13.0	60.8
e.spire	35.1	118.1
Electric Lightwave	34.3	121.5
Focal	9.3	106.7
Frontier	101.0	245.0
GST	28.9	206.5
Hyperion	25.0	191.3
ICG	93.0	446.4
Intermedia	81.3	277.7
ITCDeltacom	n.a.	56.0
McLeod	185.0	392.3
NEXTLINK	50.1	282.2
RCN	28.1	104.5
Teligent	n.a.	37.5
US LEC	49.2	302.7
WinStar	65.6	332.5
Others	172.0	727.7
Subtotal	970.9	4,131.5
(Percent of total lines)	(0.6)	(2.3)
Long-distance companies		
AT&T (Teleport)	310.0	625.0
MCI WorldCom (MFS)	530.0	1,251.0
Sprint	74.4	167.9
Subtotal	914.4	2,043.9
(Percent of lines)	(0.5)	(1.1)
TOTAL COMPETITORS	1,885.4	6,175.4
(Percent of U.S. lines)	(1.1)	(3.4)

Source: Kastan and Reingold (1999, table 8).
n.a. not available.

tors accounted for only 2.2 percent of total local exchange revenues in 1997 and 3.5 percent in 1998.[44]

Indeed, many of the new competitors bypass residential subscribers completely because these customers are so geographically dispersed and often are purchasing their local service from the regulated incumbent carriers at rates that state regulators have held below cost. As we have seen, state regulators generally set business rates much higher to generate the revenues necessary to subsidize residential connections. Moreover, businesses are likely to be much more concentrated geographically, making them attractive targets for the new competitors.

Nevertheless, recent data from FCC surveys of the incumbent local carriers show that a surprising 40 percent of all resold lines are *residential* lines.[45] One would not have expected residential resale to be particularly attractive given that the monthly gross margin on such service is only about $4 a line ($20 times a 20 percent resale discount).[46] This anomaly cannot be attributable to business-residential arbitrage since the service must remain with the residential subscriber. It is possible that the incumbent carriers have misclassified some of the lines, but this cannot explain the 1.2 million lines classified as residential resale. One possibility is that resellers are offering standard voice service to poor credit risks, who are repeatedly disconnected by the regulated incumbent carriers for nonpayment of bills, and the new, higher-valued high-speed (digital subscriber line) services to more creditworthy subscribers. Because of regulation, the incumbents' rates often must be the same to all subscribers regardless of their credit histories. The new entrants are not constrained by retail price regulation; hence, their rates may reflect the credit histories of their subscribers. In addition, the new entrants may be capitalizing on the fact that the incumbent local companies have been slow to roll out new services, partly because of concern over regulatory requirements.[47]

Since 1996 local competition has taken one of three forms: resale, use of unbundled elements, or facilities-based competition. According to an

44. FCC (2000, table 9.1). These data are obtained directly from local carriers who are required to file periodic reports on their revenues to the FCC.

45. FCC (2000, table 9.2).

46. Resale is more attractive than building one's own capacity in many residential areas because the service is obtained from the incumbent at a discount from the residential rate that is already below cost. Even at the 18–22 percent avoided-cost discount, however, it would appear that resale of residential services is not likely to be a lucrative business strategy.

47. Some of this uncertainty has been dispelled by the FCC's recent decision not to require unbundling of certain equipment used to deliver advanced services.

FCC survey, the established local carriers had provided competitors with 3.6 million lines for resale by mid-1999. In addition, the incumbents had leased 685,000 loops to their competitors, and the use of unbundled loops was increasing rapidly.[48] Given that the competitors had an estimated 6.2 million lines in service by the end of 1998, we estimate that about 1.9 million of these competitive lines—or about 1.1 percent of total U.S. lines—represented competition offered solely over an entrant's own facilities. Surely this is a paltry result more than three years after the opening of the market to competitive entry, particularly when the competitive access providers had already built a substantial share of these lines before the passage of the 1996 law.[49] As we show below, however, their enormous market capitalization suggests that the capital markets expect entrants to grow substantially in the next few years.

The slow take-up of unbundled loops is perhaps surprising in view of the low wholesale rates established for these unbundled elements in some states. As of June 1999 leased local loops constituted less than 1 percent of switched access lines in every state except Michigan, Nevada, New York, Tennessee, and Texas (table 3-2). Even in states where the incumbent carrier reports a substantial share of resold lines, entrants have shown little interest in leased loops. Part of the reason for the disinterest in this wholesale market is undoubtedly that the entrants have been waiting for an even more attractive regulatory option—the entire bundle of network facilities in a (reconstituted) package of unbundled network facilities at regulated prices that are well below the resale rate. The pursuit of this goal led to a protracted period of legal and regulatory disputes over the right of entrants to demand the entire "UNE platform," a dispute that continues. As part of its negotiations with the FCC to gain approval of its merger with NYNEX, Bell Atlantic agreed to offer the entire wholesale platform in New York, and as a result the number of leased loops has risen, from 49,000 at the end of 1998 to 138,000 in June 1999.[50] That increase, however, still represented only 1.2 percent of Bell Atlantic's 11.8 million New York loops.

The use of resale reflected in table 3-2 is somewhat misleading because it combines "total service resale," which is required by the 1996 law, with the resale of Centrex services—discount multiline business services—

48. FCC (2000, table 9.2).

49. This compares favorably with Merrill Lynch's estimate of 1.28 million "on-net" (own-facilities) lines for the CLECs as of the third quarter of 1998.

50. The FCC also required SBC to offer a UNE platform in its regions as a concession for the FCC approving SBC's acquisition of Ameritech in October 1999.

Table 3-2. *Percentage of Lines Resold or Provided as UNE Loops by Large ILECs, June 30, 1999*

State	ILEC	Percent resold	Percent UNE loops
Ala.	BellSouth	2.8	0.2
Ariz.	U S WEST	0.7	0.1
Ark.	SBC	2.4	0.5
Calif.	GTE	1.4	0.3
Calif.	SBC	1.5	0.6
Colo.	U S WEST	1.5	***
Conn.	SNET	2.4	0.1
Del.	Bell Atlantic	1.7	0.3
Fla.	GTE	2.4	***
Fla.	BellSouth	1.9	0.2
Ga.	BellSouth	2.9	0.6
Idaho	U S WEST	0.2	0
Ill.	Ameritech	2.6	0.5
Ill.	GTE	0.2	***
Ind.	Ameritech	0.9	0.2
Ind.	GTE	0.6	***
Iowa	U S WEST	11.2	***
Kans.	SBC	6.6	***
Ky.	BellSouth	2.9	0.1
La.	BellSouth	3.7	0.1
Me.	Bell Atlantic	1.8	***
Md.	Bell Atlantic	1.3	0.1
Mass.	Bell Atlantic	3.4	0.1
Mich.	Ameritech	2.1	1.0
Mich.	GTE	0	0
Minn.	U S WEST	4.7	0.3
Miss.	Bell South	4.0	0.2
Mo.	SBC	2.3	0.1
Mont.	U S WEST	0.5	0.1
Nebr.	U S WEST	1.1	0.3

(continued)

Table 3-2. *(continued)*

State	ILEC	Percent resold	Percent UNE loops
Nev.	SBC	1.3	1.3
N.H.	Bell Atlantic	3.7	0.1
N.J.	Bell Atlantic	1.2	***
N. Mex.	U S WEST	0.1	0.3
N.Y.	Bell Atlantic	2.6	1.2
N.C.	BellSouth	1.9	0.3
N.C.	GTE	0.6	***
N. Dak.	U S WEST	7.3	0.2
Ohio	Ameritech	2.1	0.9
Ohio	GTE	***	0
Okla.	SBC	2.9	0.1
Ore.	GTE	0.3	***
Ore.	U S WEST	4.2	***
Penn.	Bell Atlantic	1.5	0.7
Penn.	GTE	0.6	***
R.I.	Bell Atlantic	1.8	0.3
S.C.	BellSouth	4.0	0.1
S.Dak.	U S WEST	8.1	0
Tenn.	BellSouth	1.5	1.0
Tex.	GTE	1.3	1.0
Tex.	SBC	4.0	0.2
Utah	U S WEST	0.6	0.2
Vt.	Bell Atlantic	1.3	***
Va.	Bell Atlantic	1.3	0.1
Va.	GTE	0.1	***
Wash.	GTE	0.7	***
Wash.	U S WEST	1.9	0.1
W.Va.	Bell Atlantic	0.2	0
Wisc.	Ameritech	2.1	0.9
Wisc.	GTE	0	0.3
Wyo.	U S WEST	4.6	0

Source: FCC (2000, tables 9.3, 9.4).
***Less than 0.05 percent.

which was permissible before the 1996 law. Resale of Centrex services, a convenient mechanism for obtaining access to switches owned by incumbent local exchange carriers at economical rates in order to offer bundled local and long-distance service, apparently exists only in states served by Ameritech and US WEST. This explains the relatively large share of resold lines in Iowa, North Dakota, and South Dakota shown in the table. One company, McLeod, accounts for the overwhelming share of the resold lines in these states, and US WEST has attempted to limit the growth of such Centrex resale by filing new tariffs in each of its states that would prohibit future Centrex resale.

Wholesale Rates

The most contentious issues in the implementation of the 1996 law have been the FCC's decision to assume jurisdiction for establishing the rules for wholesale service and its prescription of forward-looking (TELRIC) prices for unbundled elements. The regulatory and legal challenges to these decisions have resulted in a confusing array of state arbitrations of interconnection agreements that are still hotly contested. Indeed, there is often no agreement among the parties as to the current level of rates for unbundled elements or wholesale discounts across the states.

The data on wholesale rates shown in table 3-3 have been assembled from a variety of industry sources and are subject to considerable dispute. These rates are for business lines, and, where the unbundled rates vary by population density, the rate given is for the most densely populated market in the state. We focus on these business rates in the dense markets because the urban business subscriber is the most important target for the new competitors. Despite the fact that rates are apparently subject to a most-favored-entrant option, allowing each entrant to select from the most favorable of the provisions already arbitrated, reported rates often differ substantially across entrants. We therefore show the rate for the largest entrants because they are likely to be the most important sources of competition. Note the large variation in wholesale rates despite the fact that the technology employed by the incumbents does not differ much across states—particularly in the largest urban areas. For example, the unbundled loop rates range from less than $5 a month to more than $30.[51]

51. The shares shown in table 3-3 reflect the regional Bells' shares of total lines for the entire state, not just the dense, urban markets. Most states have a single UNE rate for loops across the state.

Table 3-3. *Distribution of Regional Bell Unbundled Business Loop Rates (UNEs) and Wholesale Discounts for Business Service in the Continental United States, 1998*

Item	Number of states	Share of U.S. access lines (percent)
Unbundled business loop rate (dollars per month)[a]		
Less than 10	6	20.8
10–14.99	15	48.0
15–19.99	16	22.2
20–24.99	6	5.5
25 or More	4	3.6
Wholesale discount for business service (percent)		
Less than 15	9	6.2
15–17.49	11	30.4
17.50–19.99	14	32.0
20–22.49	12	22.8
22.5 or more	2	3.7

Source: Janney Montgomery Scott Inc. "The Status of Agreements between the Major LECs and CLECs: Update," Philadelphia, November 10, 1997; industry sources.

a. Rate is given for densest area.

A new entrant can lease a line in downtown Chicago for less than $5 a month, for example, but must pay more than $25 a month for a similar line in downtown Denver. Obviously no "cost model," however imprecise, guides these results.

Similarly, wholesale discounts, which are supposed to reflect the avoided costs of marketing and billing, range from 12 percent to 26 percent of the business rate. This wide range might be understandable if it were inversely correlated with retail rates since the required discount would be lower for states with high rates. However, the resale discount is directly correlated with retail rates, but the correlation is not statistically significant. Obviously, the wholesale rates that have resulted from this system of regulated negotiation do not reflect any systematic measure of cost, forward- or backward-looking.

The Supreme Court recently upheld the FCC's right to set the ground rules for establishing wholesale prices under the 1996 law.[52] This result had

52. *AT&T Corp. v. Iowa Utilities Board.*

been anticipated, and many states already had adopted some form of the FCC's forward-looking TELRIC standard. But table 3-3 shows the enormous variation in the actual wholesale rates that emerge from the state-by-state arbitration process. This result demonstrates the difficulty of using regulatory arbitrations to determine the wholesale prices for using the incumbents' network facilities. The resulting prices are the outcome of a political process wrapped in the guise of efficient regulation.

Local Competition and the Cost of Entry

Had competition developed very rapidly, the distorted local rate structure that evolved under state regulation would have come under substantial stress. But because local competition has been slow to develop, there has been little or no movement in local retail rates since the law was passed in 1996 (table 3-4).[53] In virtually every state local rates have not changed perceptibly despite the fact that they do not reflect the incremental cost of service and therefore could not survive in a competitive marketplace. Thus, one of the potential sources of large economic benefits—rate rebalancing—has been squandered for the first four years of implementing the 1996 law.

One of the major reasons for the slow pace of local entry and the limited use of leased loops is that the construction of local telecommunications networks requires substantial time and very large capital resources. Much of the investment is sunk, a factor that causes uncertainty about the future to have a significant effect on investment incentives.[54] Furthermore, the FCC has determined that the wholesale prices of network elements should be set below the true economic cost, reducing the incentive for entrants to invest in their own networks. This disincentive is directly contrary to the goals of the 1996 Telecommunications Act. Figure 3-2 shows the market capitalization of all listed incumbent local companies, long-distance carriers, and new entrants. Note that the market capitaliza-

---

53. In earlier exercises of "deregulation," there was often substantial volatility and a sharp decline in prices charged by the erstwhile regulated carriers; see Winston (1998). Because competition has developed slowly in local telecommunications and retail rates remain regulated, this volatility has not yet emerged in U.S. telecommunications.

54. See, for example, Dixit and Pindyck (1994) for a further discussion of the effect of uncertainty and sunk costs on investment incentives.

Table 3-4. *Average Monthly Residential and Single-Line Business Rates in Urban Areas, October 15*

Dollars per month

Rate	1993	1994	1995	1996	1997	1998	1999
Residential	19.95	19.81	20.01	19.95	19.88	19.76	19.87
Single-line business	42.57	41.64	41.80	41.81	41.67	41.28	41.00

Source: FCC (2000, tables 14.1, 14.2).

tion of the twenty-eight new entrants listed in the figure was about $155 billion in March 2000, or about four times that of the airline industry.

Most of these entrants are only beginning to build their local networks, and most are concentrating their initial effort on only a few states. Yet, despite this slow progress and geographical concentration, they are already a very large presence in capital markets. Entry can easily require

Figure 3-2. *Market Capitalization, March 2000*

Billions of dollars

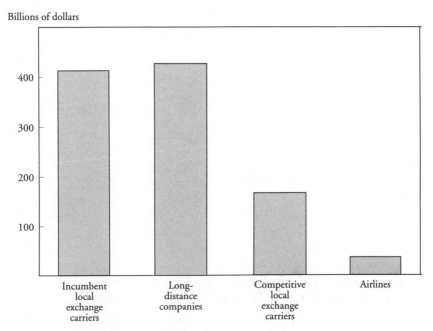

Source: quote.yahoo.com (March 31, 2000).

$1,000 or more per home passed for fiber-optics systems, including start-up losses. Because technology is changing very rapidly and a large share of this investment may be truly sunk, buildout plans must be cautiously conceived. Nevertheless, the current capitalization of the new entrants suggests that investors expect them to serve a substantial number of subscribers. If the present value of the cash flows from the average ultimate subscriber is $3,000, for example, the market value of competitive local exchange carriers in March 2000 reflected the market's expectation that they will eventually serve more than 50 million homes.

The size of many of these new local entrants and their ability to raise capital—all but a few have a market capitalization of $1 billion or more—calls into question a regulatory strategy that is based on the need to subsidize entrants' access to incumbents' facilities. Had the regulatory climate not sown confusion, discord, and innumerable court challenges, capital formation by new entrants might have been even greater than that revealed in figure 3-2. Equally important, in the absence of the ability to rely on resale and the leasing of network facilities at below-cost rates from incumbents, the new entrants would undoubtedly have moved more quickly to build their own networks, mobilizing even more capital and converting it into modern network facilities

Long-Distance Competition

The AT&T divestiture in 1984 sought to encourage competition in long-distance markets by placing entrants and incumbents on an equal footing with regard to access (interconnection) conditions and charges. In essence, the AT&T decree provided long-distance entrants what the reciprocal compensation requirements of the 1996 law provided for local entrants.

The result of the 1984 equal-access provisions on long-distance competition in the United States appears to have been dramatic. As table 3-5 shows, AT&T began to lose market share rapidly after 1984. Even though competition had begun in the mid-1970s, AT&T still had more than 90 percent of long-distance carrier revenues at the time of the divestiture. In the next ten years, however, its share fell from 90.1 percent to 55.2 percent. In the first three years after the divestiture, AT&T lost approximately 12.8 percent of its market share (11.5 percent divided by 0.901)—a far greater

Table 3-5. *Market Shares of Revenues for U.S. Long-Distance Carriers, 1984–97*

Percent

Year	AT&T	MCI	Sprint	WorldCom	All others
1984	90.1	4.5	2.7	. . .	2.6
1985	86.3	5.5	2.6	. . .	5.6
1986	81.9	7.6	4.3	. . .	6.3
1987	78.6	8.8	5.8	. . .	6.8
1988	74.6	10.3	7.2	. . .	8.0
1989	67.5	12.1	8.4	0.2	11.8
1990	65.0	14.2	9.7	0.3	10.8
1991	63.2	15.2	9.9	0.5	11.3
1992	60.8	16.7	9.7	1.4	11.5
1993	58.1	17.8	10.0	1.9	12.3
1994	55.2	17.4	10.1	3.3	14.0
1995	51.8	19.7	9.8	4.9	13.8
1996	47.9	20.0	9.7	5.5	17.0
1997	44.0	19.0	9.5	6.5	20.9
1998	43.0	25.6[a]	10.5	a	20.9

Source: FCC (2000, table 11.3).
a. MCI/WorldCom.

share loss than has occurred in the local markets in the first three years after the passage of the 1996 Act.

U.S. long-distance rates continue to fall in the face of increasing competition and declining access charges. The FCC estimates that average revenue per domestic interstate minute of long-distance service fell from 15 cents in 1992 to 11 cents in 1998.[55] About 2 cents of this decline is attributable to declining access charges collected by the local carriers and universal service charges imposed by the FCC. The remainder reflects competition and increased productivity. Most of this "competitive" decline appears to be concentrated in business rates, not residential rates. On average, residences paid 17.6 cents a minute in 1996, 17.0 cents in 1997, and 15.3 cents in 1998.[56] Rates for business calls, which account for about 60 percent of all long-distance calls, averaged about 8 cents a minute in 1998, still somewhat above the long-run in-

55. Lande (1999, table 9).
56. Data obtained from PNR and Associates, Jenkintown, Pennsylvania.

cremental cost of service—access charges plus 1.5 cents a minute, or 5.5 cents a conversation minute.[57] Residential rates remain far above the long-run incremental cost of physically delivering the service, creating the need for further market entry, but entry from the most likely sources—the regional Bell companies—has been blocked by continued disputes over the Bell companies' compliance with the detailed regulatory "checklist" in the 1996 Act.

The forgone welfare gains from denying the Bell companies entry into long-distance services are considerable. For example, assume that such entry had lowered interstate residential long-distance rates by 4 cents a minute in 1998 (which still would leave those rates substantially above business rates.) Given that residences spent $44.1 billion on long-distance services in 1998, of which two-thirds is interstate long-distance, this reduction would have generated consumer gains of $8.6 billion, including a transfer from producers of $7.7 billion and a reduction in deadweight consumer loss of $900 million.[58] Given that intrastate long-distance is about one-third of long-distance services, the consequent liberalization of intrastate long distance could have generated another $4 billion in consumer gains.[59]

The Wireless Sector: Competition without Regulation

Until the mid-1990s, competition in U.S. commercial wireless services was slow to develop. For more than a decade the United States had only two wireless (cellular) providers in each market because the FCC allocated only two 25 megahertz (MHz) licenses to each market. Regulation in many large states led to higher prices than would have occurred under competition. In addition, unlike Europe or Canada, the United States licensed wireless services on a geographically fragmented basis, making it difficult for wireless companies to put together national or even regional wireless networks. In 1993, however, Congress forced a major change in U.S. wireless policy by instructing the FCC to auction spectrum, in part

57. Lande (1999, table 10) on access charges. The cost per minute for long-distance services is from Crandall and Waverman (1998).

58. Estimates of residential spending are from the Bureau of the Census, *Annual Survey of Communications, 1998* (1999).

59. The 1996 law allows full liberalization of intrastate long-distance markets once Section 271 approval is granted to the Bell companies or three years have elapsed.

to help solve the U.S. government's budget deficit but essentially to deregulate cellular pricing.[60] These auctions began in December 1994 and have resulted in the assignment of 120 MHz of additional wireless spectrum for "personal communications services" (PCS) throughout the country. In addition, an entrepreneurial company, Nextel, has succeeded in transferring another 10–15 MHz of spectrum from a dispatch-mode service to a commercial wireless service that competes with cellular and PCS service providers.

Wireless Rates

The first of the new PCS services began in late 1995, and a large number of companies have begun building facilities. All but 28 of the top 100 metropolitan markets in the United States now have at least five wireless competitors—two cellular providers, two to four PCS services, and Nextel.[61] The effect of the resulting competition on wireless rates has been stunning (figure 3-3). Throughout the 1984–95 period, inflation-adjusted cellular rates had fallen at a rate of 3 to 4 percent a year.[62] Between 1995 and 1999, however, real cellular rates fell at a rate of 17 percent a year as PCS providers offered service at per minute prices that were more than 50 percent lower than existing cellular rates. There is evidence that with open entry just one new player is sufficient to drive rates sharply lower.[63] As the wireless industry evolves from its current structure into one with six or seven competitive national players, further major beneficial effects are likely on both rates and service quality.

The capital requirements for building the new PCS systems are considerable. Altogether the PCS providers have been spending between $1.5 billion and $2.2 billion a year on their infrastructure. The established cellular companies have been spending even more, upward of $3 billion a year, to convert their infrastructure from analog to digital. And both have been spending heavily to subsidize a portion of the annual $6 billion investment in consumer handsets.[64] All told, wireless companies have been spending more than $12 billion a year during the past three years.[65] Were

60. In 1993 about half the states regulated cellular prices at either the wholesale or retail level.
61. See Mutschler and Wuh (1999, p. 13) for data on the number of carriers by market.
62. Hausman (1999a).
63. Crandall and Gertner (1999).
64. Leibowitz and others (1999), tables 14B, 14C, 15A, and 15B.
65. Cellular Telecommunications Industry Association, semi-annual surveys.

Figure 3-3. *Real per Minute Wireless Prices, 1993–99*

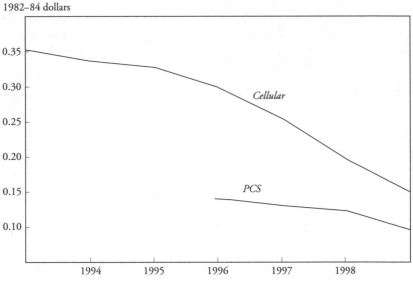

1982–84 dollars

Source: Leibowitz and others (2000).

this investment directed to wireline services, it could have resulted in providing new facilities to serve perhaps 30 million subscribers—far more than the CLECs and CAPs currently serve. Competition in a very capital-intensive wireless sector followed immediately upon the liberalization of entry conditions. Subscriber rates fell dramatically, and they continue to fall as the new PCS companies fill out their networks.

The only new regulation the 1996 Telecommunications Act placed on the wireless industry was the imposition of "reciprocal compensation" on wireless-wireline interconnection. Before 1996 these rates for exchanging traffic were often in excess of 2 cents a minute; today, they range between 0.5 and 0.7 cents a minute because wireless companies are afforded the same interconnection rates as the new CLECs. Otherwise, competition has increased dramatically without unbundling, resale, or other new forms of regulation. Indeed, wireless services are essentially fully exempt from wholesale and retail price regulation. The result has been a major decline in real wireless prices.

Wireless rates are continuing to decline, perhaps at an accelerating rate. In May 1998, AT&T introduced a flat-price nationwide calling plan that allowed a subscriber to make calls to and from anywhere in the continental United States for a single rate of 11 cents to 15 cents a minute, depending on the volume of calling. AT&T eliminated roaming charges under this plan.[66] The other carriers followed with 10-cents-a-minute plans, and Bell Atlantic even has one plan that offers nationwide calling at only 8.33 cents a minute. These sharp declines in the price of wireless calling are now sparking interest in developing wireless as an alternative to wireline service. Indeed, AT&T is promoting its service in Texas as the alternative to a subscriber's second line.

Subscriber Penetration

The United States has lagged behind some European countries in cellular penetration, in large part because of its fragmented wireless industry and therefore the need for subscribers to roam onto other systems at high prices in areas where their carriers have no facilities. The development of national wireless service by AT&T, Sprint, and Nextel as others, such as Bell Atlantic, AirTouch, SBC, Voicestream, and U.S. Cellular, expand their footprints has led to national pricing without roaming charges. While subscriber penetration is still only about 30 percent of the population, it is now growing rapidly.

As long as the United States subsidizes residential wireline connections, U.S. wireless penetration may remain below that realized by Hong Kong, Italy, and the Scandinavian countries, but the full effect of the sharp decline in U.S. wireless rates has not yet been realized. Nor has the United States been able to implement "calling-party-pays" tariffs, thereby encouraging wireless subscribers to leave their lithium-ion powered handsets on continuously to receive calls.

Wireline-Wireless Substitution

Substantial casual empirical evidence indicates that wireless service is a substitute for traditional wireline telephone service in several countries. Subscriber line growth has stopped in several Scandinavian countries and is likely to turn negative as wireless service becomes virtually universal. Some forecast that many European countries will have more than 70

---

66. Roaming charges are charges assessed by wireless carriers to offer service to the customers of carriers from other parts of the country.

Table 3-6. *Average Household Bills for Most Intensive Users of Wireless,
1997 and 1998*
Dollars per month unless otherwise specified

Wireless spending percentile	Average 1997 wireline bills	Average 1997 wireless bills	1997 ratio: wireless/ wireline	Average 1998 wireline bills	Average 1998 wireless bills	1998 ratio: wireless/ wireline
70–75	84.73	47.36	0.56	80.85	46.72	0.58
75–80	87.65	53.78	0.61	88.27	53.13	0.60
80–85	92.03	62.81	0.68	90.58	62.18	0.69
85–90	101.60	77.11	0.76	95.54	75.17	0.79
90–95	122.31	100.86	0.82	108.18	98.08	0.91
95–100	133.37	223.63	1.68	123.03	194.22	1.58

Source: PNR and Associates, Jenkintown, Pa.

percent penetration of wireless service, meaning that virtually every adult will have a portable wireless handset.[67] Our preliminary analysis suggests that wireless services may already be a weak substitute for wireline telephone service in the United States. First, it is clear that heavy users of wireless services are also intensive users of wireline services, and their ratio of wireless to wireline expenditures generally increased between 1997 and 1998 (table 3-6). Households generate large telephone bills through heavy use of out-bound long-distance services. The evidence in table 3-6 thus shows that as their long-distance calling increases, their use of wireless services also increases. Moreover, the ratio of their wireless expenses to their wireline expenses appears to be rising over time despite falling wireline long-distance rates because wireless rates have been falling even more rapidly. These patterns are suggestive of a growing substitution of wireless for wireline services.[68] We expect this substitution to grow even stronger once the new low-priced bulk pricing plans for wireless have been fully marketed. As real wireless prices continue to fall and the real costs of

67. Mutschler and Wuh (1999, p. 32).

68. Preliminary estimates of a logit model of the probability of a household subscribing to a cellular (or PCS) service in 1998, using PNR data, find that the probability of wireless subscription is directly related to the level of intraLATA rates in the state in which the subscriber resides. This relationship is stronger in 1998 than in 1997, as we would expect. However, we have been unable to estimate the effect of wireline prices on cellular *usage* because of problems in the minutes-of-use data in the PNR data sets.

residential wireline connections rise because of the rebalancing forced by local competition, the usage of wireless service should increase substantially from its current 6 percent of total minutes of use in the United States.

Another form of wireless telecommunications could compete with wireline telephony, particularly in areas of low population density. "Fixed" wireless service, which connects fixed subscribers to the network through signals transmitted through the radio spectrum from terrestrial towers, is already in use in many developing countries in areas of low density. Fixed service could be deployed to a much greater degree in the United States if universal service pricing policies did not artificially hold rural rates below the long-run incremental cost of the wireline service. Were current telephone rates set efficiently, fixed wireless services might develop rather rapidly and provide substantial potential and actual competition for even the lightly populated areas of the country.[69]

Payphone Use

Decreased wireless prices and increased wireless penetration have already had a significant effect on payphone usage. The number of payphones has decreased substantially during the past three years.[70] With integration of networks, including voice and data networks to allow easy conversion from e-mail to voice mail, and the ability to view e-mail on hand-held mobile devices, a mobile telephone will likely become the chief instrument for voice messages in the future. Especially in a business setting, the ability to avoid voice mail tag is likely to lead to significant substitution of mobile voice for current wireline voice usage. One detriment to even higher mobile usage is the relatively high tax rates levied on mobile usage by a combination of federal, state, and local tax authorities.[71]

Regulation and Investment

The 1996 Telecommunications Act provides extensive new regulation of the nation's existing local-exchange carriers but leaves the wireless sector

69. Unfortunately, the 1996 law allows states to exempt rural areas from competitive entry. Therefore, even if current rates were rebalanced to economically efficient levels or explicit, transferable subsidies were imposed to cover access deficits in rural areas, many states might still refuse to allow rural areas to enjoy the benefits of competition.

70. Jerry A. Hausman, "Reply Declaration to the FCC," December 1998.

71. Hausman (forthcoming).

to develop on an unregulated basis. In addition, the 1996 law provides a substantial modicum of rate deregulation for the cable television industry and allows cable companies to provide traditional and new advanced telecommunications services free of the wholesale and retail regulation that applies to their rivals in the local-exchange sector. All three groups—the local-exchange companies, cable television, and wireless service providers—are important potential sources of new technologies and facilities for delivering broadband Internet connections. Indeed, AT&T has invested more than $100 billion in cable systems as part of a strategy to deliver a full range of video, data, and voice services to residential customers. The local-exchange companies have begun to deploy their own broadband service over their copper-wire distribution lines, called digital subscriber-line service. And wireless companies continue to invest in new digital technologies capable of offering ever greater bandwidth and features.

It is still too early to estimate the effects of the regulatory climate on investment strategies in any detail. A brief look at recent investment trends suggests, however, that regulation may be a substantial drag on investment in the traditional telephone industry. Despite the very large potential market for new, advanced broadband services for Internet connections, wireline carriers—incumbent local exchange companies, long-distance carriers, and the new competitive carriers—have increased their capital spending only modestly in recent years. At the same time, capital spending by the cable-broadcast sector and by wireless companies has soared (figure 3-4). Between 1993 and 1997, real spending in the cable-broadcast sector increased at an annual rate of 26 percent, largely due to digital upgrades of cable systems, while wireless spending increased by more than 40 percent a year. During this period the wireline carriers increased their capital spending at only 6 percent a year. Surprisingly, the rate of increase was virtually the same for the incumbent local companies and their principal potential rivals—the long-distance carriers and the competitive carriers. Moreover, in 1998, the year in which deployment of digital subscriber lines began in earnest, investment by incumbent local companies increased only marginally.[72] The slow growth in capital spending by entrants and incumbents alike in a sector that has recently been opened to competition should set off warning alarms that something is amiss. This difference in the

---

72. FCC, *Statistics of Communications Common Carriers,* 1998/99 edition. The 1998 data for the entire sector are not yet available from the Bureau of Economic Analysis, so we are unable to report spending for wireline carriers other than the incumbent local carriers.

Figure 3-4. *Real Investment in the Communications Sector, 1985–97*

Millions of 1992 dollars

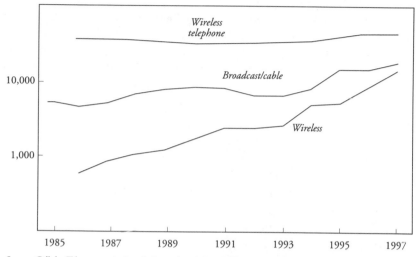

Source: Cellular Telecommunications Industry Association; FCC; Department of Commerce.

investment behavior of the regulated and the unregulated sectors of the communications industry provides further evidence that FCC regulation of new services and FCC-state regulation of wholesale and retail rates is retarding capital formation.

Competition in U.S. telecommunications markets is only beginning in the local wireline access and exchange market. The complex regulatory structure developed to manage local competition has been extremely controversial and has created years of regulatory strife and litigation. "Regulated competition" may well be an approach that harms consumers while regulators attempt to help new competitors. Relying upon a flawed system of cost-based regulation to provide entrants with extremely favorable access to incumbents' facilities, regulators are attempting to micromanage the liberalization process in a manner that is quite unprecedented in the recent history of U.S. deregulation. Moreover, there is very little evidence that this management of competition is working very well. Rather, it appears to be mired down in a hopeless exercise of setting wholesale rates and limiting incumbents' ability to exploit the value of their own networks, stunting the incentives to invest in new facilities by existing carriers, and delaying investments by entrants as they wait for regulators to provide them with access to the full complement of incumbents' facilities at below-cost prices.

By contrast, competition in the totally deregulated wireless market is flourishing, and competition in the partially deregulated long-distance market has increased (although the recently announced merger between MCI/WorldCom and Sprint could change that assessment). Long-distance rates, particularly business rates, are falling steadily. Residential rates are still substantially above long-run incremental cost, pointing out the need for further entry. Wireless rates are falling even more dramatically. New wireless pricing plans are emerging and wireless carriers are experimenting with new services in a totally deregulated market. It appears likely that wireless will soon be a sufficient source of competition for at least conventional voice and data wireline services to permit a substantial degree of deregulation of the nation's telecommunications service providers, but it is unlikely that such deregulation can or will occur, given the detailed mandates of the 1996 Telecommunications Act. Nor is it likely that a reconsideration of the 1996 law by Congress would lead to better legislation and an improvement in the prospects for deregulation.

A recurring theme in this chapter is that detailed cost-based regulation of wholesale rates is not a satisfactory approach for stimulating competition in this network industry. Rather, we would prefer an attempt by regulators to undo the regulatory-created barriers to entry built into the *retail* rate structure. As long as large numbers of subscribers—particularly residential subscribers in all but the most dense areas of the country—are provided local service at rates below long-run incremental cost, entrants will have little incentive to offer these subscribers service. It would be better for regulators to attempt to eliminate the pricing distortions that they have already created than to erect an entire new set of distorted wholesale rates that will be difficult to eliminate in the future. An ounce of regulatory forbearance is surely much to be preferred over a pound of regulatory cure.

References

Baumol, William. 1999. "Option Value Analysis and Telephone Access Charges." In *Real Options: The New Investment Theory and its Implications for Telecommunications Economics*, edited by James Alleman and Eli Noam. Kluwer Academic.
Crandall, Robert W., and Robert H. Gertner. 1999. "Declaration on Behalf of Bell Atlantic

Mobile, Inc., in the Matter of 1998 Biennial Regulatory Review—Spectrum Aggregation Limits for Wireless Telecommunications Carriers, WT Docket No. 98-205." FCC, January 25.

Crandall, Robert W., and Leonard Waverman. 1998. Affidavit submitted in support of Application of Ameritech Michigan for Provision of In-Region, InterLATA Services in Michigan. Submitted to the FCC.

———. 2000. *Who Pays for Universal Service When Subsidies Become Transparent?* Brookings.

Dixit, Avinash K., and Robert Pindyck. 1994. *Investment under Uncertainty.* Princeton University Press.

FCC (Federal Communications Commission). 2000. *Trends in Telephone Service.* March.

Jerry A. Hausman. 1996. "Proliferation of Networks in Telecommunications." In *Networks, Infrastructure, and the New Task for Regulation,* edited by Donald L. Alexander and Werner Sichel. University of Michigan Press.

———. 1997. "Valuing the Effect of Regulation on New Services in Telecommunications." *Brookings Papers on Economic Activity: Microeconomics:* 1–54.

———. 1998. "Taxation by Telecommunications Regulation." *Tax Policy and the Economy* 12: 29–48.

———. 1999a. "Cellular Telephone, New Products and the CPI." *Journal of Business and Economics Statistics* 17 (April): 188–94.

———. 1999b. "The Effect of Sunk Costs in Telecommunication Regulation." In *Real Options: The New Investment Theory and Its Implications for Telecommunications Economics,* edited by James Alleman and Eli Noam. Kluwer Academic.

———. 1999c. "Regulation by TSLRIC: Economic Effects on Investment and Innovation." *Multimedia und Recht* 3: 22–26.

———. Forthcoming. "Efficiency Effects on the U.S. Economy from Wireless Taxation." *National Tax Journal.*

Hausman, Jerry A., and Howard Shelanski. 1999. "Economic Welfare and Telecommunications Regulation: The E-Rate Policy for Universal Service Subsidies." *Yale Journal on Regulation* 16 (Winter): 19–52.

Hausman, Jerry A., and J. Gregory Sidak. 1999. "A Consumer-Welfare Approach to Mandatory Unbundling of Telecommunications Networks." *Yale Law Journal* 109 (December): 417–506.

Kastan, Mark, and Daniel Reingold. 1999. "Telecom Services–Local, In-Depth Report." New York: Merrill Lynch.

Lande, Jim. 1999. "Telecommunications Industry Revenue: 1998." Federal Communications Commission, Common Carrier Bureau.

Leibowitz, Dennis H., and others. 1999. "The Global Wireless Communications Industry, Winter 1999–2000." New York: Donaldson, Lufkin and Jenrette.

Mutschler, Linda J., and Paul Wuh. 1999. "The Next Generation III: Wireless in the U.S." New York: Merrill Lynch.

National Association of Regulatory Utility Commissioners. 1998. "Bell Operating Companies Long-Distance Message Telephone Rates." Washington, D.C.

Perl, Lewis. 1985. "Social Welfare and Distributional Consequences of Cost-Based Telephone Pricing." Paper presented at the Thirteenth Annual Telecommunications Policy Research Conference, Airlie, Va. April 23.

Wenders, John T., and Bruce L. Egan. 1986. "The Implications of Economic Efficiency for U.S. Telecommunications Policy." *Telecommunications Policy* 10 (March): 33–40.

Winston, Clifford. 1998. "U.S. Industry Adjustment to Economic Deregulation." *Journal of Economic Perspectives* 12 (Summer): 89–110.

PAUL L. JOSKOW

4

Deregulation and Regulatory Reform in the U.S. Electric Power Sector

The U.S. electric power sector is in the midst of major changes in its structure, the way that it is regulated, and the role that competition plays in allocating resources to and within the sector. These reforms are more substantial than many had anticipated only a few years ago, and the pace of change is accelerating. This paper examines the nature and origins of these changes and provides an initial assessment of their costs, benefits, future trends, and unresolved issues.

The paper begins with a brief discussion of the industry structure and regulatory framework that characterized the sector during most of the twentieth century and the economic performance of the sector after World War II. It then describes the initial efforts in the 1980s and early 1990s to open the electricity industry to competitive suppliers of generating services. Next it reviews the economic and political pressures that emerged in the early 1990s for more fundamental reforms, which focused on increasing the role of competition in the supply of electric generation services. This

The author is grateful to Alfred Kahn, Alvin Klevorick, Elizabeth Moler, David Newbery, Sam Peltzman, John Rowe, Mathew White, and Cliff Winston for comments on an earlier draft of this paper. The author also thanks Margaret Kyle and J. J. Prescott for their assistance with the research. He is grateful for research support from the MIT Center for Energy and Environment Policy Research.

discussion develops the architecture of the basic reform model, adopted by a number of pioneer states and supported by changes in federal regulation, that underpins both wholesale and retail competition in the supply of generation services. It then examines recent trends in generation divestiture, mergers between electric utilities, and between electric and gas pipeline and distribution companies, and the development of competitive merchant generating plants.

An important aspect of this reform process is the development of new institutional arrangements to govern access to and the operations of transmission networks, which provide the essential platform supporting competition among decentralized generators of electricity. To provide a concrete example of the nature and complexity of this task, I discuss the structure and performance attributes of the transmission network and wholesale power market institutions that began operating in California in early 1998.

The paper then turns to a discussion of the early experience with retail competition in California, Massachusetts, and Pennsylvania. Reform in the electricity sector is unusual in that the stimulus for the most radical reforms has come from the states rather than from the federal government, although federal regulators and Congress have played an important supporting role. One result of this state-by-state process is that reform is moving at very different paces in different regions of the country even though electricity trading regions encompass large geographic areas covering many states. In some cases, retail competition initiatives are moving forward faster than the wholesale market and transmission reforms that are necessary to support an efficient retail competition regime. This mismatch between wholesale and retail market reforms can lead to performance problems. I conclude with a discussion of the early evidence on electricity market performance.

Governance Structures in Electricity before Deregulation

To best understand the roles of competition, deregulation, and restructuring in today's electric power sector, one should begin with an understanding of the industry structure and regulation framework that characterized the industry during most of the twentieth century.[1]

1. A more detailed discussion of the traditional industry structure, its regulation, and early initiatives to introduce competition can be found in Joskow (1989), Joskow (1997), and Joskow and Schmalensee (1983).

Physical and Economic Attributes of Electricity Supply and Demand

The supply of electricity is generally divided into several separate functions: generation, distribution, power procurement and retailing functions, and transmission. Electricity is generated using falling water, internal combustion engines, steam turbines powered with steam produced with fossil fuels, nuclear fuel, and various renewable fuels, wind-driven turbines, and photovoltaic technologies. In most developed countries numerous generating plants are typically dispersed over a large geographic area. Electricity is distributed to residences and businesses at relatively low voltages using wires and transformers along and under streets and other rights of way. A set of power procurement and retailing functions related to distribution includes making arrangements for supplies of power from generators, metering, billing, and various demand management services. The dividing line between distribution and retailing is still murky and controversial. The transmission of electricity involves the "transportation" of electricity between generating sites and distribution centers, the interconnection and integration of dispersed generating facilities into a stable synchronized network, the scheduling and dispatching of generating facilities that are connected to the transmission network to balance demand and supply in real time, and the management of equipment failures, network constraints, and relationships with other interconnected networks.

The attributes of electricity demand, electricity supply, and physical constraints associated with the operation of synchronized alternating current (AC) networks are highly relevant not only for understanding the organizational structure of the electric power sector that has evolved over the last century but also for designing transmission network and competitive wholesale power market institutions with good performance attributes. A modern AC transmission network makes it possible to meet continually changing demand levels efficiently by substituting increased production from facilities with low marginal costs (say, in New Mexico) for production from those with high marginal costs (say, in California). An efficient network also economizes on the reserve capacity required for any given level of reliability (responses to equipment outages and unanticipated swings in demand) by effectively aggregating demand (or "loads") and reserve generating capacity over a wide geographic area and by providing multiple links between geographically dispersed demand and generating sites to ensure a high probability of service continuity when individual transmission links fail. To accomplish these tasks, the network must be operated to maintain its frequency and voltage parameters within narrow bands and to respond to rapidly changing system conditions on the demand and supply sides, especially short-term demand swings and unplanned equipment outages. In addition to providing energy to run customer appliances and equipment, generating facilities are called upon almost continuously to provide a variety of ancillary services that help the network adjust to the ebb and flow of demand and unexpected outages of transmission and generating facilities.[2]

Electricity usually cannot be stored or inventoried economically, and demand varies widely from hour to hour during any single day and from day to day during the year. The aggregate short-run elasticity of demand is very small. Moreover, there is generally no meaningful direct physical relationship between a specific generator and a specific consumer and no way to curtail an individual customer's consumption when specific generators fail to perform. Electric power networks are not switched networks like railroad or telephone networks, where a supplier makes a physical delivery of a product at point A that is then physically transported to a specific customer at point B. A free-flowing AC network is an integrated physical machine that follows the laws of physics (Kirchoff's Laws), not the laws of financial contracting. Electricity goes into a common pool of electric energy, and demand by consumers draws energy out of that common pool. The network operator must ensure that the pool stays filled to a constant level, balancing inflows and outflows continuously and managing congestion on the network.

The aggregate generation of electricity and its consumption must be balanced continuously, subject to congestion constraints, for the entire network to meet specific physical parameters (frequency, voltage, stability) and constraints (thermal limits and contingency constraints) on network operations. Electricity must be manufactured in a generating plant virtually contemporaneously with its consumption; it is the ultimate in just-in-time manufacturing. When a generator turns on and off, it affects system

---

2. Ancillary services include spinning reserves, which are provided by generating facilities that are operating at less than their full capacity and that can increase output quickly in response to a call from the network operator. Nonspinning reserves are generating units that are not currently operating but that can be brought into service fairly quickly (within thirty minutes, for example). Standby reserves are similar, but their response time is slower (say, sixty minutes). Frequency regulation requires generators to increase and decrease output virtually instantly in response to variations in frequency from 60 hertz. Blackstart capability refers to generating plants that can be self-started after the network has crashed and can be used to bring the network back into service.

conditions throughout the interconnected network. A failure of a major piece of equipment in one part of the network can disrupt the stability of the entire system if the network operator does not have resources available to respond quickly to these contingencies. Moreover, efficient and effective remedial responses to equipment failures can involve coordinated reactions of multiple generators located far from the site of the failure. These attributes create potential network externality and "commons" problems.

Market Structure and Regulation circa 1980

The U.S. electric power sector evolved largely with firms that were (and in most regions of the country still are) vertically integrated into generation, transmission, distribution, and retailing and that held de facto exclusive rights to serve retail consumers within defined geographic areas. These firms were generally subject to "cost of service" or "rate of return" regulation by state public utility commissions.[3] Figure 4-1 provides a simple picture of the structure of the U.S. electric power industry around 1980.

Although electric power industries throughout the world were vertically integrated, the organization of the U.S. industry was atypical in several key ways. The most striking differences were the large number of electric companies providing service to the public and the primary role of private rather than state-owned companies. The bulk of the resources in the U.S. sector were controlled by more than one hundred privately owned firms of varying sizes. Thus, *horizontal* integration was not nearly as extensive in the United States as it was in other countries.[4]

From a physical perspective, the U.S. sector (combined with portions of Canada and northern Mexico) is composed of three large, synchronized AC networks: the Eastern Interconnection, the Western Interconnection, and the Texas Interconnection.[5] None of these networks is controlled by a single entity, however. Instead, more than 140 separate "control areas" are

3. The economic rationale for vertical integration is discussed in more detail in Joskow (1996b).

4. In addition to the vertically integrated privately owned utilities, there are thousands of (generally small) unintegrated or partially integrated public and cooperative distribution entities that buy power from the private utilities as well as from state, cooperative, and federal power production and marketing entities using the transmission networks of surrounding private utilities. There are also a few large municipal utilities that are vertically integrated and look much like a typical private utility (the Los Angeles Department of Water and Power is an example). Collectively, these public and cooperative entities still account for more than 20 percent of the electricity generation and distribution in the United States.

5. There are small direct current ties connecting the Western and Eastern systems as well.

Figure 4-1. *Traditional Industry Structure*[a]

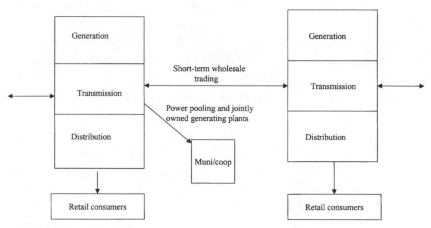

a. Muni/coop = municipal utilities and cooperatives.

superimposed on the three networks, and individual vertically integrated utilities, or groups of utilities operating through power pooling arrangements, are responsible for generator dispatch, network operations, and reliability on specific portions of each of the three physical networks. To harmonize and rationalize this sprawling system, the U.S. industry has developed a complex set of standard operating protocols and bilateral and multilateral agreements designed to maintain reliability, to facilitate coordinated operations between interconnected transmission systems, to facilitate trades of power between control areas, and to minimize free-riding problems, while maintaining dispersed ownership and control of vertically integrated "pieces" of the relevant networks.

The decentralized structure of the U.S. electricity sector fostered the early development of competitive *wholesale* markets, through which utilities buy and sell electricity among one another to reduce the costs of supplying their franchise customers. Wholesale trade expanded rapidly in the 1970s, initially in response to large differences in the short-run marginal cost of hydroelectric, coal, oil, and natural gas generating units as well as to variations in demand and capacity availability among utilities in the same region. By the 1980s a set of fairly active wholesale electricity markets had emerged in the United States.[6] In all cases, these were wholesale

6. See Joskow and Schmalensee (1983) and Joskow (1989) for a more detailed discussion of wholesale power markets.

transactions between utilities. Virtually all retail consumers received a "bundled" product (generation, transmission, distribution, and retailing services packaged together) from the local monopoly distributor (whether vertically integrated or not) with prices based on the average total cost of power generated by the plants owned by the distribution utility plus power purchased under contract from third parties.

Potential Benefits of Restructuring and Deregulating the System

It is only natural to hypothesize that a primary motivation for major structural and regulatory reforms of the electricity sector would be a long historical record of poor economic performance. After all, the institution of regulated monopoly has a bad reputation. Cost-plus regulation dulls incentives, and government-granted monopolies induce rent seeking and lead to taxation by regulation.[7] Several supply-side indicators show, however, that the electric power sector in the United States has performed fairly well over time. In particular, it has supplied electricity with high levels of reliability, investment in new capacity has been readily financed to keep up with (or often exceed) demand growth, system losses (both physical and those due to theft of service) are as low as or lower than those in other developed countries, and electricity is available virtually universally. The traditional system was efficient and reliable in dispatching generating plants; making cost-reducing, short-term energy trades between generating utilities; maintaining network reliability; and dealing with congestion, unplanned outages, and system emergencies. This record contrasts sharply with the performance of the electricity sectors in many other countries, especially developing countries and many developed countries that rely on state-owned utilities.

Average real electricity prices in the United States fell rapidly from the early 1900s until the early 1970s. Indeed, during this time period, the U.S. electric power sector had one of the highest rates of productivity growth of any major industry in the U.S. economy. From the mid-1970s until the mid-1980s, however, real prices for electricity increased sharply

7. Of course, electric utility regulation was never pure cost-plus regulation. Both regulatory lag and opportunities for regulators to monitor and disallow costs ensured that there were some incentives to control costs. See Joskow and Schmalensee (1986).

in response to increases in basic energy prices, high interest rates, tightened environmental standards, and investments in capital-intensive nuclear power plants. In the mid-1980s, average real electricity prices began to fall again as input prices declined, and they continued to fall during the 1990s; in some areas of the country, however, electricity costs and prices remained well above their historical low values.[8] These continuing high prices became an impetus for restructuring in several states. The average price of electricity in the United States in 1997, before major reforms were implemented, was 6.85 cents a kilowatt hour (kWh). The average price charged to residential customers was about 8.4 cents/kWh, and the price to industrial customers was about 4.5 cents/kWh. These prices were and are at the low end of the range of prices for developed countries.[9] But the average price data hide large interstate and interregional differences in electricity prices.

Despite these generally favorable performance attributes, a variety of apparent short-run, medium-run, and long-run inefficiencies are targets of opportunity for structural and regulatory reforms and the creation of competitive generation markets. Decentralized competitive wholesale markets for electricity are most likely to have significant beneficial effects in the medium and long term in the following areas:

Generation investment decisions and construction costs. Construction costs of similar generating units vary substantially across utility companies, a fact that cannot be readily explained by differences in underlying cost opportunities.[10] Poor cost control incentives created by price regulation in a monopoly environment may explain some of these variations. Because vertically integrated monopolies served defined geographic areas, companies that were particularly good at managing the construction of generating plants could not expand into other geographic areas. Nor were generating utilities that did not manage generation construction projects very well subject to severe penalties or driven out of the business. Smaller utilities with less experience may have been less capable of managing more complex technologies than larger utilities and were also less innovative.[11] More important, the large investments in nuclear generating

---

8. Joskow (1987, 1989).

9. Energy Information Administration (1999, table 11); and International Energy Agency (1997, tables 32, 34). The difference between the residential and industrial prices largely reflects differences in load factor and the voltage level at which electricity is supplied.

10. Joskow and Rose (1985); Lester and McCabe (1993).

11. Rose and Joskow (1990).

technology made by U.S. utilities during the 1970s and 1980s turned out to be uneconomical compared with fossil-fueled generation supply alternatives. Whether these investments were bad decisions to begin with or simply bad outcomes, the result is that many utilities were saddled with nuclear power plants whose accounting costs (used for regulatory purposes) were far above their competitive market values. Competitive generation markets should increase the efficiency of investments in new generating plants and place the risk of both managerial decisions and changes in market conditions initially on the suppliers of generation service.

Politicized resource planning processes. In some regions, the Northeast and California, in particular, the process through which utility investment and power contracting decisions were made became highly politicized during the late 1980s.[12] Utilities came under pressure to invest in or contract for power supplies from cogenerators and renewable energy sources at prices far in excess of the least-cost alternatives available. These projects came into operation during the late 1980s and early 1990s, causing electricity costs and prices to rise significantly in the affected states. One of the potential benefits of creating competitive decentralized markets for wholesale power is to bring these politicized resource planning processes to an end and to create an environment that stimulates the lowest-cost generation sources, consistent with environmental regulations, to enter the system.

Operating costs of generating units. The operating costs of generating plants depend on the cost of fuel, the availability of the unit (that is, the fraction of the year that it is not being repaired and is available to supply electricity), and the plant's thermal efficiency. Unlike the situation in England and Wales before privatization and restructuring, U.S. utilities have not been forced to buy costly fuel in order to support domestic fuel producers and their employees. Both availability and thermal efficiency across fossil and nuclear generating units vary significantly, however, even after controlling for the underlying attributes of the technology that was chosen.[13] Moreover, some utilities appear to be systematically better operators than others. The regulatory process penalized and rewarded operating performance only indirectly, although several states began to focus on performance-based incentives for performance during

12. Joskow (1989).
13. Joskow and Schmalensee (1987); Lester and McCabe (1993).

the 1980s.[14] Again, the market mechanisms for driving firms to best practice maintenance and operating protocols were blunted by the institution of regulated monopoly.

Retirement of uneconomical generating plants. Some have argued that U.S. utilities have continued to operate some nuclear plants and old fossil plants even though it would have been economical to close them. This is the case because regulatory rules traditionally treated the remaining capital costs of "abandoned plant" in a way that is less rewarding to shareholders than continuing operations, *so long as* the regulators do not catch them operating the plant inefficiently and do not assess an even more costly penalty for failing to close an inefficient plant. Forcing these plants to succeed or fail based on the revenues they can earn in competitive markets may lead some plants to close earlier than would have been the case under traditional regulatory arrangements and accelerate investments in more efficient generating technologies.

Employment practices and wages. The experience with restructuring, privatization, and deregulation around the world suggests that public enterprises and private firms subject to price and entry regulation employ too many workers (that is, they have low levels of labor productivity). Recent efforts by U.S. utilities to reduce costs, in part, by reducing employment levels, suggests that there are significant opportunities for increasing labor productivity. In some formerly regulated industries, wages fell after deregulation in the face of more competition, especially from nonunionized suppliers.[15] There is limited evidence that wages for production workers in the regulated sector are higher than in other sectors, controlling for various indicators of human capital.[16] At the same time, senior managers of regulated private utilities are paid significantly less than managers with similar (measurable) attributes would earn in unregulated businesses of similar size.[17] The potential gains from improvements in labor productivity and wage concessions must be kept in perspective, however. In the United States, wages and benefits (including pensions) account for only about 12 percent of the total cost of supplying electricity.[18]

Pricing inefficiencies. There are wide variations in the care that utilities and regulators have taken to establish electricity price structures that provide

14. Joskow and Schmalensee (1986).
15. Joskow and Rose (1989).
16. Katz and Summers (1989).
17. Joskow, Rose, and Shepard (1993).
18. Energy Information Administration (1997, table 12).

good price signals and associated consumption incentives to consumers, given the relevant marginal supply costs and the budget constraints under which these entities operate. U.S. utilities were slow to offer time-of-use pricing options. Perhaps more important, the regulatory system based on average costs led to prices that were poorly aligned with the relevant marginal costs. Specifically, tariffs were designed to recover the operating and fixed costs of the supplier, based on historical investment decisions and their associated costs. As a result, prices tended to rise with excess capacity and to fall when capacity was short, just the opposite of how a market would work. This type of "average cost" bias may be inherent in any credible regulatory scheme that satisfies traditional rent extraction, production cost efficiency, and investment viability constraints.[19] Regulators made little use of Ramsey-Boiteux or nonlinear pricing to reduce the distortions associated with utilities' overall budget constraints. The development of public spot and futures markets for electricity should produce transparent information on short-term price fluctuations and expected forward price levels at various locations on the network. Accordingly, one of the potential efficiency benefits of competitive wholesale markets combined with retail competition is that retailers will install real-time meters, communications, and control equipment at customer locations and work with consumers to adjust consumption behavior to reflect changing electricity prices in the wholesale market.

Stimulating innovation in electricity production and utilization equipment. Unlike the U.S. telephone industry, electric utilities generally are not vertically integrated into the manufacture of electric appliances or power supply equipment. This equipment is manufactured by companies like GE, Westinghouse, Toshiba, and ABB. Customers are free to choose their own appliances and equipment for using electricity. If there is a regulatory problem slowing down innovation associated with the appliances and equipment purchased from competing suppliers by retail consumers of electricity, it can be traced to the limited use of time-of-use pricing that reflects variations in the marginal cost of supplying electricity at different times of the day. Equipment manufacturers will not develop new appliances and equipment that can exploit opportunities for energy conservation in response to price variability if potential consumers of that electricity do not see these price signals. The speed and direction of technological innovation related to electric generating technology depends, in part, on utility procurement and investment decisions. Some systematic variation

19. Gilbert and Newbery (1994).

also occurs in the rate at which utilities adopt new generating technologies.[20] Moreover, the growth of a competitive independent power sector in the United States (discussed later) has clearly stimulated innovation and speeded up diffusion of more efficient generating technologies. Absent the demand for these technologies by cost-conscious power developers, it is likely that their development and diffusion would have been significantly slower under the old regulated monopoly regime.

How much do all of these potential inefficiencies add up to, and how well will the reforms being implemented succeed in ameliorating them? The bulk of electric utility costs (such as depreciation, interest payments, taxes, deferred cost items, and long-term fuel and purchased power contracts) are fixed in the short run. Wages and benefits account for about 12 percent of total costs, and fuel for another 15 percent. Moreover, the system has efficiently dispatched generating plants, managed congestion, and maintained reliability. For these reasons, I have argued elsewhere that the *short-run* benefits from promoting competition in generation are relatively small but that the *long-run* benefits from doing so are potentially significant.[21] The benefits associated with lower construction and operating costs overall in the supply of generation over time, improved incentives to close inefficient plants, better investment decisions, improved retail price signals, and so forth are potentially large and can more than offset some additional imperfections in generator dispatch, network coordination, and constraint management that may accompany horizontal and vertical decentralization. This happy outcome depends on designing sound transmission network, competitive wholesale power market, and retail market institutions and on mitigating serious market power problems efficiently where they arise in power or transmission markets.

Federal Actions to Stimulate Competition in Wholesale Power Generation Markets

Privately owned utilities are regulated by both state and federal regulatory agencies. Each state has a public utility commission that defines service obligations, determines prices, and approves major investments in generation, transmission, and distribution facilities. Regulated prices are

20. Rose and Joskow (1990).
21. Joskow (1997).

determined pursuant to ratemaking principles whereby a utility's base prices are set to reflect its "reasonable" operating costs, depreciation of capital equipment, taxes, and a "fair rate of return" on the depreciated original cost of its "prudent" capital investments or rate base. The prices under this accounting cost-of-service ratemaking are not reset continuously with changing demand and cost conditions, and the associated "regulatory lag" provides some efficiency incentives compared with a pure cost-plus system.[22]

Under the Federal Power Act of 1935 as amended, the Federal Energy Regulatory Commission (FERC) shared regulatory responsibilities with the states. Its price regulation authority is limited, however, to the regulation of "wholesale power" transactions and interstate transmission service provided by a utility to third parties. Wholesale power transactions are defined as sales of energy produced by a generating company to a distribution company or marketing intermediary (which may or may not also be in the generation business). That is, they are transactions between utilities. Interstate transmission service has typically been used to support wholesale power transactions or to allow a distribution utility to gain access to generation service from a generating plant in which it has an ownership interest, but no direct physical transmission interconnection. FERC also has jurisdiction over the interstate transmission service that is typically required to consummate direct sales of unbundled generation service between generators and retail customers, as is now being contemplated by a growing number of states.

FERC does not have jurisdiction over bundled power sales to retail customers or over internal transfers of energy from generating plants to transmission and distribution facilities and then on to retail customers within a single utility operating company; these internal transfers are under the jurisdiction of each state. Thus, under the industrial and regulatory structure that evolved during the twentieth century in the United States, it is the states, rather than the federal government, that have had the primary regulatory authority over electricity investments, operating costs, and retail prices paid by end-use consumers.

Title II of the Public Utility Regulatory Policies Act (PURPA) played an important role in stimulating the entry of independent power producers in the 1980s and helped to set the stage for the more dramatic reforms of the late 1990s. PURPA was enacted in 1978 primarily to encourage

---

22. Joskow and Schmalensee (1986).

improvements in energy efficiency through expanded use of cogeneration technology and to create a market for electricity produced from renewable fuels and fuel wastes, not by a desire to restructure the electricity sector. Its effects, however, were to begin the process of creating an independent generation sector and the market and regulatory institutions to support a competitive market for new generating resources.

Title II of PURPA required utilities to purchase power produced by certain qualifying facilities (QFs), primarily cogenerators and small power plants using renewable fuels. Figure 4-2 depicts the electric utility industry around 1985 after QFs began to enter the system. Several states embraced PURPA with gusto, requiring utilities in these states to sign long-term contracts (twenty to thirty years) with QFs at what later turned out to be extremely high prices compared with the costs of power in competitive wholesale markets. The costs of these contracts in turn were reflected in regulated retail prices as a cost pass-through. PURPA made it possible for a large number of nonutility companies to enter the electric generation business as owners of QFs.[23] Roughly 60,000 megawatts (MW) of QF capacity came into the sector during the 1980s and early 1990s and eventually accounted for 10 percent of total U.S. generating supplies. This capacity was concentrated in California, New Jersey, New York, Pennsylvania, Texas, and the six New England states.[24]

PURPA had four important effects on more recent reforms. First, it changed prevailing views about vertical integration. In particular, it became clear that nonutilities could build and operate generating facilities cost effectively. Second, the long-term contracts that utilities were compelled to sign with QFs in several states had pricing provisions that turned out to require payments far in excess of the competitive market value of electricity supplied by the QFs under contract. Third, the growth of a competitive independent power market clearly stimulated innovation and sped up diffusion of high-efficiency gas-fueled generating technology. Fourth, it created an interest group—independent power producers—that desired to find ways to develop more power projects in states that had not enacted regulations favorable to QFs; to shed PURPA's restrictions

23. Utilities and public utility holding companies were allowed to own no more than a 50 percent interest in a QF. However, some of the most successful QF development and operating companies are subsidiaries of utility holding companies (an exempt holding company could retain its single state exemption and still have interests in QFs located anywhere in the United States).

24. Author's estimate based on Edison Electric Institute (1997, tables 1, 9).

Figure 4-2. *Traditional Industry Structure plus PURPA*[a]

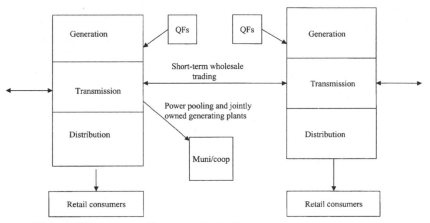

a. QFs = qualifying facilities; muni/coop = municipal utilities and cooperatives.

on technology, size, and fuel use; to have an opportunity to compete more directly against existing generating plants owned by the private utilities; and to amend onerous federal restrictions on who could own independent power projects.

Expanding Competitive Opportunities for Independent Producers

In 1988 FERC began to revise its pricing regulations in an effort to encourage entry of independent producers that were not QFs into the electricity sector, as well as to encourage utilities with excess capacity to sell it to third parties under long-term contracts.[25] These efforts reflected two FERC policy decisions: first, that encouraging utilities to buy and sell generation services in competitive wholesale markets, rather than always building, owning and operating generating plants themselves, would reduce costs to consumers; and, second, that it was inefficient to limit competitive opportunities for independent producers to those that met PURPA's size, thermal efficiency, and fuel restrictions.

25. In 1988 FERC issued three then-controversial notices of proposed rulemaking that dealt with wholesale power and transmission service pricing as well as the regulatory treatment of independent power producers. FERC never issued final rules, but it subsequently implemented many of the policies de facto through case-by-case rulings.

By 1991 FERC had been largely successful in achieving these goals. Utilities seeking new generating resources were now free to rely on competitive procurement for incremental generating resources from private power producers or proximate utilities with excess generating capacity if they were encouraged to do so by their state regulators. FERC, however, had no authority to force utilities to purchase electricity from non-QF independent power suppliers or from other utilities with excess capacity. States like California, Massachusetts, New Jersey, and New York encouraged utilities to procure power competitively from all available sources, rather than relying on building their own new generating capacity that would be subject to cost-based regulation. Most other states were much more cautious about moving further away from the traditional vertical integration and cost-based regulation model.

Restrictions on the availability of transmission and related network services owned and controlled by vertically integrated utilities probably also slowed the development of fully competitive wholesale markets for power. Under the Federal Power Act of 1935, FERC could not order a utility to provide interstate transmission services or related network services or to build facilities to support such transactions. FERC could only regulate the prices at which transmission service could be sold. The potential problems here for independent producers were compounded by the balkanization of the interconnected networks in most regions with pieces owned and operated by many different utilities: an economical transaction could involve a "contract transmission path" requiring "wheeling" across the transmission systems owned by several utilities. In this case, transmission service could be difficult to arrange, and transmission charges for use of each "end-to-end" transmission system were "pancaked" on top of each other, increasing the cost of transferring power from one location to another.[26]

Finally, the Public Utility Holding Company Act of 1935 (PUHCA) placed severe restrictions on the ability of utilities to own independent power projects through unregulated affiliates remote from their service areas, on nonutilities owning IPP projects, and on foreign acquisitions by U.S. utilities. PURPA provided important exemptions to these restrictions, but they applied only to generating projects meeting its QF criteria.

---

26. Under traditional regulation, the price for wheeling electricity across two transmission systems was about twice as much as wheeling the same amount of electricity the same distance on a single transmission system.

Congress cured some of these problems when it passed the Energy Policy Act of 1992.[27] It permitted utilities and nonutilities to have ownership interests in independent power producers, allowed U.S. utilities to own electric utility assets in other countries, and expanded FERC's authority to order utilities to provide transmission (or wheeling) service to support wholesale power transactions. Under the 1992 law a new class of electricity generators, called exempt wholesale generators, was created; these generators could, directly or indirectly through one or more affiliates, own or operate facilities dedicated exclusively to producing electricity for sale in wholesale markets. The law also provided that buyers and sellers of wholesale power could petition FERC to order transmitting utilities to provide wheeling service for wholesale power transactions, even if meeting such requests required the utility to expand its transmission facilities. FERC in turn was directed to establish pricing regulations that promoted the efficient generation and transmission of electricity and that allowed utilities to recover the full economic cost of the transmission service provided. In response to utility concerns, the law made clear that FERC had no authority to order a utility to make unbundled transmission service available to serve a *retail* customer. Figure 4-3 depicts the structure of the industry envisioned by the major proponents of the reforms embodied in the 1992 law.

In light of more recent developments, it is interesting to note that the 1992 law was built around the traditional model of a regulated monopoly distribution company that has the exclusive right to serve retail customers within its franchise area. The law did not require utilities to open up their retail markets to competitive suppliers, nor did it require utilities to buy power from independent producers other than QFs. It did give FERC the tools to support state initiatives that might promote more radical restructuring leading to more direct competition against incumbent generators and for retail customers. When the law was passed, however, most utilities thought that it would make only incremental changes in the basic structure of the industry. They would soon be surprised.

Expanding Access to Transmission Systems

The next step in the development of efficient competitive wholesale power markets was to ensure that power producers and buyers had access

27. P. L. 102–486, Title VII, October 24, 1992.

Figure 4-3. *Traditional Industry Structure plus PURPA*
plus 1992 Energy Policy Act[a]

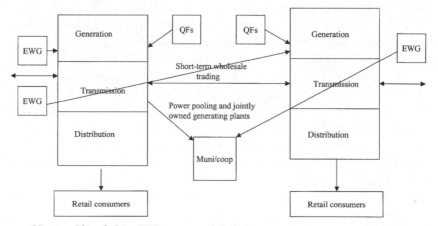

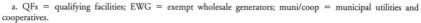

a. QFs = qualifying facilities; EWG = exempt wholesale generators; muni/coop = municipal utilities and
cooperatives.

to transmission services to actually deliver and receive the power. FERC's
initial attempts to expand access to transmission services met with little
success. Utilities were not required to file generic tariffs that specified the
transmission services they would offer and the maximum prices for those
services; instead they responded to requests for transmission services on a
case-by-case basis. Services offered, and their associated prices, remained
fairly vague, and different utilities interpreted the regulations in different
ways. As a result, requests for transmission services sometimes turned into
lengthy and contentious negotiations.

Both FERC and transmission service customers grew frustrated with
the slow pace at which transmission service was being made available to
support wholesale market transactions, and FERC continued to receive
complaints about discriminatory terms and conditions (real or imagined)
being offered for transmission service. Moreover, California's electricity
restructuring initiatives, which started in April 1994, began to make FERC
realize that its transmission access and pricing rules might have to support
far more radical changes in the structure of the utility industry—the
functional separation of the generation and transmission of electricity from
distribution service and the opening of retail electric service to competition. FERC also realized that the restructuring would raise a variety of new
issues regarding state and federal jurisdiction over transmission, distribu-

tion, wholesale power sales, and the treatment of "above-market" costs of generating capacity and QF contracts (what came to be called the "stranded-cost" problem).

In 1995 these considerations led FERC to initiate rulemakings on transmission service that ultimately served as the basis for two major sets of new rules issued by FERC in 1996.[28] These two rules now serve as the primary federal framework for the provision of transmission service, ancillary network support services, and information about the availability of these services to support both wholesale and retail competition in the supply of generating services.

Order 888 requires all transmission owners to file with FERC proforma open access tariffs that define the terms and conditions of transmission services that will be made available to all wholesale customers. Order 888 specifies the types of transmission services that must be made available, the maximum cost-based prices that can be charged for these services, the definition of available transmission capacity and how it should be allocated when there is excess demand for it, the specification of ancillary services that transmission owners must provide and the associated prices, requirements for reforms to power pooling arrangements to comply with Order 888, and provisions for stranded-cost recovery. All transmission owners and power pools have now filed open access transmission tariffs with FERC.

Order 888 recognizes the sanctity of existing commercial, contractual, and regulatory arrangements associated with the historical use of transmission systems and is generally sensitive to smoothing the transition from the old regime to the new regime. Importantly, Order 888 establishes federal principles governing the recovery of stranded costs (discussed in more detail below). For utility-owned generating plants, stranded or "strandable" costs are defined conceptually as the difference between the net book value of a generating plant used for setting cost-based regulated prices and the market value of that plant if it were required to sell its output in a competitive market. For a QF contract, stranded costs are generally defined as the difference between the present value of the contractual payment obligations and the present value of the competitive market value of the electricity delivered under the contracts. FERC established the public

28. These rules are Order 888, "Promoting Wholesale Competition through Open Access Non-Discriminatory Transmission Services by Public Utilities; Recovery of Stranded Costs by Public Utilities and Transmitting Utilities," and Order 889, "Open Access Same-Time Information Systems." Final Rule issued April 24, 1996, 75 FERC ¶ 61,080. Order 889: Final Rule issued April 24, 1996, 75 FERC ¶ 61,078.

policy case for stranded-cost recovery in light of the long-established regulatory rules in effect when the investments and contractual commitments were made and for the public policy interest in facilitating restructuring and creating competitive wholesale power markets.[29]

Although FERC's position on stranded-cost recovery was based primarily on its assessment of its legal obligations and equity considerations, it almost certainly reflected a set of more practical considerations. Specifically, a major impediment to incumbent utilities' accepting more fundamental changes in the competitive environment and cooperating in creating the institutions necessary to support full wholesale and retail competition was their concern about stranded-cost exposure. FERC, and ultimately most state commissions that have considered the stranded-cost issue, effectively sent utilities with stranded-cost problems the following message: "Play ball by opening up your transmission and distribution systems and by taking actions necessary to create competitive wholesale and retail markets quickly, and regulatory policy will treat requests for reasonable provisions for stranded-cost recovery favorably. Moreover, this deal may not be on the table forever."

Order 888 did not attempt to resolve the problems created for transmission service customers by the large number of transmission owners, all operating under separate Order 888 tariffs, which existed in many regions of the country. So, for example to make a trade between Indiana and Pennsylvania, a trader might still have to deal with several transmission owners to get a complete "contract path" from the generator supplying the power to the customer. However, FERC recently issued regulations (Order 2000) that strongly encourage the creation of large regional transmission organizations (RTOs) to resolve problems created by the balkanized control of transmission networks and alleged discriminatory practices faced by generators and energy traders seeking to use the transmission networks of vertically integrated firms under Order 888 rules.[30]

Order 889 requires each public utility or its agent (a power pool, for example) that owns, controls, or operates facilities used to transmit electric energy in interstate commerce to create or participate in an "open access same-time information system." This system must provide information, by

29. Verifiable stranded costs net of all reasonable mitigation options.

30. *Regional Transmission Organizations,* 89 FERC ¶ 61,285 (1999). Order 2000 technically makes participation in an RTO voluntary, but there are carrots and sticks available to FERC that will create significant pressure for utilities to join RTOs. Order 2000 does not mandate a particular organizational form for an RTO, however.

electronic means, regarding available transmission capacity, prices, and other information that will enable transmission service customers to obtain nondiscriminatory transmission service in a time frame necessary to make effective use of the transmission system to support power transactions. The rule also required public utilities to implement standards of conduct to separate transmission and unregulated wholesale power merchant functions to ensure that a vertically integrated transmission owner's wholesale market transactions are not advantaged by virtue of preferential access to information about the transmission network. Utilities must also treat third parties the same as their wholesale power marketing affiliates, offering both the same terms.

Pressures for More Fundamental Change

Pressure for more fundamental changes began to grow soon after passage of the 1992 Energy Power Act, which sought to stimulate competition while still largely retaining the traditional structure of the industry. A variety of interest groups, including the new independent power producers, envisioned a new model in which generation would be fully separated from transmission and distribution, regulated distribution and transmission charges would be "unbundled" from generation and retail service charges, wholesale generation service prices would be deregulated, and generators would compete de novo in regional markets both to supply distribution companies purchasing on behalf of their retail customers (full wholesale competition with exclusive retail supply) and to supply retail customers as well ("retail wheeling") either directly or through financial intermediaries.

This alternative full "wholesale competition" plus "retail unbundling and competition" model for the electric power industry was based on the same basic principles that governed the restructuring of the electricity sector in England and Wales in 1990 and the restructuring of the natural gas and telecommunications sectors in the United States. Competitive services such as generation would be separated from natural monopoly services such as transmission and distribution, and the regulated monopoly services would be made available and priced on an unbundled basis to retail consumers or their procurement agent. All generators would compete in unregulated wholesale markets to serve retail demand. Retail customers or their agents would be guaranteed nondiscriminatory access to the monop-

Figure 4-4. *Competitive Wholesale plus Retail Markets*[a]

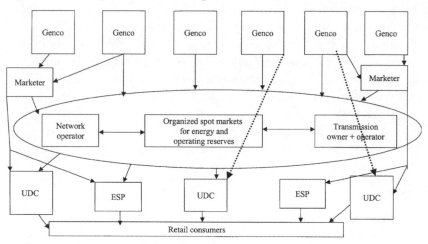

a. Genco = generating company; UDC = utility distribution company; ESP = electric service provider.

oly transmission and distribution services at regulated rates so that they could shop directly in the wholesale market or through competing retail supply agents, which purchase electricity in wholesale markets and resell it to final consumers (figure 4-4).

To understand the political and economic pressures that emerged for more radical changes in the electric power industry, it is useful to understand the cost components of regulated retail electricity prices for the typical vertically integrated utility before reforms were enacted. Let:

$$P_R = C_T + C_D + C_G + C_R + DSM,$$

where P_R equals total regulated (bundled) price of retail service, C_T equals average total accounting cost of transmission service, C_D equals average total accounting cost of distribution (wires) service, C_G equals average total accounting cost of owned-generation and power contracts including contracts with independent producers, C_R equals average cost of customer services (such as billing and customer care), and DSM equals costs of various "public benefit" programs such as energy efficiency subsidies, renewable energy subsidies, and subsidies for low-income consumers. Table 4-1 displays the regulated price (P_R) for electricity for residential and industrial customers in a representative set of the states for 1997 (these

Table 4-1. *Average Revenue per Kilowatt Hour from Residential and Industrial Consumers* [a]

Cents per kilowatt hour

State	Residential		Industrial	
	1997	1998	1997	1998
Connecticut	12.13	11.95	7.76	7.70
Maine	12.75	13.02	6.36	6.61
Massachusetts	11.59	10.60	8.78	8.18
Rhode Island	12.12	10.91	8.52	7.61
New Jersey	12.08	11.39	8.11	7.94
New York	14.12	13.66	5.20	4.95
Pennsylvania	9.90	9.93	5.89	5.63
Delaware	9.22	9.13	4.82	4.65
Illinois	10.43	9.85	5.29	5.11
Indiana	6.94	7.01	3.91	3.95
Ohio	8.63	8.70	4.16	4.30
Wisconsin	6.88	7.17	3.72	3.86
Iowa	8.21	8.38	3.95	3.99
Kansas	7.71	7.65	4.51	4.46
Missouri	7.09	7.08	4.46	4.43
North Dakota	6.27	6.49	4.38	4.30
Florida	8.08	7.89	5.04	4.81
Georgia	7.74	7.67	4.13	4.23
South Carolina	7.51	7.50	4.00	3.69
West Virginia	6.26	6.29	3.47	3.78
Kentucky	5.58	5.61	2.80	2.91
Alabama	6.74	6.94	3.71	3.89
Arkansas	7.80	7.51	4.45	4.16
Texas	7.82	7.65	4.05	3.94

(continued)

prices are similar to those prevailing in 1995 when the pressures for more radical reforms intensified).[31] Of particular note are the large differences in prices across the states, with the states in the Northeast and California having much higher prices than the average for the rest of the country.

31. Industrial prices are typically much lower than residential prices because industrial customers take power at higher voltages and do not use the costly low-voltage distribution facilities that serve

Table 4-1. *(continued)*

| | Residential | | Industrial | |
State	1997	1998	1997	1998
Arizona	8.82	8.68	5.05	5.12
California	11.50	10.60	6.95	6.59
Montana	6.40	6.50	3.66	3.19
New Mexico	8.92	8.85	4.42	4.47
Wyoming	6.22	6.28	3.46	3.38
Oregon	5.56	5.82	3.23	3.50
Washington	4.95	5.03	2.59	2.64
U.S. average	8.43	8.26	4.53	4.48

Source: Energy Information Administration (1997, 1998).

a. These data will not be meaningful after 1998 unless the Energy Information Administration changes the way it collects retail sales data and calculates prices, because the data do not now distinguish customers taking all of their electricity from a utility distribution company from those that take generation services from an energy service provider and distribution and transmission services from the distribution company.

Some of this price difference reflects inherent differences in the costs of providing electricity in different regions of the country, differences in population density, and differences in weather and electricity utilization patterns.

A significant fraction of these price differences, however, especially as they relate to the generation component (C_G), reflects the costs associated with historical generation investment and contracting decisions, costs that had been included in prevailing regulated retail electricity prices. So, for example, in 1999 the competitive market price (P_{CG}) for electric generation service (averaged over a year) was in the range of 2.5–3.5 cents per kWh. In the mid-1990s, the regulated prices for generation service in the highest priced areas of the country were in the 6.0–7.0 cents per kWh range. The difference between the regulated cost of generation service reflected in retail prices and the competitive market value of electricity ($C_G - P_{CG}$) represents a "generation service price gap" and a potentially strandable cost that utilities would have had to absorb if they were required to sell their

residences, have higher load factors (capacity utilization), and have lower thermal losses. Some of the difference may also result from some price discrimination reflecting the higher demand elasticities of some industrial customers, especially large customers that can self-supply electricity.

generation service at its market value rather than at its regulated cost-based price.[32] The differences between the regulated costs and market values for generation service are largely, but not entirely, differences in sunk costs and long-term contractual commitments. (Note that many utilities, in states such as Kentucky and Wyoming, have regulated prices *below* the competitive market value of electricity. That is because utilities in these states relied heavily on cheap and relatively old coal-fired generating plants whose original capital costs had largely been depreciated and because regulated prices reflect historical accounting costs rather than the economic value of these generating plants.)

As Mathew White has observed, whatever the public interest rationale for adopting the reform model (see figure 4-4), the primary political stimulus for these reforms was the gap that existed between the regulated embedded cost of generation services (C_G) and the market value of those services (P_{CG}).[33] This price gap in turn primarily reflected the costs of earlier investments in nuclear power plants; the burdens of long-term contracts with QFs, where prices were set at levels far above the competitive market value; and most important, the subsequent abundant supply and very low price of natural gas available throughout the United States combined with the development of high-efficiency gas-fueled electricity generators (combined cycle gas turbine, or CCGT).[34] CCGT plants have much smaller minimum efficient scale than the coal and nuclear plants upon which the industry had relied, are easier to site, can be built more quickly and with better cost controls, are more thermally efficient, and produce less pollution. CCGT plants thus have significantly reduced the long-run marginal cost of generating electricity.

Organized customer groups (primarily industrial customers) in states with a large price gap ($C_G - P_{CG}$) recognized that they would benefit if they could obtain the right to buy unbundled distribution and transmission service at a regulated price ($C_D + C_G$) from the local utility and then use these delivery services to acquire generation services directly (or through intermediaries) in the wholesale market at prices far below the

32. How much they would have to absorb would, of course, depend on the intensity of competition they faced if their wholesale and retail generation service prices were deregulated.

33. White (1996).

34. Development of the CCGT technology, in turn, can be credited in part to the demand for it in some QF facilities. Perhaps more important, though, were the developments in efficient jet engine technology developed for aircraft, which were then applied directly to combustion turbines that were the key innovation in the CCGT technology.

regulated prices for generation service embedded in bundled regulated retail prices. An unbundled retail competition model also gave independent power developers an opportunity to go after *all* of the electricity demand then served by incumbent utilities at above-market prices, rather than just serving utilities' *incremental* generating capacity needs through what were effectively resale arrangements. To potential wholesale energy marketers, some of whom got their start in the rapidly developing deregulated wholesale and retail markets for natural gas, a larger competitive generation market created new opportunities to sell their newly acquired transaction and risk-hedging skills.

Strandable-cost estimates associated with the price gaps varied from about $100 billion to about $200 billion nationwide, with these strandable costs heavily concentrated in California, New England, New York, New Jersey, Pennsylvania, Illinois, Arizona, and a few other states.[35] Regulators estimated that the strandable costs for the electric utilities in Massachusetts were roughly $9 billion, or about double the equity in these companies.[36] In California, strandable costs were estimated to be about $25 billion, again more than twice the equity investment on the companies' books.[37] In both cases the estimated strandable costs were roughly equally divided between nuclear power plant investments and QF contract costs.

State Electricity Competition and Restructuring Initiatives

In light of these facts, it should not be surprising that industrial customer groups, independent power plant developers and electricity marketers actively promoted a full wholesale and retail competition model that did not include provisions for recovering stranded costs. Utilities, and initially some environmental groups, aggressively opposed a full retail competition model,

35. It is useful to distinguish between "strandable costs," which are potentially not recoverable by a utility if it sold its generation at market prices, and costs that actually have to be written off (are stranded) as a result of the actual competition and cost recovery rules eventually adopted. For example, Moody's estimated strandable costs at about $130 billion in 1995, most of which, by 1999, had been either mitigated through asset sales or recovered when regulators and legislators allowed utilities to impose nonbypassable distribution charges. "Moody's: Stranded Costs Sink to about $10 Billion," *Electricity Daily,* October 29, 1999, p. 2.

36. "DOER Report: 1998 Market Monitor," Division of Energy Resources, Commonwealth of Massachusetts, September, 1999, 25.

37. Author's calculations.

while representatives of residential consumers focused on finding ways to ensure that small customers received the same benefits from restructuring and competition that the large industrial customers received. Nor should it be surprising that the battle was fought initially in those states where the price gap and associated strandable costs were largest.

California Starts the Ball Rolling

California was the first state to respond to pressures from industrial customers to reduce the price of electricity and from independent power producers to increase opportunities to widen the markets for their power. California's restructuring initiative was instrumental in defining the basic framework for the restructuring that more than twenty states have since followed and that several more states (and the U.S. Congress) are considering adopting in some form (table 4-2). High electricity rates became a major issue in California in the early 1990s, where general concerns about the future of the state's economy were exacerbated by a severe recession. Industrial customers aggressively sought regulatory and tax relief to help them reduce their costs to remain competitive with firms in other states.

In April 1994, the California Public Utilities Commission (CPUC) issued a report (known as the "Blue Book") that laid out a set of major proposed structural and regulatory reforms for the electric power sector, including a schedule to phase in retail competition (also called "retail direct access" and "retail customer choice").[38] The commission also proposed that traditional cost-of-service and rate-of-return regulation for distribution service be replaced with performance-based regulation; that generation be unbundled from transmission and distribution services; and utilities be allowed to recover the "uneconomic" portion of their embedded generation costs and QF contract obligations—their strandable costs—through a competitive transition charge (CTC) that all retail consumers would be obligated to pay.[39] Although the three major private utilities initially resisted the proposals for unbundling and retail competi-

---

38. California Public Utilities Commission, "Proposed Policy Statement on Restructuring California's Electric Services Industry and Reforming Regulatory Policy," San Francisco, April 20, 1994.

39. Several of the then-sitting commissioners have also told me that their visit to England and Wales in early 1994 to study the competitive electricity system that had been created there in 1990 greatly influenced their decision to endeavor to create a similar system in California.

Table 4-2. *Comprehensive State Retail Competition Programs Adopted as of December 1999*

Year adopted	State	Start date	Date all consumers are eligible	Average private utility price in 1997 for states listed (cents/kWh) [a]
1996	California	April 1998	April 1998	10.4
	New Hampshire	1998	1998 (delayed)	
	New York	1998	2001	
	Pennsylvania	Jan. 1999	Jan. 2000	
	Rhode Island	Jan. 1998	Jan. 1998	
1997	Illinois	Oct. 1999	May 2002	8.3
	Maine	March 2000	March 2000	
	Massachusetts	March 1998	March 1998	
	Montana	July 1998	July 2000	
1998	Arizona	Oct. 1999	Jan. 2001	9.5
	Connecticut	Jan. 2000	July 2000	
1999	Arkansas	Jan 2002	June 2003	6.8
	Delaware	Oct. 1999	Oct. 2000	
	Maryland	July 2000	July 2002	
	New Jersey	Nov. 1999	Nov. 1999	
	New Mexico	Jan. 2001	Jan. 2002	
	Ohio	Jan. 2001	Dec. 2005	
	Oregon	? [b]	? [b]	
	Texas	Jan. 2002	Jan. 2002	
	Virginia	Jan. 2002	Jan. 2004	

a. The average price per kilowatt hour in the remaining states in 1997 was 5.6 cents.
b. Oregon's law excludes residences; the start date for other customers is expected some time in 2000.

tion, they soon focused their attention on gaining approval of the strandable-cost provisions.[40] In early 1996 the commission issued its long-awaited restructuring decision, which was subsequently refined and adopted by the state legislature.[41]

The restructuring and competition programs adopted by most states

40. Major differences of opinion have also emerged regarding the institutional changes required to support a fully competitive electricity sector (Joskow, 1996b).
41. California Public Utilities Commission, Decision 95–12–063 (December 20, 1995) as modified by Decision 96–01–009 (January 10, 1996). The restructuring law was AB 1890, approved in September 1996.

have included many of the same elements as those adopted in California, although some significant variations occur from one state to another. Typically, these state programs include:

Resolution of stranded-cost recovery issues. A critical part of the structuring "deal" in most states is a set of provisions that gives incumbent utilities an opportunity to recover a large fraction of their stranded costs through a charge levied on all retail customers as a component of the price of regulated monopoly distribution service. States have extracted varying concessions from utilities in return for permitting the utilities to recover stranded costs. California, New York, and the New England states have either required or given utilities strong financial incentives to divest their generating facilities (to value their stranded costs) and to reduce the risks associated with future recovery. New Jersey and Pennsylvania have placed much less pressure on utilities to divest their generating facilities and have relied more on ex ante administrative determinations and ex post valuations to come up with values for recoverable stranded costs. The Texas restructuring law appears to require utilities to divest at least some of their generating capacity.

Market pricing of wholesale generation service and market valuation of generating assets. Once utilities have taken the prescribed steps to recover stranded costs, those that continue to own generating facilities must look to the market for revenues to cover operating costs and any residual sunk costs of their generating assets. In effect, generating plants are de-regulated, and cost-of-service regulation of generation prices comes to an end.

Unbundling of services. Monopoly transmission, distribution, and various "public benefits" charges are unbundled from the costs of generation services. Regulations providing for "customer choice" of their generation service suppliers are introduced. Access to the utility's distribution system for delivery of electricity at a separate regulated delivery charge gives retail consumers the opportunity to purchase unbundled generation service from competing energy service providers.

The creation of wholesale market institutions. These institutions are designed to support sales by competing generators and purchases by distribution companies, energy service providers, and marketers in competitive markets in a way that respects the special physical attributes of electricity and the need to maintain the reliability of the transmission network. These institutions include organized markets for energy and ancillary network support services, network congestion management protocols, and physical and financial metering and settlement mechanisms that recognize that electricity is supplied to and withdrawn from a common pool, so that one supplier's electrons cannot be physically distinguished from another's.

The creation of various "public benefits" programs to stimulate energy efficiency and renewable energy technology and to subsidize rates for low-income families. These programs are paid for through charges added to the monopoly distribution prices paid by all retail consumers who use the distribution network.

The development and application of incentive, or performance-based, regulatory mechanisms to replace traditional cost-of-service regulation of residual monopoly distribution services. These schemes typically involve the application of a variant of a price-cap mechanism. These mechanisms are designed to give distribution utilities incentives to control costs and to relieve the regulatory agency of the need to reset distribution rates frequently.

Mandatory retail price reductions (3–15 percent) for all or a subset of customers, whether or not they choose to be supplied with generation service from an electric service provider or continue to purchase electricity from their local UDC. These rate reductions are paid for from the cost savings from securitization, sales of generating assets at prices above the book value historically used to set regulated prices, and by squeezing the profits of the utilities, as discussed later. (So, stranded-cost recovery may really be less that 100 percent.) In some states, regulated rates would have fallen anyway under then-prevailing regulated pricing arrangements, so the mandatory rate reductions (or rate freezes) may not be as financially painful to the utilities as may first meet the eye.

As table 4-2 shows, the first states to restructure their power sectors in 1996 and 1997 were primarily those with high electricity prices, utilities with significant potential stranded costs, and earlier aggressive policies to encourage QFs (Montana is the primary outlier, and restructuring initiatives there appear to have been promoted by the state's single large private utility). In 1999 several states that did not have extremely high (relatively) electricity prices and stranded costs (such as Arkansas, Maryland, Ohio, Oregon, and Texas) adopted comprehensive restructuring programs. It should be noted, however, that these later programs often involve a much more gradual phase-in of retail access and customer choice, and involve much less pressure on utilities to divest their generating assets. Overall, it is still the case that the states that have adopted comprehensive reform initiatives are those with above-average embedded generation costs and have utilities with sufficient potential stranded cost problems that the resolution of these problems became a useful bargaining chip for state policymakers. Although some low-cost states, such as Wisconsin and Wyoming, have rejected restructuring programs, others are well along the path toward passing restructuring laws that provide for wholesale and retail competition.[42]

At this point the reader may wonder how a state could adopt a policy that both provided stranded-cost recovery for utilities and provided rate decreases for consumers that would not have been realized under the old regime. Theoretically, the combination of stranded-cost recovery and the ability of consumers to buy electricity at its competitive market value should net out to zero (except perhaps for timing) because stranded costs represent the difference between the market value of a utility's generating plants and their book value.

How is this magic accomplished? Several factors are at work here. First, several utilities have in fact recovered less than 100 percent of their stranded costs through this process, earning less on the portion of their generating assets that have been deemed to be stranded than they earned under the old regime. Second, some of the rate reductions that have been advertised as resulting from restructuring would have been realized under the previous regulatory arrangements as a result of lower fuel, depreciation, and QF costs. Third, generation divestiture has yielded market values that were far higher than utilities and their regulators had expected (more on this point later).[43] The credits against stranded costs have reduced significantly the balance that is reflected in consumer rates and this has not (yet) been balanced by higher wholesale market prices. Fourth, most states have adopted stranded-cost securitization programs which create financing cost and tax savings that are passed on to customers. Finally, some of the rate reductions involve deferring recovery of some costs. These deferred costs will ultimately find their way back into distribution charges or stranded-cost charges.

---

42. "West Virginia Adopts Dereg Plan to Send to Legislature," *Megawatt Daily*, February 1, 2000, 1; "Oklahoma to Consider Final Restructuring Bill," *Megawatt Daily*, February 7, 2000, 1.

43. If the prices paid for divested assets reflect anticipated efficiencies that the new owners will bring to the system, retail customers will benefit overall. If the prices paid for the divested assets merely reflect higher wholesale prices that the new owners expect to realize when they sell electricity in the unregulated market, this suggests that stranded costs had been overestimated because competitive wholesale market prices had been underestimated.

Trends in Restructuring

The competition and regulatory reform initiatives by the federal government and various states have fostered important structural changes in the electric power industry as well. Among these are divestiture of generating plants, mergers of electric utilities with each other and with gas pipeline and distribution companies, and entry of merchant generating plants.

Divestiture of Utility Generating Plants

One of the surprising outcomes of the state reform programs has been a significant amount of "voluntary" divestiture of generating facilities by incumbent vertically integrated utilities. Some states adopted stranded-cost recovery mechanisms that provided favorable financial outcomes to utilities that market-valued their generating assets by auctioning them off to third parties rather than relying on administrative procedures to value the assets. Some states also encouraged utilities to divest generating assets to deal with perceived vertical market power problems associated with common ownership of generating and transmission assets; California encouraged divestiture in response to concerns about horizontal market power in wholesale power markets. Finally, as state restructuring programs deregulated generation services and required utility-owned generating plants to rely on market prices to cover their costs (net of any stranded-cost allowances), some utilities simply decided to focus their business strategies on regulated transmission and distribution service. Accordingly, they decided to get out of the generation business by selling their plants to companies that had decided to focus on the merchant generating plant business.

Table 4-3 provides data on utility divestitures of generating assets from 1997 through late December 1999. Nearly 90,000 MW of generating capacity has been sold or is for sale, accounting for more than 15 percent of the generating capacity owned by private utilities in the United States.[44] Clearly, divestiture has been concentrated in those regions where state electricity restructuring and competition programs have been enacted and where incumbent utilities had significant stranded-cost burdens. Indeed, aside from Montana, and a pending sale to respond to horizontal market power problems raised in connection with a merger involving American Electric Power

44. There were 582,000 Mw of private utility generating capacity in 1997; see Edison Electric Institute (1997, table 1).

Table 4-3. *Generation Divestitures, 1997–99*
Megawatts

State/region	1997	1998	1999	For sale	Totals
California	10,077	7,853	0	4,230	22,160
New England	6,009	4,552	4,394	4,296	19,251
New York	0	5,222	6,775	2,080	14,077
Penn., N.J., Md.	0	6,898	3,942	5,320	16,160
Illinois	490	1,108	10,350	0	11,948
Other	0	1,556	0	3,580	5,136
Totals	16,576	27,189	25,461	19,506	88,732

Source: Energy Information Administration, Dow Jones, trade press, company releases and regulatory filings.

and Central and South West Corporation, utilities in states with no significant stranded-cost problems or with no comprehensive state restructuring program have divested no generating assets so far. Utilities in New England, New York, California, and Illinois have sold off, or are in the process of selling off, almost all of their fossil generating capacity. Some utilities in New Jersey, Pennsylvania, and Delaware have divested generating assets, while others have resisted pressures to do so.

Table 4-4 lists all sales of utility fossil and hydroelectric (mostly fossil) generating capacity for which I was able to obtain both the sale price of the assets and their net book value used for regulatory purposes. I am confident that these data are representative of the larger population of fossil and hydro generating assets sales. Recall that a utility's potentially strandable costs are equal to the difference between the net book value of the plant used for determining regulated prices and the market value of the plant. This is the case because cost-of-service regulation uses a rate base equal to the original cost of the plant net of depreciation.[45] Annual capital charges included in the regulated prices charged to customers are then supposed to be equal to the annual depreciation of the plant's book value plus a return on the rate base equal to the firm's cost of capital times the net book value of the plant (with adjustments for taxes). If these regulatory cost accounting and pricing procedures work perfectly, then the net present value of future revenues (net of operating costs) earned by the plant should equal its net book value at every point in time.[46]

45. Joskow and Schmalensee (1986).
46. Schmalensee (1989).

Table 4-4. *Market and Book Values for Divested Hydro and Fossil Generators*

Millions of dollars except where noted

Seller	Buyer	Book value	Market value ($/kW)	Market value as a percentage of book value
NEP	PG&E GEN	1,100	1,590 (397)	1.44
SCE	Various	421	1,115 (148)	2.65
PG&E	Southern	430	801 (296)	1.86
Boston Edison	Sithe	450	536 (271)	1.19
CMP	FPL	340	846 (714)	2.49
ComEnergy	Southern	79	462 (470)	5.85
EUA	Southern	40	75 (268)	1.87
MainePS	WPSPower	12	37 (309)	3.08
Montana Power	PPL Global	650	988 (635)	1.52
Niagara Mohawk	Orion	250	425 (643)	1.70
SDG&E	NRG/Dynegy	94	356 (296)	3.78
Niagara Mohawk	NRG	370	355 (261)	0.96
GPU/NYSEG	Edison Mission	560	1,800 (950)	3.21
GPU	Sithe	815	1,680 (408)	1.98
ConEd	Keyspan	300	597 (275)	1.99
ConEd	NRG	250	505 (347)	2.02
ConEd	Orion	275	550 (296)	2.0
Unicom	Edison Mission	1,100	4,800 (510)	4.36
NU	NRG	87	460 (206)	5.29
NU	NUGen	125	865 (650)	6.92
DQE	Orion	1,100	1,710 (654)	1.55

Source: Dow Jones, trade press, company releases, and regulatory filings.

Two things are immediately evident from table 4-4. First, the market price per unit of capacity varies widely.[47] Second, the fossil and hydroelectric generating portfolios that have been auctioned off have almost universally been sold at a price that is in excess, sometimes far in excess, of the

47. In general, coal-fired plants and hydroelectric facilities have sold for higher prices than older oil- and natural gas–fired facilities. Assets have also fetched higher prices in regions where wholesale prices are expected to be high (and volatile) during peak periods in the next few years (the Midwest and the Pennsylvania–New Jersey–Maryland (PJM) power pool, for example). This can be inferred from the futures contracts for delivery at various locations in the United States, which are traded on the New York Mercantile Exchange.

book value of the plants, suggesting either that the regulated charges for these plants were less than the competitive market value of the electricity they supply[48] or that the new owners expect to operate the plants more efficiently, or a combination of both.[49] This indicates that the stranded-cost problems were not associated with utility portfolios of fossil and hydroelectric generating assets. Most state restructuring plans require utilities to credit the excess of market price over book value against any stranded costs associated with nuclear plants, QF contracts, and other categories of stranded costs. Accordingly, the sales of these assets at prices in excess of their book values have made a significant contribution to reducing the projected stranded costs associated with the entire generation portfolios of utilities, including nuclear facilities and QF contracts.

The major buyers of the divested generating plants are affiliates of U.S. utilities that have entered the merchant plant business and are buying and building generating plants around the United States to supply the competitive wholesale markets that are emerging. Two major buyers (AES and Sithe) are independent companies that got their start as owners and operators of QFs and independent power plants during the 1980s.[50] Several of these companies (both utility affiliates and independents) also own generating plants in other countries that allow independent power projects.[51]

One of the surprises associated with this divestiture process is that a market for deregulated nuclear power plants has emerged. Two companies—Entergy (a public utility holding company with vertically integrated utility subsidiaries in Arkansas, Louisiana, Mississippi, and Texas) and AmerGen (a joint venture between PECO, a vertically integrated utility serving the Philadelphia area, and British Energy, the owner and operator of all of the nuclear plants in England and Wales[52])—have actively sought to purchase nuclear plants from their vertically integrated utility owners and to operate them as merchant plants, which are not subject to economic regulation. (The plants, of course, would still be regulated for safety.) As this is

48. Under traditional regulatory cost accounting, the present discounted value of the future cash flows from a generating plant selling at regulated prices would be 1.0.

49. In addition, it appears that some buyers have attributed significant value to the sites that the generating plants are on in anticipation of adding additional generating capacity at these sites.

50. Sithe began to sell its generating assets in 2000. Reliant announced that it would purchase Sithe's generating plants in New Jersey and Pennsylvania in February 2000.

51. These countries include China, England and Wales, India, Indonesia, Ireland, Pakistan, Spain, and several countries in South America.

52. British Energy itself emerged from the restructuring and privatization of the electricity sector in England and Wales.

written, sales agreements have been made for eight nuclear power plants, with sales prices ranging from $16 per kilowatt (kW) to more than $350 per kW. (The reported values are difficult to interpret because the terms of the reported sales vary with regard to the treatment of fuel stocks, additional contributions to nuclear decommissioning funds, and associated purchased power contracts that some of the buyers have taken back.)[53] Any way you slice it, however, the sales prices for nuclear plants are far below their net book values used for regulatory pricing purchases in the past, which are as high as $2,000 per kW. As a result, nuclear plants account for a large share of stranded costs. Looking to the future, however, the aggregation of existing nuclear assets into a smaller number of companies that can run the plants safely and economically and that have powerful financial incentives to close the plants if the "going forward" costs rise relative to expected revenues is likely to represent a significant benefit of restructuring and competition in the electricity sector.

Utility Mergers and Acquisitions

Regulatory reform and the expansion of competitive opportunities in other previously regulated industries, such as telecommunications, railroads, airlines, and trucking has been accompanied by a significant amount of merger activity. The electric power industry appears to be following this trend.

Between 1935, when the Federal Power Act and the Public Utility Company Holding Act were passed, and the early 1990s, there were very few major mergers between electric utilities or between electric utilities and natural gas pipeline and distribution companies.[54] Federal and state regulatory policies were hostile to mergers between proximate utilities. More-

53. As Kahn (1999) has observed, adjusting for these factors suggests that these plants have sold for very close to zero or even negative prices. For example, he shows how the $121 million sales price announced by Boston Edison for its Pilgrim nuclear power plant might be interpreted as Boston Edison actually paying the buyer $176 million to take the plant when the value of fuel and Boston Edison's additional contributions to decommissioning funds are taken into account. Entergy also recently announced the purchase of about 1,800 Mw of nuclear assets from the New York Power Authority. The press headlines reported that "New York Sells Nukes to Entergy for $806 Million," *Megawatt Daily*, February 15, 2000, 1. After taking account of the value of fuel, the mortgage provided by the seller, the value of intangible assets, and a power contract with the seller, however, the purchase price of the plant was no more than about $350 million.

54. There are, however, many combination gas and electric utilities, primarily dating from before the 1930s.

over, the Public Utility Holding Company Act restricted mergers between electric utilities that did not operate as part of a single integrated system and placed an absolute ban on mergers between electric and gas utilities when the mergers involved registered holding companies. As a result, many regions of the country had a large number of relatively small vertically integrated utilities.

Deregulation of wholesale power markets, incentive regulation of distribution and transmission service, investment opportunities around the world, and diversification opportunities in telecommunications and natural gas have led many utilities to look to mergers for cost savings and increased scale to support investments in other markets. In response to the growing interest in mergers, the regulatory environment in which utility mergers are evaluated has changed considerably in the last few years. In late 1996 FERC revised its merger evaluation standards to be (arguably) more compatible with the Justice Department's guidelines for horizontal mergers, and its reviews now focus primarily on the effects a proposed merger might have on competition in generation markets and on whether the merger might unduly complicate the regulation of the remaining regulated components of the merging firms.[55] Several state commissions have encouraged utilities to merge to reduce costs and have allowed utility shareholders to retain a substantial share of any cost savings resulting from mergers. The Energy Policy Act of 1992 removed many restrictions on foreign acquisitions by U.S. utilities, and the Securities and Exchange Commission has become much more flexible in accommodating mergers between utilities that are not closely integrated geographically, as well as mergers between electric and gas utilities that had previously been almost completely banned.[56]

The result has been a dramatic acceleration in the number of mergers between electric utilities and between electric and gas utilities in recent years. Table 4-5 lists the electric utility mergers initiated between 1995 and February 2000 and indicates the primary states where the merging utilities operate.[57] Most of these mergers have been between relatively small utilities

---

55. *Inquiry Concerning the Commission's Merger Policy under the Federal Power Act: Policy Statement,* Order 592, Issued December 18, 1996, 77 FERC ¶ 61,263.

56. As part of its enforcement of the Public Utility Holding Company Act over the years the SEC had forced many electric utility holding companies to divest all of their gas utility and gas pipeline subsidiaries.

57. Between 1988 and 1994, nine electric utility mergers were consummated. Five involved mergers of very small proximate utilities, and one was an acquisition of a utility through a bankruptcy proceeding.

Table 4-5. *Electric Utility Mergers, 1995–99*

Merging companies (states)	Announcement	Completion[a]
Wisconsin Energy (Wis.) + NSP (Minn.) (Primergy)	1995	Terminated (1997)
BG&E (Md.) + PEPCO (D.C., Md.)	1995	Terminated (1997)
PS Colorado (Colo.) + Southwestern PS (Texas) (New Century Energies)	1995	1997
Ohio Edison (Ohio) + Centerior (Ohio) (FirstEnergy)	1996	1997
Delmarva (Del.) + Atlantic City Elec (N.J.) (Connectiv)	1996	1998
Union Electric (Mo.) + CIPSCO (Ill.) (Ameren)	1996	1998
WPL (WI) + IES (Iowa) + Interstate Power (Iowa) (Alliant)	1996	1998
Allegheny (Pa.) + DQE (Pa.)	1997	In litigation
AEP (Ohio, W. Va., Ky., Ind.) + CSW (Texas, Okla.)	1997	2000
LG&E (Ky.) + KU (Ky.)	1997	1998
Western Resources (Kan.) + KCP&L (Kan.)	1997	Terminated (1/2000)
Sierra Pacific (Nev.) + Nevada Power (Nev.)	1998	1999
ConEd (N.Y.) + Orange & Rockland (N.Y.)	1998	1999
Cal Energy (Independent) + MidAmerican (Kan., Mo.)	1998	1999

(continued)

Table 4-5. *(continued)*

Merging companies (states)	Announcement	Completion [a]
AES (Independent) + CIPSCO (Ill.)	1998	1999
Boston Edison (Mass.) + CommEnergy (Mass.) (NSTAR)	1998	1999
Scottish Power (Scotland) + Pacificorp (Ore., Utah, Wyo.)	1998	1999
National Grid (UK) + NEES (Mass., R.I., N.H.)	1999	2000
NEES (Mass.,R.I.,N.H.) + EUA (Mass., R.I.)	1999	2000
UtilCorp (Mo.) + St. Joseph L&P (Mo.)	1999	In process
UtilCorp (Mo.) + Empire Dist Elec (Mo.)	1999	In process
Dynegy (Independent) Illinova (Ill.)	1999	2000
New Century (Colo., Texas) + NSP (Minn.)	1999	In process
ConEd (N.Y.) + NU (Conn., Mass., N.H.)	1999	In process
PECO (Pa.) + UNICOM (Ill.)	1999	In process
EnergyEast (N.Y.) + CMP (Maine)	1999	In process
CP&L (N.C., S.C.) + Florida Progress (Fla.)	1999	In process
Sierra Pacific (Nev.) + Portland General Electric-Enron (Ore.)	1999	In process

Source: Dow Jones, trade press, company releases, and filings.
a. Completion data are as of June 23, 2000.

serving proximate geographic areas and typically have been motivated by cost-savings opportunities. A few involve consolidations of utilities that are not in close proximity to one another and largely reflect strategic values perceived by their respective managements (although the participants typically claim that these mergers will realize significant cost savings as well). Two recent mergers involve acquisitions of U.S. utilities by foreign utilities seeking to enter the U.S. market. Two other mergers involve companies that started out as independent power producers (AES and Dynegy) and have decided to acquire small vertically integrated utilities with low-cost generating capacity.

A significant number of mergers between electric utilities and gas pipeline or gas distribution utilities have also occurred in the last three years. This type of "convergence" merger was virtually impossible a decade ago, when federal and state regulatory policies discouraged them on the grounds that electricity and gas were competing sources of energy. Be that as it may, some gas and electric companies see opportunities for joint marketing of natural gas and electricity transportation services and for direct sales to end-use customers seeking to take advantage of unbundling and open access reforms that have been introduced in both sectors.[58]

Competitive Entry of Merchant Generating Plants

Competitive entry of new unregulated generating facilities owned by developers that assume construction and operating cost risks and that have incentives to use the lowest-cost technologies is likely to be one of the most important long-term benefits of competitive electricity markets.[59] One of the consequences of the uncertainties about the direction of electric sector

58. Regulators have been concerned about potential vertical market power problems emerging as a result of mergers between electric utilities with downstream generation businesses and natural gas pipelines that control supplies of natural gas used by actual or potential competing generators in the same downstream markets. The fact that natural gas–fired generating plants are generally the lowest-cost entrants into wholesale power markets has heightened these concerns. FERC's open access pipeline regulations and open access rules applied to gas distribution utilities in some states have led to the unbundling of the transportation of natural gas from the sale of commodity natural gas in ways symmetrical to the separation of generation from transmission and distribution in electricity. As a result, in states that have adopted these policies for both gas and electricity suppliers, joint ownership of transportation services should, ideally, not reduce end-use customers' opportunities to buy electricity and natural gas commodities from competing upstream suppliers. Nevertheless, open access rules cannot be monitored perfectly. As a result, regulators have attached conditions to some of these mergers to ensure that credible and enforceable open access policies are in place.

59. Joskow (1997).

restructuring between 1992 and 1997 was little investment in new generating capacity. As a result, reserve margins declined steadily.[60] From 1992 to 1997, U.S. generating capacity increased by about 4 percent, with QFs and independent producers accounting for half that growth, while electricity consumption increased by more than 14 percent. Demand growth since 1997, driven primarily by economic growth and unusually warm summer weather, has made it clear that the supply of generating capacity is now getting very tight—as shown by extraordinarily high wholesale market prices in many regions of the United States during the last two summers and by projections of supply shortages in some regions of the country for the next few years.

The growing demand for electricity, high wholesale market prices, and the gradual development of credible institutional arrangements that allow new generators to enter the market to compete in wholesale energy markets has stimulated substantial interest in the construction of new unregulated merchant generating facilities by independent power developers. In New England alone, developers of more than 30,000 MW of generating capacity (in a system with about 24,000 MW of generation resources today) have indicated an interest in entering the market.[61] In California, developers of more than 10,000 MW of merchant plant capacity have filed permit applications with the California Energy Commission for specific power plant projects, and another 5,000 MW of new generating capacity has been announced.[62] The Electric Power Supply Association reports that as of October 1999, there were 121,700 MW of merchant plant announcements, up from 56,500 MW in October 1998.[63] Most of the announced merchant plants are combined-cycle or single cycle generating facilities that rely on natural gas as a fuel and use advanced combustion turbine designs that have dramatically increased thermal efficiency.[64]

Of course, announcing the intention to build a merchant plant and actually completing a new plant are very different things. New entrants

60. North American Electric Reliability Council, "Reliability Assessment," Princeton, N.J., various years; and Edison Electric Institute (1997, tables 1, 8).

61. Division of Energy Resources, Commonwealth of Massachusetts, "DOER Report: 1998 Market Monitor," September, 1999, Appendix F.

62. California Energy Commission, Sacramento [www.energy.ca.gov (2/6/00)].

63. Electric Power Supply Association, "Doubling of Announced Merchant Plant Capacity Shows Market Confidence Is on the Rise, EPSA Says," Press Release, Washington, D.C., October 27, 1999.

64. See, for example, *Public Utilities Fortnightly*, January 20, 2000, 26–30.

must still find suitable sites, obtain siting and environmental permits, and find financing. The entire process from start to completion is shorter than it once was but still takes three years or so. Combustion turbines installed at existing sites can be developed much more quickly, in as little as one to two years. Many of the announced plants are unlikely to become real operating power plants. Nevertheless, a significant number of new projects are moving forward with construction and I expect that they will begin to come into service by summer of 2000.[65]

Transmission and Wholesale Markets in California: An Example

The core of most electricity sector reforms is the creation of reasonably competitive wholesale spot and forward markets for electric energy, capacity, and a variety of operating reserve services (also referred to as ancillary services), plus free entry of new generating capacity to make sales in these unregulated power markets. As in other commodity markets, these markets play the traditional role of balancing supply and demand and allocating supplies among competing generators in the short run and provide economic signals for entry of new suppliers in the long run. Wholesale electricity market mechanisms also play another important role, however: they provide the generation resources—and economic signals for using these resources efficiently—that the operator of an electric power transmission network depends on to maintain the reliability and power quality of the network (frequency, voltage, and stability) and to manage congestion and related network constraints at the same speed at which electricity supply and demand attributes change, which is very fast.

These resource allocation functions were traditionally performed within vertically integrated firms using internal scheduling, dispatch, and emergency response protocols that depended on a combination of computer optimization routines, marginal cost signals, and Band-Aids applied by system operators to deal with unusual circumstances. These short-run operating functions and the associated physical attributes of electric power systems are perhaps the primary factors that led to vertical integration

65. Hard data on independent power projects under construction and development are quite poor because the Department of Energy does not collect good information on these plants, and they are not captured in the standard forecasts prepared by the North American Electric Reliability Council until after they are under construction.

between generation and transmission. They are also the most challenging resource allocation activities to mediate through market mechanisms.[66] In this regard, it must be recognized that vertical integration and multi-lateral agreements between proximate vertically integrated utilities solved real technical and economic coordination problems, but they largely re-placed competition with public or regulated private monopolies. An important technical challenge associated with a system based on decen-tralized competition at the generation level is to design the system in a way that preserves the operating and investment efficiencies associated with vertical and horizontal integration while mitigating the significant costs that the institution of regulated monopoly has created. Improve-ments in network control technologies, communications, and computing speed are important for responding to this challenge, but so too are fundamental changes in the institutional arrangements that govern the electric power sectors.

Competitive generation markets on electric power networks are most appropriately conceptualized as spatial markets with demand (or loads) and differentiated generators dispersed across the network's geographic expanse. These demand and supply locations are generally referred to as "nodes" on the network. Although the generation suppliers produce more or less the same product—electric energy, they are differentiated from one another along three major dimensions: marginal costs of production; trans-portation costs, affected by congestion and thermal losses; and the speeds with which generators can adjust their output from one supply level to another, including starting up from zero. The transportation costs vary widely with supply and demand conditions at all nodes on the network. In addition to energy, generators also can produce ancillary network ser-vices, as described earlier. So, the basic framework for thinking about competition among generators should be based on a fairly complicated spatial competition model with competing multiproduct firms at different locations that are "separated" by congestion costs and thermal losses. The suppliers of generation service are asymmetric, the costs of transportation vary widely over time as congestion varies, and the elasticity of supply around the competitive equilibrium varies widely over time as demand that must be met by just-in-time production fluctuates between very low and very high levels.

All of the credible models for creating new competitive electricity

66. Joskow (1997).

markets recognize that there must be a single network operator responsible for controlling the physical operation of a control area, coordinating generator schedules, balancing loads and resources in real time, acquiring ancillary network support services required to maintain reliability, and coordinating with neighboring control areas. In the United States there also seems to be general agreement that the many control areas that now exist should be consolidated into a smaller number of regional control areas to better internalize network externalities and to reduce transactions costs associated with buying and selling power over large geographic areas.

There is much less agreement about precisely what the network operator's role should be in organizing wholesale markets for energy and ancillary network support services, how congestion should be managed, the ownership structure for the network operator, and how the network operator should be regulated. The management of the interactions between the power markets and the operation of the transmission network (in particular the management of network congestion and reliability) are particularly challenging problems because of the existence of transmission constraints whose location and severity vary over time, potential network externalities arising from the interrelationships between generators and loads at different nodes on the network, and the need to balance supply and demand at every node on the system continuously to maintain the network's reliability and necessary physical operating parameters, such as voltage and frequency.

The process that led to the restructuring of the power sector in California was characterized by a heated debate between what came to be called the "bilateral contracts" paradigm and the "poolco" or "nodal pricing" paradigm. The two approaches envision different roles for the network operator in creating and managing organized public markets for energy and ancillary services and different methods for managing scarce network transmission capacity.[67] The bilateral contracts model envisioned the network operator playing a relatively limited role that focused on reliability and "last minute" balancing of supply and demand and associated congestion management. The nodal pricing framework vested the network operator with a much more active role in both the energy markets and the management of network congestion. The network operator would manage bid-based forward and real-time public markets

67. Joskow (1996b).

for delivery of power to determine hourly market clearing day-ahead and real-time prices at different locations. Simultaneously, the network operator would manage congestion based on the supply and demand bids at different locations submitted when the unconstrained "least cost" allocations cannot be realized as a result of network congestion. The debate between the two models reflected a mix of rent seeking by entities with an interest in inefficient markets, different views on how the physical attributes of electric power networks constrained trading behavior and associated market institutions, and plenty of ideology. This debate continues today as the wholesale market restructuring process spreads across the country, although the nodal pricing framework now appears to be gaining ascendancy.

The Structure of the California Wholesale Market

California's restructuring program required the state's incumbent private utilities to create two nonprofit corporations: the California Independent System Operator (CAISO) and the California Power Exchange (CALPX).[68] The utilities had to turn the operation of their transmission networks over to CAISO; CAISO and CALPX were responsible for operating public markets with transparent market clearing prices for electric energy and ancillary services and for managing congestion using market mechanisms. This institutional structure is quite ambitious compared with the designs of wholesale markets created earlier in Argentina, Chile, and England. The California design places greater reliance on individual generator owners to make decentralized unit commitment and dispatch decisions to supply energy and ancillary services and to manage congestion based on their own self-interests, and it provides more bidding, dispatch and pricing flexibility than do most of the earlier organized electricity markets. These earlier markets ultimately rely more on the network operator to control generator commitment and dispatch based on bids reflecting marginal generating costs. The discussion of the California transmission

---

68. New wholesale market and transmission institutions managed by independent system operations have also been created in New England, New York, and the Pennsylvania–New Jersey–Maryland (PJM) power pool. New York and PJM rely heavily on a nodal pricing model; New England relies on a model that mixes the attributes of the system in England and Wales with separate ancillary service markets like those in California. The market institutions in New England have encountered many problems and are likely to be reformed significantly in the near future.

and wholesale market institutions indicates that creating competitive electricity markets is a fairly complex and challenging undertaking.

CAISO RESPONSIBILITIES.   CAISO is the core institution that governs the operation of a large portion of the transmission system in California and the system's use as a platform for wholesale and retail market trading of electricity (see figure 4-5 for a depiction of California's wholesale electricity market institutions). A nonprofit, public benefit corporation organized under the laws of California, CAISO is nonetheless subject to regulation by FERC under its rules governing transmission operators (Orders 888 and 889) and a set of "independence" criteria applicable to independent system operators. CAISO is responsible for operating the transmission networks owned by the three major investor-owned utilities in California,[69] is responsible for coordinating these operations with interconnected transmission systems in the Western System Coordinating Council (WSCC),[70] and operates a control center to do so. CAISO has adopted protocols that allow generators directly connected to the transmission facilities it operates, as well as generators that can move their power over neighboring transmission systems to points of interconnection with CAISO's network, to be scheduled to serve demand, or load, supplied over CAISO's network through intermediaries called scheduling coordinators.

CAISO accepts hourly schedules from scheduling coordinators for day-ahead and hour-ahead supply and demand and then manages the operation of the system in real time based on market information it receives from sellers and buyers and the physical constraints of the network. Because demand and supply realized in real time can vary from day-ahead or hour-ahead schedules, CAISO operates a real-time energy balancing market into which generators can submit bids to supply more energy or to reduce the energy they have scheduled to supply to the network. CAISO also manages transmission congestion through its day-ahead scheduling process and in real time. To manage congestion economically, it relies on hourly adjustment bids and supplemental energy bids

69. It was hoped that municipal transmission owners in California would also join CAISO and that it would expand to include transmission owners in neighboring states. This has not yet happened.

70. The WSCC is a regional reliability council that covers all of the states (roughly) west of the Rocky Mountains, western Canada, and portions of northern Mexico. Significant imports of energy into California and (less significant) exports of energy from California occur continuously. The volume and direction of trade varies widely with changing demand patterns in the WSCC and the availability of supplies from generating facilities, especially hydroelectric supplies.

Figure 4-5. *Structure of California Independent System Operator (CAISO) and California Power Exchange (CALPX)*[a]

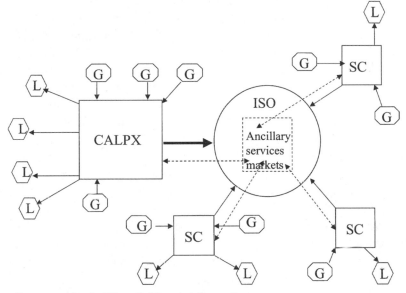

a. G = generator; L = load (demand); SC = scheduling coordinators.

submitted by generators. When congestion arises, the marginal supply cost at different nodes on the network varies.[71] California has adopted a "zonal" congestion management system, which allows separate market-clearing energy and ancillary services prices to emerge in northern and southern California (separated by a transmission path called path 15)[72] and at each point of interconnection between CAISO's facilities and those of neighboring transmission operators.[73] (Different protocols are used to manage intrazonal congestion, but I will not discuss these protocols here, except to note that managing such congestion efficiently has become a significant challenge in California.) Scheduling coordinators that schedule supplies

71. Joskow and Tirole (forthcoming).

72. In February 2000, CAISO created a third congestion zone, carving it out of the original southern zone between transmission paths 15 and 26.

73. PJM and the New York independent system operator (ISO) have implemented full nodal pricing systems. New York's wholesale market and congestion management system first became operational on November 17, 1999. The New England ISO also intends to implement a nodal pricing and congestion management system. These systems follow closely the nodal pricing models developed by Bill Hogan (1992, 1993).

from one zone to another must make congestion payments to CAISO during periods of congestion. These payments are equal to the difference in the clearing prices, based on adjustment bids, on either side of any congested interface times the quantity being scheduled across it. These payments are then rebated to the entities that hold financial transmission rights on the congested paths (see below).

To maintain the short-term reliability of the network, CAISO is also responsible for acquiring various ancillary services from generators—frequency regulation, spinning reserves, nonspinning reserves, and replacement reserves—to respond to unanticipated changes in demand and transmission or generating plant outages. CAISO operates day-ahead and hour-ahead markets for each of these reserve services for each hour of the day. These markets select generators that agree to hold generating capacity with specified physical attributes (primarily adjustment speeds and communications capabilities) in reserve to be available in a particular hour to respond to instructions from CAISO to supply energy. Generators selected in these ancillary services auctions are paid a market-clearing reservation price to hold the capacity in reserve and are then paid for any energy they are subsequently called on to supply.

Finally, CAISO is responsible for developing protocols for financial settlements between generators supplying the network and agents for consumers using energy from the network, effectively determining energy and ancillary services imbalances and the associated financial responsibilities of each coordinator that schedules over the facilities operated by CAISO.

THE CALIFORNIA POWER EXCHANGE.   California's restructuring program created a separate "voluntary" public market for trading energy for each hour of the day on a day-ahead and hour-ahead basis.[74] This organization, the California Power Exchange, or CALPX, serves as a scheduling coordinator for purposes of interacting with CAISO. Under the restructuring law, California utilities use CALPX to place all of the day-ahead demand from retail customers that have not chosen to be supplied by an energy service provider. The utilities must also bid into CALPX all of the energy supplied from any generating units they continue to own or power supplied to them under long-term contracts. Other generators and demand-

---

74. The existence of a separate power exchange distinguishes the California structure from most other organized electricity markets. ISO-New England, PJM, and New York ISO operate both day-ahead energy and ancillary services markets. That is, there is no separate organized public power exchange in these regions.

serving entities (such as marketers, municipal utilities in California, or utilities in other states) may voluntarily trade in the CALPX. Market-clearing prices, quantities, and aggregate bid curves are publicly available for each hour of the day.

OTHER SCHEDULING COORDINATORS.   Energy marketers may register as scheduling coordinators with CAISO. They must adhere to CAISO's operating and payment rules and meet credit requirements. A coordinator can organize its own portfolio of supply resources and load obligations and schedule its portfolio for physical delivery with CAISO. Scheduling coordinators rely on bilateral financial contracts with buyers and sellers (or owned generation) to assemble their portfolios and are then supposed to submit balanced schedules (supply schedule equals demand schedule) for each hour to CAISO. The prices coordinators pay to generation suppliers or charge to buyers and the methods they use to manage congestion are internal to each coordinator, and such information is not public.

MARKET OPERATIONS.   The day-ahead market accounts for the vast bulk of the trade mediated by CALPX and for 80–90 percent of the energy traded over CAISO's facilities. The CALPX day-ahead market is a forward market that defines financial obligations of winning bidders. Early in the day before delivery, generators participating in CALPX submit (upward sloping) supply portfolio bids (quantity and price schedules) to CALPX for each (or any) hour of the following day. Distribution companies and wholesale market intermediaries also submit demand bids for each hour of the following day. CALPX stacks up the supply-side and demand-side bids for each hour and identifies the highest bid that clears the market. This bid determines the day-ahead price at which the winning buyers and sellers are committed to trade during each hour of the following day. That is, CALPX runs a uniform price auction for energy for each hour of the following day. Figure 4-6 shows the aggregate day-ahead supply and demand bids and market-clearing prices for a typical day and hour. The figure reflects bids submitted to CALPX on August 25, 1998, for supplies delivered during the hour beginning at 3 p.m. the next day. The day-ahead market clearing price for that hour is just under $70 per megawatt hour (MWh).[75] Once

75. Note that the slope of the aggregate demand curve reflects a day-ahead demand elasticity. Some of the apparent demand elasticity reflects demand that simply gets shifted to the real-time market to take advantage of caps on real-time prices. The rest is demand by utilities or marketers with generation portfolios that will supply from their own resources rather than buy from the market if the price gets high enough.

Figure 4-6. *CALPX Aggregate Supply and Demand Bids,*
August 26, 1998, 3 P.M.

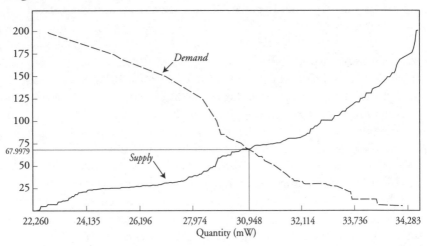

Source: California Power Exchange (www.calpx.com/prices).

the winning bidders are chosen, the generators are required to tell CALPX
the specific generators that have been designated to meet their supply
commitments, and CALPX uses this information to develop a "preferred
schedule" of specific generators and associated expected supplies for each
hour of the following day. Generators also submit adjustment bids to
CALPX at this time, which indicate at what price they are willing to
increase or reduce their supplies from their day-ahead schedules.

CALPX and the other scheduling coordinators then submit their
preferred generation schedule for each hour of the following day to
CAISO, along with generators' adjustment and ancillary services bids.
CAISO puts all of the preferred schedules together and determines
whether the transmission network has the capacity to accommodate all of
these schedules without creating interzonal congestion that must be managed. If the network has the capability to do so, then CAISO informs
CALPX and other scheduling coordinators that their day-ahead energy
schedules are accepted and provides a preliminary schedule of, and prices
for, ancillary services. If expected interzonal network congestion makes it
impossible for CAISO to accommodate the preferred schedules, CAISO
informs them that that the schedules must be adjusted. CAISO provides
the other scheduling coordinators with a suggested set of schedule revisions
based on adjustment bids they have submitted, as well as the associated

congestion prices applicable to their interzonal schedules, and allows them to reschedule energy and ancillary services based on this information. The other scheduling coordinators are free to resolve their congestion in any way they choose, including trading with one another. The scheduling coordinators then resubmit this second set of schedules and adjustment and ancillary services bids to CAISO, which uses the adjustment bids it has received from CALPX to resolve interzonal congestion for its portfolio. If CAISO determines that the transmission network still cannot accommodate the adjusted schedules, it applies its own schedule revisions to the other coordinators' schedules based on the adjustment bids they have submitted.

Once these steps are completed, CAISO specifies a final set of day-ahead schedules for energy and ancillary services, day-ahead ancillary service prices, and congestion charges for each hour of the following day. CALPX posts a symmetrical set of zonal day-ahead prices for energy for each hour. To conclude the day-ahead scheduling process, CAISO determines whether there are any unmet local reliability needs and can then order schedule changes to meet them by calling on "reliability-must-run" (RMR) generators with which it has contracts. (A similar process is used to adjust hour-ahead schedules, but the volumes in the hour-ahead—or day-of—markets are generally small.)

TRANSMISSION PRICING. The responsibility for paying for the operating, maintenance, and sunk costs of the transmission network is currently that of the distribution entities whose retail customers receive power over CAISO's facilities. These charges, included in each retail customer's base distribution charges as they have always been, are known as "license plate" transmission charges because they give retail consumers or their agents (including the distribution company providing default service) access to any generator supplying to the market over the transmission facilities operated by CAISO. Existing generators in California or generators located outside California that can deliver energy to a point of interconnection with CAISO do not pay transmission service charges, unless there is congestion on a path over which their supplies are scheduled. When that happens, the coordinators scheduling for the affected generators pay day-ahead or real-time congestion charges (or both). The congestion rents were initially rebated to the transmission owners, and these revenues then reduced the transmission charges paid by retail consumers. CAISO has created tradable financial transmission rights, which entitle the holders to a share of these transmission rents. The first vintage of these rights was auctioned off in mid-November 1999. The revenues from the auction will be credited back against the sunk costs of transmission and reduce the charges to retail consumers. (Interconnection of new generators and transmission expansion are controversial works in progress as this is written.)

Energy Market Behavior

CAISO and CALPX began operating on April 1, 1998. Figure 4-7 provides information for the hourly demands served by CAISO on three representative days: a relatively low demand day in April 1999; a moderate demand day in July 1999; and a high demand day in September 1999. As expected, demand is substantially higher during the day than at night, and a very high load day can have a peak demand that is almost double that on a low load day.[76] Figure 4-8 shows the associated day-ahead prices in CALPX for each of the hours of the days reflected in figure 4-7. To help to interpret the prices in figure 4-8, figure 4-9 displays a hypothetical short-run marginal cost function (competitive supply curve) for energy that could be made available to the energy and ancillary services markets during an "average" hour. The marginal cost can be as low as zero at very low demand levels, especially during the hydro spill season in the late spring and early summer when supplies of electricity are abundant. The relatively flat portion of the curve reflects generators with marginal supply costs in the $25–$35 per MWh level. The inelastic portion of the curve reflects the marginal costs of operating peaking generators with a marginal supply cost in the $35–$60 per MWh range, including start-up costs.[77] At some point, capacity is exhausted and the supply curve becomes vertical.

The hourly prices displayed in figure 4-8 are higher in July than in April, reflecting the higher loads in July. The availability of more hydro-electric energy in early July increased supply and moderated the price differences. The peak hour prices jump considerably during the high demand hours on September 10, 1999. This is far above the marginal supply cost of any generator in the WSCC. Indeed, the $250 price cap imposed by CAISO on real-time prices (through September 30, 1999, when the price cap was raised to $750 per MWh) is effectively capping the

---

76. In addition, demand is lower on weekends and holidays than on standard weekdays, other things equal.

77. Borenstein, Bushnell, and Wolak (1999).

Figure 4-7. *CAISO Load, by Hour*

Load (megawatts)

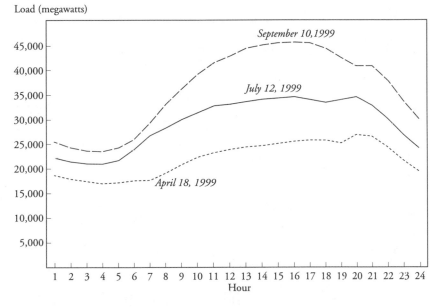

Source: CALPX (www.calpx.com).

prices in the day-ahead market as well as during high demand conditions, since demand can arbitrage between the day-ahead and real-time markets with modest penalties.

Table 4-6 displays day-ahead prices in CALPX, the real-time prices in CAISO, and prices for day-ahead bilateral contracts for energy sold in southern California for the first twenty-one months the new California markets were in operation.[78] The monthly average prices are further broken down between peak (sixteen hours each day) and off-peak (eight hours each day) periods. The monthly patterns described earlier can be seen in the data for the whole period. Prices are higher during the day than at night. Prices are generally higher during the summer than the spring, fall, or winter months, although prices were very high in early October 1999 because of a late heat wave and the raising of the real-time price cap from $250 to $750

78. The unconstrained CALPX clearing prices were obtained from the exchange's web site. The real-time prices for the southern zone (SP15) were obtained from CAISO's web site [www.caiso.com (5/15/00)]. The bilateral contract prices for delivery in southern California were obtained from Economic Insights, Inc. I am grateful to Economic Insights, Inc., in Portland, Ore., for providing me with these data for the last few years.

Figure 4-8. *CALPX Day-Ahead Price, by Hour*

Price (dollars per megawatt)

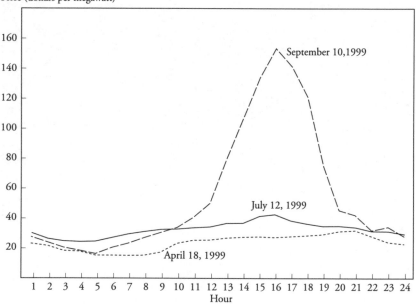

Source: CALPX (www.calpx.com).

per MWh. Prices appear to have been lower during the summer of 1999 than the summer of 1998, even when I controlled for demand and fuel price variation.[79] The bilateral market prices (based on private surveys of traders) move roughly in step with the equivalent CALPX prices, suggesting arbitrage between the CALPX and bilateral day-ahead markets, although the data for bilateral transactions are not good enough to draw more refined conclusions about the extent of price arbitrage. Similarly, real-time energy prices move roughly with day-ahead energy prices, although there appear to be systematic differences between day-ahead and real-time prices, suggesting that price differences are not being fully arbitraged away.[80] Moreover, as expected (but not displayed here), real-time prices are considerably more volatile than are day-ahead prices.

79. Based on preliminary econometric analysis of CALPX prices, which I am now completing.

80. Real-time prices appear to be systematically lower than day-ahead prices during the spring of 1998 and systematically higher than day-ahead prices during the summer of 1998. Price differences appear to be more fully arbitraged away since then, although this question is worthy of further analysis. See Borenstein and others (1999).

Figure 4-9. *Competitive Electricity Supply Curve*

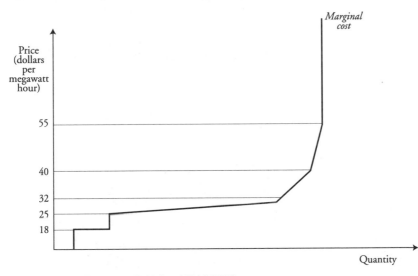

Source: Author and Borenstein, Bushnell, and Wolak (1999).

Short-Run Market Performance

The performance of California's electricity markets has been subject to extensive scrutiny because the institutional arrangements approved by FERC (wisely) included a requirement that CAISO create a market surveillance committee and that CALPX create a market monitoring committee. Both committees have independent members, primarily academic economists, and have issued several reports and papers based, in part, on proprietary data available only to CAISO and CALPX. In evaluating the performance of California's electricity markets, it must be recognized that these institutions have been operating for less than two years and that numerous refinements have been introduced during this time period. It is thus too early to perform the kind of comprehensive assessment that Newbery and Pollitt have completed for England and Wales.[81]

HORIZONTAL MARKET POWER.   During periods of low and moderate demand, California's energy markets appear to be quite competitive, with

81. Newbery and Pollitt (1997).

Table 4-6. *Day-Ahead Wholesale Market Prices in California, by Month, 1998 and 1999*

Dollars per megawatt hour

Year	Month	Unconstrained CALPX clearing prices[a]			Bilateral prices[a]			CAISO real time prices[b]		
		All hours	Peak	Offpeak	All hours	Peak	Offpeak	All hours	Peak	Offpeak
1998	4	22.60 (23.32)	25.24 (25.59)	17.33 (17.89)	20.15	25.11	15.19	20.30	23.30	14.27
	5	11.65 (12.5)	14.23 (14.85)	6.48 (6.93)	12.71	16.74	8.68	10.08	12.66	4.91
	6	12.09 (13.26)	15.39 (16.26)	5.50 (6.06)	10.65	15.49	5.81	8.38	10.35	4.45
	7	32.42 (35.58)	37.69 (40.6)	21.87 (22.94)	24.92	34.21	15.63	27.62	33.67	15.53
	8	39.53 (43.42)	46.72 (50.37)	25.14 (25.72)	35.26	45.70	24.81	43.53	53.41	23.75
	9	34.01 (36.96)	38.74 (41.79)	24.55 (25.07)	30.66	38.33	22.99	35.13	40.97	23.44
	10	26.65 (27.28)	29.00 (29.35)	21.94 (22.31)	22.77	26.52	19.02	27.66	31.80	19.41
	11	25.74 (26.45)	28.04 (28.52)	21.15 (21.5)	21.24	24.89	17.59	24.08	27.67	16.91
	12	29.13 (29.98)	31.25 (31.94)	24.89 (25.41)	21.74	24.98	18.49	26.13	29.41	19.59
	Total	26.01 (28.53)	29.63 (32.15)	18.78 (19.72)	21.28	26.28	16.29	24.81	29.30	15.83
1999	1	20.96 (21.65)	23.22 (23.63)	16.44 (16.86)	19.94	22.35	17.53	19.50	21.53	15.43

2	19.03 (19.59)	21.20 (21.49)	14.68 (14.99)	17.39	20.41	14.36	18.98	21.39	14.15
3	18.83 (19.31)	20.91 (21.12)	14.66 (14.97)	16.97	21.02	12.93	20.09	22.93	14.42
4	24.01 (24.67)	26.33 (26.68)	19.38 (19.87)	21.71	26.14	16.93	25.42	28.02	20.19
5	23.61 (24.74)	26.87 (27.65)	17.10 (17.71)	21.81	27.37	16.26	19.66	21.47	16.04
6	23.52 (25.76)	28.01 (29.87)	14.55 (15.6)	19.48	28.32	10.65	21.87	26.16	13.28
7	28.92 (31.52)	33.49 (35.66)	19.80 (20.63)	26.62	35.94	17.30	22.22	27.81	11.05
8	32.31 (34.71)	37.11 (39.02)	22.72 (23.44)	28.29	36.15	20.44	34.47	41.43	20.56
9	33.91 (35.15)	37.33 (38.19)	27.08 (27.54)	28.59	32.51	24.68	33.09	39.37	20.53
10	47.56 (49.01)	53.33 (54.23)	36.02 (36.43)	36.16	40.45	31.67	42.50	49.08	29.39
11	36.91 (38.29)	41.53 (42.39)	27.66 (28.09)	22.50	26.65	18.09	31.95	38.01	19.83
12	29.66 (30.17)	31.47 (31.83)	26.05 (26.34)	26.37	30.26	22.48	32.01	33.21	29.61
Total	28.23 (30.04)	31.68 (33.25)	21.31 (22.15)	23.70	28.91	18.42	26.87	30.92	18.75

Source: Author's calculations based on data from California Power Exchange, California Independent System Operator, and Economics Insights, Inc.

a. Numbers in parentheses are volume-weighted averages.

b. Prices given are for the southern zone.

day-ahead prices reasonably close to estimates of marginal cost. This is generally the case whether or not congestion is observed.[82] When demand gets very high, however, the market is clearing at prices far above the marginal cost of the most expensive generators in the region. Because these markets do not yet have any real demand elasticity, it is evident that as demand grows and supply gets very tight, generators realize that a small amount of capacity withholding, even with moderate levels of concentration, can lead to large price increases. All of the studies indicate that during periods of very high demand, unilateral behavior leads to prices that are significantly above competitive levels.[83] The preferred long-run solution is to bring more price-sensitive demand directly into the day-ahead and real-time markets by getting more customers on real-time pricing programs, and to relax current restrictions that limit the ability of California's utilities to enter into fixed-price forward contracts for energy months or years before delivery. The short-run solution is to impose price caps on the real-time markets operated by CAISO to keep the prices from running away to infinity. CAISO has had price caps in effect on real-time balancing energy since the markets began operating, and it imposed price caps on ancillary services markets in July 1998, when prices reached $10,000 per MW.[84] These bid caps effectively cap day-ahead prices in CALPX as well, because buyers can submit price-sensitive bids to the day-ahead market that effectively shift demand to the real-time market when prices rise to levels approaching the caps.[85]

ANCILLARY SERVICES MARKETS.   In every electricity market outside the United States that I am familiar with, most ancillary services are procured simultaneously with energy. Suppliers submit bids specifying prices and

82. Congestion tends to occur in the North to South direction as a result of abundant supplies of hydroelectric energy in the Northwest and northern California in the spring and early summer, when demand is relatively low. Congestion tends to occur in the South to North direction in the fall and winter at night when cheap energy from the Southwest is (effectively) being exported to the Northwest through California. The high-priced periods in the summer of 1998 did not generally coincide with significant congestion. Demand was high everywhere in the WSCC, and there was little energy for export to California from the Northwest and Southwest.

83. Borenstein, Bushnell, and Wolak (1999); CAISO Annual Report (1999); CAISO MSC Report (1999).

84. CAISO Annual Report (1999, ch. 3).

85. CALPX itself has an administrative cap of $2,500/Mwh. I have observed generators routinely placing bids into CALPX with a small amount of capacity offered at $2,500. The suppliers must be hoping that some demand-serving entities are not smart enough to arbitrage the cap on real-time prices.

quantities at which they are willing to supply, along with relevant technical parameters for their generating units, and the network operator effectively does a simultaneous "least-cost" procurement of energy and ancillary services. So, for example, assume that the expected system demand for an hour is 10,000 MW. Based on the supply bids submitted, the network operator would buy 10,000 MW of energy and perhaps about 1,200 MW of reserve services with the mix of response times and locations it requires to manage the reliability and power quality attributes of the network. To oversimplify a bit, the lowest bidders are selected to supply energy, the next lowest to supply frequency regulation, the next lowest to supply spinning reserve, and so on. These algorithms yield prices for ancillary services that reflect simple opportunity cost principles. These opportunity costs are usually very low, since these units are the highest ones in the bid stacks. (Differences in physical capabilities of different generators complicate these pricing relationships, but I will not dwell on these complications here.) This integrated procurement approach seems to work just fine in other organized markets, and indeed there is almost no mention of these reserve services in the literature discussing the markets in Argentina, Chile, and England and Wales, all of which have been fairly widely studied.

CAISO initially took a different approach, setting up separate day-ahead and hour-ahead markets for these services. These markets initially performed very poorly: prices were much higher than expected, rising to more than 15 percent of total energy costs during the summer of 1998; moreover, there was often no rational relationship between prices for different products and their relative quality.[86] The combination of separate sequential markets and zero price elasticity of demand for ancillary services has exacerbated market power problems, especially since the supply of some of these services is highly concentrated during some system conditions.[87] The problems are most severe during high demand periods and when congestion isolates northern and southern California.[88]

By the fall of 1998 it was agreed that the ancillary services markets in California had to be redesigned to reflect a "rational buyer" approach that allows the network operator to adjust its purchases of individual ancillary services, so that CAISO does not buy a low-quality service when it can buy

---

86. CAISO Annual Report (1999, ch. 3), CAISO MSC Report (1999).

87. CAISO Annual Report (1999, ch. 3). In New England, the market rules for ancillary services have also distorted bidding behavior, which has led to unbounded prices; see Cramton (1999).

88. CAISO MSC Report (1999). Administrative limits have been placed on imports of some ancillary services from outside CAISO's network for technical reasons.

a high-quality service at a lower price. Some reforms along these lines were made in mid-1999, along with several other changes in the procurement of ancillary services. Perhaps as a result of these reforms, costs of ancillary services declined significantly in California in 1999. The system would work better if ancillary services procurement were further integrated with the energy market.

A somewhat different problem is related to the *quantity* of reserve services that CAISO was procuring in the market during its first year of operation. One of the costs of relying on competitive markets for generation services, especially the self-commitment and scheduling philosophy that characterizes the California market design, is that network operators are less certain about the supplies and the loads (but mostly the supplies) that will actually be available to them in real time. Their response to these commitment uncertainties has been to purchase unusually large quantities of ancillary services, a move that has increased costs and further exacerbated performance failures in the ancillary services markets themselves. Some of these costs may be transitory as network operators grow more confident, but some of them are simply a cost of moving from a vertically integrated system to a decentralized competitive market system.

LOCATIONAL MARKET POWER AND THE RELIABILITY-MUST-RUN CONTRACTS. Network congestion or reliability constraints sometimes effectively create a geographic market for energy or ancillary services in which there is little or no competition. When the wholesale market institutions were created in California, it was recognized that to maintain reliability, CAISO would have to depend on generators at specific locations on the network to operate under certain system conditions. This led to concerns that these generators would have "local market power" and would charge very high prices to provide service at the direction of CAISO, no matter what prices they had bid into the energy or reserve markets To mitigate this problem, CAISO entered into contracts with these generators specifying a maximum price the generators would be paid when CAISO had to call them "out of market" to meet reliability needs. More than 15,000 MW of generating capacity, including a large fraction of the cycling capacity that is frequently at or near the margin on the supply curve where the energy and ancillary services markets clear, was eventually given the "reliability-must-run" designation (RMR) and operated subject to these contracts.

Unfortunately, the original RMR contracts were structured very poorly. Indeed, in the process of trying to mitigate the direct effect of local market power, the original RMR contracts caused costly distortions in the broader energy and ancillary services markets.[89] The problems were magnified by the very large fraction of cycling capacity that was covered by these contracts. The original contracts were amended effective June 1, 1999, and now are structured with a fixed annual "option payment" and a per MWh call price equal to each unit's variable operating costs. The principles for determining the levels of the fixed option payments remain a matter of dispute as this is written.[90] It is too early to tell how these contracts have affected market behavior and performance because a number of other changes to the ancillary services markets went into effect during the summer of 1999 as well.

Locational market power problems can arise on any electric power network; they are not unique to California and are probably more prevalent than is generally assumed. Locational market power issues have been identified and mitigation mechanisms have since been implemented by other independent supply operators (ISOs) in the United States as well as in England and Wales. In light of the problems engendered by California's approach to these problems, it would be worthwhile to better understand the conditions in which serious local market power problems are likely to emerge and the properties of alternative mitigation mechanisms.

CONGESTION MANAGEMENT.   California's interzonal congestion management protocols appear to work reasonably well. During the first year of operation, day-ahead import congestion occurred at the California-Oregon border during 18 percent of the hours and (north to south) on path 15 connecting northern and southern California about 14 percent of the hours. Import congestion occurred on other paths less than 10 percent of the hours. Export congestion (generally south to north) occurred much less frequently and primarily during offpeak hours. Total congestion charges were about $35 million during the system's first twelve months.[91]

The management of intrazonal congestion is much less transparent and the costs difficult to calculate because CAISO relies heavily on RMR con-

---

89. Bushnell and Wolak (1999).

90. I submitted testimony in the FERC proceedings that should resolve this issue.

91. CAISO (1999, ch. 5). The auction for financial transmission rights conducted by CAISO during November 1999 yielded revenues of $41 million for fourteen-month rights. This is consistent with the historical congestion revenue data. It appears that congestion costs increased in 1999, but I have not yet analyzed the 1999 congestion cost data.

tracts to manage intrazonal congestion.[92] When units with RMR contracts are not available to mitigate intrazonal congestion, significant gaming by generators has been observed at strategic locations. This is an area where CAISO's protocols require further refinement. In late 1999 CAISO proposed changes in its intrazonal congestion management protocols to deal with perceived local market power problems. While recognizing that these problems identified were real, FERC rejected portions of the proposal because it said CAISO was approaching a growing number of congestion management issues in a piecemeal fashion. FERC ordered CAISO to develop a comprehensive set of reforms to its congestion management protocols.[93]

WHOLESALE MARKET PRICE TRENDS.   Has the introduction of these new and complex institutional arrangements in California led to lower wholesale market prices? In England and Wales, despite persistent market power problems, wholesale electricity prices have declined during the 1990s as the competitive wholesale market has matured. Are we observing similar responses to the expansion of competitive opportunities in wholesale markets in California? This is a hard question to answer, because it is not clear which prices to compare "before and after" the introduction of the new market institutions in California. Moreover, hydroelectric supplies, gas prices, and demand have varied over time, and new entrants have not yet completed any new generating plants. Nevertheless, it is useful to examine the data that are available.

A bilateral contract market for day-ahead deliveries has existed in the WSCC for many years, and I have been collecting survey data for daily transactions in this market since 1996. Table 4-7 displays the average day-ahead peak period bilateral contract prices for deliveries to southern California for January through December for the years 1996 through 1999. CAISO and CALPX began operating in April 1998, so prices can be compared across time. There does not appear to be any evidence that the new market arrangements have led to significant changes in wholesale prices. If anything, wholesale prices have increased since April 1998, although one must use caution in drawing strong conclusions from these data since demand and supply conditions vary over time. Because demand

92. CAISO distinguishes between local market power problems handled with RMR contracts and the management of intrazonal congestion when there are too few suppliers to get competitive adjustment bids. Conceptually, these problems appear to be effectively the same, although there may be differences in severity, duration, and predictability.

93. 90 FERC 61,006 issued January 7, 2000.

Table 4-7. *Day-Ahead Bilaterial Contract Prices at Peak Period for Delivery to Southern California, 1996–99*

Dollars per megawatt hour

Month	1996	1997	1998	1999
January	13.0	18.7	23.1	22.3
February	11.8	12.7	18.3	20.4
March	10.6	15.2	21.2	21.0
April	11.9	17.4	25.1	26.1
May	11.7	24.1	16.7	27.4
June	13.4	21.8	15.5	28.3
July	19.0	25.1	34.2	35.9
August	21.9	31.0	45.7	36.1
September	18.4	32.7	38.3	32.5
October	21.4	26.5	26.5	40.4
November	24.1	25.5	17.9	26.7
December	26.1	25.2	25.0	30.3
Unweighted average	16.8	23.1	25.7	28.9

Source: Calculated from daily reports provided by Economic Insights, Inc. Does not include CALPX transactions. CALPX became operational in April 1998.

has grown relatively rapidly and because no new generating plants have come on line yet, prices should be rising over time, other things equal.

When the very high ancillary services costs, the RMR contract costs, and the costs of creating and operating CAISO and CALPX (several hundred million dollars so far) are taken into account, it would be hard to make a convincing case that California's new wholesale market institutions have, so far, led to lower wholesale power and transmission costs. The best that can be said is that the start-up costs and market inefficiencies associated with these new market arrangements are an investment that one hopes will yield greater societal benefits in the longer run as competition affects the costs and performance of existing generating facilities and new merchant plants that enter the market and as demand side innovations associated with retail competition develop and diffuse.

Retail Competition and Customer Choice

A great deal of the popular discussion about electricity sector restructuring, competition, and regulatory reform has focused on providing customer choice for all retail consumers—small, medium, and large. As noted earlier, customer choice or retail wheeling programs separate the distribution of electricity, which remains a regulated monopoly, from the financial arrangements for acquiring electric generation services in competitive wholesale markets and reselling these services to end-use retail consumers. Utility distribution companies (UDCs) provide the first service. Independent unregulated electricity providers (known as electric service providers, or ESPs) provide the second service, relying on the UDCs' distribution facilities to deliver the electricity. ESPs need own no physical electricity production or distribution facilities; they are primarily financial intermediaries that acquire electricity in the competitive wholesale market and resell it at retail to residential, commercial, and industrial consumers. ESPs may provide their own metering, billing, and customer care services, may rely on UDCs to provide some or all of these services, or may outsource them to third parties. Customers who do not switch to an ESP can generally continue to be supplied with electric energy by a UDC —through a default or standard offer service option—based on a regulated price. The performance of retail customer choice programs depends on the existence of competitive wholesale markets, the retailing costs associated with marketing and billing for electricity, customer switching costs, and the intensity of competition among retailers.

Retail competition programs must confront two sets of issues. First, wholesale market prices vary widely from hour to hour, yet the vast bulk of retail consumers of electricity are now billed based on meters that do not record hourly consumption and that are read monthly or semimonthly. If an ESP serves customers without hourly meters, how are the ESP's financial obligations for energy and ancillary services purchased through the wholesale market to be determined? How are the ESPs to match the consumption of their retail customers against supplies from generators with which the ESPs have power supply contracts? In the absence of hourly metering, financial settlements must depend on consumption estimation protocols—called load profiling—that allocate each retail customer's monthly meter readings into consumption estimates for each hour in the previous month. These load profiles are estimated by giving hourly meters to samples of representative consumers, developing a profile of the proportion of their recorded monthly consumption that is consumed in each hour of the month, and then assuming that each individual consumer with similar characteristics has the same hourly consumption patterns as the sample group. All ESPs and distribution utilities providing default or standard offer service must agree to adhere to the same load-profiling rules to ensure that the aggregate energy consumed from the network is attributed to some responsible ESP or UDC and that this consumption can be matched with supplies from generators with which the ESPs and UDCs have contracts or supplies they have acquired through anonymous spot market purchases. Obviously, this is not an ideal measurement situation. Individual consumers have no incentives to respond to hourly price signals. Moreover, the load-profiling and settlements systems are costly and time consuming to implement effectively.

Second, it is important to step beyond the public rhetoric about retail competition and recognize that there is a simple and low-cost way to ensure that retail electricity consumers get the *price-related* benefits of spot market competition among generation suppliers. Retailing costs (metering, billing, customer services, and the like) represent a very small part of the average customer's electricity bill—less than 5 percent.[94] The physical attributes of electricity production and delivery make it very easy for a distribution company to give all retail electricity consumers the equivalent of direct access to the wholesale spot market for electricity. All the UDC need do is register its customers' demands in an organized wholesale market and bill their metered consumption at the wholesale price plus losses and any associated retail service costs. Accordingly, the societal benefits of retail competition programs turn on the value-added services provided by ESPs to consumers over and above what can they can realize in a simple and inexpensive way through direct access to the wholesale market through their local UDC. The success of retail competition should be measured by the valued-added services it brings to the system, not by the fraction of customers who decide to buy from an ESP rather than buy directly in the wholesale market through their UDC.

A retail competition program must start by unbundling competitive services (generation service supplies and their associated costs) from regulated monopoly services (transmission, distribution, and designated stranded-cost charges). In the old regime, the typical regulated bundled electricity price was built up from various cost elements as follows (simplifying somewhat):

$$P_T = C_g + C_T + C_D + C_{RCS} + DSM = \text{average UDC bundled price/kWh,}$$

94. Joskow (2000).

where C_g equals average accounting costs of utility owned–generation plus QF contract costs; C_T equals average accounting costs of transmission service; C_D equals average accounting costs of distribution service; C_{RCS} equals average accounting costs of retail customer services, or RCS; and DSM equals charges for energy efficiency and other public benefit (low-income) programs.

As discussed earlier, state electricity restructuring programs do at least four things that affect these base regulated prices. First, they include a scheme to measure and collect allowed stranded costs. Second, they impose a mandatory price reduction for at least some groups of customers whether they choose a competitive retailer or not. Third, they develop an unbundled rate design that separates charges for services or payment obligations (such as transmission and distribution services and energy efficiency subsidy payments) that all customers must pay, regardless of whom they choose as a retail electricity supplier, from services and costs that are open to competition (such as generation services). Finally, the distribution utility is required to offer a regulated default or standard offer option to allow customers who do not choose to use an ESP to continue to receive basic energy service from the UDC. So the prices consumers face after restructuring have the following basic structure:

$$P_{UDC} = S_g + C_T + C_D + (1-a)C_{RCS} + DSM = \text{average regulated price for non-bypassable transmission and distribution services,}$$

$$P_{DS} = P_{DG} + aC_{RCS} = \text{UDC default service prices for competitive services or the "price to beat" for ESPs,}$$

and

$$P_{UDC} + P_{DS} \leq P_T \quad \text{(reflecting the policy of assured price reductions for a large fraction of retail customers whether they choose an ESP or not),}$$

where all of the definitions are as above and S_g equals the stranded-cost component; P_{DG} equals the default or standard offer price for basic generation services; and a equals the fraction of retail service costs open to competition.

From the perspective of an ESP competing primarily on the basis of the price of commodity electricity, the magnitude of the default service price relative to its own costs of providing these services is of great importance. Different states have taken alternative approaches to setting the relevant charges. For example, California's laws effectively require that the default service price reflect a direct passthrough of the prices paid by the UDC to CALPX and CAISO for energy purchased in these markets to supply default service customers (ancillary services and RMR costs are included in transmission charges and are paid by all customers) plus a small charge for avoidable RCS costs. The reasoning is that once the customers have paid for the stranded costs of the generating plants, they are entitled to get electricity at its competitive market value. Since CALPX and CAISO are competitive wholesale markets for electricity with transparent prices, they represent a natural benchmark for the competitive market value of electricity. Thus, to compete successfully based only on price, an ESP must be able profitably to beat the CALPX and CAISO prices, something that is very difficult to do.

Another example is provided by Massachusetts, which focused its attention on minimizing stranded-cost obligations (by requiring complete divestiture of generating plants), providing utilities with a credible commitment that if they divested, they would recover any residual stranded costs; giving all customers significant and immediate retail price reductions (10 percent in 1998 and another 5 percent in 1999); and gradually providing consumers with incentives to shop for an ESP. It adopted a "standard offer" approach, which set an eight-year trajectory of values for P_{DG} that starts at an estimate of the annual wholesale market price in 1998 (2.8 cents per kWh) and then rises over time to levels that were anticipated to be above the wholesale market price (5.1 cents per kWh in 2004). The idea was that over time, the rising standard offer price would create more "margin" against which ESPs could easily compete to move consumers off standard offer services. As it turned out, the initial value for P_{DG} was probably somewhat below the actual wholesale market prices in 1998 and 1999 and far below the wholesale market price by summer 2000. In addition, the Massachusetts restructuring legislation prohibits unbundling of billing, customer service, and other RCS services before 2001.[95]

In contrast, Pennsylvania chose an approach that was focused much more on providing stranded-cost recovery to utilities and creating good

95. See [www.magnet.state.ma.us/dpu/restruct/competition/index.htm (5/15/00)].

market opportunities for ESPs than on quickly reducing retail prices for all customers.[96] The mandated retail rate reductions in Pennsylvania were much smaller than those in Massachusetts and (for residential customers) California. The value of P_{DG} was set above the expected wholesale market value of electricity; the size of the premium (known as a "shopping credit") varied from utility to utility, reflecting differences in the magnitude of their stranded costs rather than the market value of wholesale power. Because the stranded-cost component of the nonbypassable UDC charges in Pennsylvania was determined in an administrative proceeding rather than through market valuation of generating assets, one can view the premium either as representing a policy of putting some of each utility's stranded costs out to be competed away by ESPs or as providing an opportunity for the utilities to earn more than 100 percent of their stranded costs if retail competition is not too intense and if a large fraction of the retail customers continue to take default service from the UDC at a price that exceeds its competitive market value.

Tables 4-8, 4-9, and 4-10 display information on the number of customers who have switched to ESPs in each of these states. It is evident that customers in Pennsylvania have generally taken much greater advantage of the opportunity to reduce their rates by giving their business to ESPs than have customers in California and Massachusetts. It is also worth noting that in Pennsylvania, larger customers have been able to take much greater advantage of retail competition than have smaller customers, despite the large residential shopping credits in some areas. Moreover, in California and Massachusetts, where the default and standard offer service provide little if any margin over the wholesale price, ESPs have still been able to attract a surprisingly large fraction of the largest customers. This suggests that ESPs can and do offer large customers value-added services in addition to providing them with commodity electricity they acquire in the wholesale market.

The shopping credits in Pennsylvania have clearly given residential customers greater incentives to switch to ESPs, although the vast majority have continued to take bundled service from their local UDC. The fact that more residential customers have switched in Pennsylvania, however, does not necessarily imply that residential customers are better off than they would have been if the Pennsylvania regulators had required UDCs to offer *all* residential customers the opportunity to buy directly at the wholesale

96. New Jersey has adopted a similar approach.

Table 4-8. *Retail Customers Switching to ESPs in Massachusetts, as of November 1999*[a]

Customer	Percent of retail sales
Residential	0.17
Small commercial	1.7
Medium commercial	5.0
Large commercial	20.7

Source: Division of Energy Resources, Commonwealth of Massachusetts, November, 1999.
a. Retail choice began on April 1, 1998.

price as is the case in California or to buy under a default service option as in Massachusetts. Customers who have not switched are paying both stranded-cost charges and a generation service price in excess of its wholesale market value. In Philadelphia, for example, the discount of the total UDC default rate offered by the most successful ESP was only about 0.5 cents per kWh in 1999, while the discount would have been roughly 1.2 cents per kWh if all customers could have bought at the wholesale market price. Overall, the 10–15 percent rate cuts implemented in California and Massachusetts for *all* residential customers have conveyed much more significant benefits to these customers than has Pennsylvania, where the largest customers have received most of the benefits of restructuring so far.

Overall, it is not at all obvious to me that smaller customers reap any net social gain from retail competition without real-time meters compared with a regime where they are given direct access to the competitive whole-sale market by their UDCs. Significant costs are associated with developing

Table 4-9. *Retail Customers Switching to ESPs in California as of December 15, 1999*[a]

Customer type	Percent of demand	Percent of customers
Residential	2.0	1.7
Commercial		
Less than 20 kW	4.2	3.4
20–500 kW	14.6	6.5
Industrial		
More than 500 kW	32.0	20.1

Source: California Public Utilities Commission, Direct Access Reports, December 1999.
a. Retail choice began on January 1, 1999.

Table 4-10. *Retail Customers Switching to ESPs in Pennsylvania as of January 7, 2000*[a]

Percentage of load served by ESPs

Company	Residential	Commercial	Industrial
PECO	17.5	39.15	58.7
PP&L	2.8	33.3	42.1
GPU Energy	6.7	58.2	67.3
Duquesne	13.6	41.3	13.4
Allegheny	1.5	20.1	21.1

Source: Pennsylvania Office of Consumer Advocate.
a. Retail choice began on January 1, 1999.

load profiling and settlements protocols to match up monthly metered consumption for individual consumers with wholesale market prices that vary hourly. ESPs must incur significant additional advertising, promotion, and marketing costs. Moreover, there is no evidence that ESPs are yet providing small customers with much, if anything, in the way of value added services (such as real-time pricing) over and above what consumers would get by buying directly in the wholesale market through their UDC. The major value added services being offered to small customers are "green power" (energy supplied from designated environmentally friendly generating technologies, such as solar and wind power) and bundling of electricity, gas, telephone, and Internet services (one-stop shopping). Perhaps new technologies will reduce the costs of marketing, billing, real-time metering, and control for smaller customers in the future. ESPs will then be in a position to offer value added services to residential and small commercial consumers, so the option of buying from an ESP under appropriate terms and conditions should still be available to all retail consumers.[97]

The societal benefits of retail competition per se are more apparent so far for larger commercial and industrial customers than for residential and small commercial consumers. Successful ESPs are offering them a whole package of energy management and energy procurement services covering electricity, natural gas, on-site generation, and price and weather risk-hedging products. A growing fraction of larger customers can be expected to

97. For example, the Internet is now being used to sell and bill for electricity sold by ESPs to residential consumers. See [www.essential.com (5/12/00)] and [www.utility.com (5/12/00)]. Perhaps some day Internet technology will be capable of remote metering of real time use as well.

switch to ESPs in states with retail competition programs, even in the absence of additional subsidies or incentives to switch provided by state regulators.

Conclusions

Electricity sector restructuring, regulatory reform, and the diffusion of wholesale and retail competition is still a work in progress in the United States. Federal laws and regulations have created the opportunity for states to restructure their electric power sectors and the role of wholesale and retail competition in it. However, the creation of transmission and wholesale market institutions to govern efficiently fully competitive wholesale electricity markets has proven to be a significant challenge. The optimal design of energy market trading and settlement rules, market mechanisms for the acquisition of ancillary services, transmission pricing and congestion management, institutions governing the interconnection of new generators, and the expansion of the transmission network capacity all remain uncertain and controversial.

California's transmission and wholesale market institutions have encountered numerous problems. A large number of market design changes have been implemented or proposed to try to fix these imperfections. There is some evidence that the changes in market design and contractual arrangements are mitigating the performance problems and reducing the costs of operating these markets. This is encouraging, but additional design changes are needed to fix remaining problems. The New England ISO experienced similar problems during its first year of operation and intends to implement major changes in market design and congestion management during the next year. The wholesale market and congestion management system implemented in PJM has had the smallest number of problems, largely because it is not very different from the power-pool dispatch and operating mechanisms that were used when PJM was a large traditional power pool relying on central economic dispatch based on marginal cost pricing principles. Neither New England nor PJM has subjected its market and transmission institutions to the kind of scrutiny that characterizes California. The Midwest, a region where wholesale competition has grown dramatically, but where transmission and wholesale market institutional reforms have been minimal, has experienced serious network operating problems during the last two summers and some extremely high spot market prices. Efforts to resolve these problems are accelerating.

It is clear that designing good wholesale market and transmission institutions remains an intellectual challenge and an even bigger implementation challenge. Nevertheless, all things considered, these wholesale markets seem to work reasonably well during the vast majority of hours when demand is not too high and the network is reasonably unconstrained. Of course, it is true that in these conditions, the market institutions do not have to work too hard to allocate resources reasonably efficiently. I remain optimistic that the most serious problems that have emerged when demand is high and network congestion is significant can be fixed if regulators can come to understand the nature of the problems, give the system operators the time to fix them, and provide the tools to mitigate the adverse impacts of these problems on market participants while they are being fixed.

That markets are imperfect and market and transmission institutions need continuing improvement does not mean that the effort to create competitive electricity is not socially worthwhile. Costs may be associated with imperfect electricity markets, but these costs must be weighed against the benefits associated with replacing the imperfect institution of regulated monopoly with market mechanisms. Because the public interest rationale for restructuring has been to benefit consumers, it is natural to ask the following question: Are there any visible *consumer* benefits yet from restructuring, regulatory reform, and deregulation of the U.S. electric power sector against which we can balance the set-up costs and market inefficiencies that have been experienced in California, New England, and elsewhere? This is perhaps an unfair question since the major reforms are so new, and start-up costs and problems were anticipated. Nevertheless, it is a question worth asking, reflecting upon, and revisiting as time goes by.

One obvious potential benefit is associated with the retail price reductions seen in California, Massachusetts, and other states that have already implemented reforms. So far, however, these price reductions are not the direct result of wholesale or retail competition. They are more properly attributed to regulatory and legal obligations placed on utilities to reduce prices in conjunction with the resolution of stranded-cost obligations, securitization of stranded costs, and cost pressures created by the introduction of incentive regulation programs that place pressure on all utility costs. In theory, regulators and legislators could have accomplished the same reduction more directly through the regulatory and legislative process without going to the expense and trouble of creating institutions like

CAISO and CALPX. In practice, without the threat of pending wholesale and retail competition and the potential loss of billions of dollars in above-market strandable costs, it is unlikely that utilities would have been so receptive to these cost pressures. More important, the prospect of selling generating assets to third parties, which in turn could use them to produce electricity for sale in unregulated markets, helped to reduce the burden of stranded costs and support the price reductions seen so far.

Larger electricity consumers are seeing benefits from retail competition in the growing number of states where it is available to them. Although these benefits are hard to document, they appear to take the form of lower energy prices and better energy procurement and energy management services that the best ESPs are supplying to these consumers. I remain skeptical, however, that small residential customers without hourly meters will benefit directly from retail competition over and above the benefits that they can obtain by direct access to the wholesale market through their UDCs. I also am concerned that some smaller consumers may actually be harmed by retail competition because the large advertising, marketing, and billing costs that ESPs incur must eventually find their way into the prices that retail customers pay for service.

It has been my view that the primary benefits of a well-designed competitive electricity sector will come from better incentives to improve the operating performance of existing generators, to retire generators that cannot make a go of it from market sales revenues, to control construction and operating costs of new generators coming into the market, and to innovate in generating technology. The decision regulators made to use stranded-cost recovery as a bargaining chip to induce utilities to divest their generating plants was quite fortuitous. A large stock of unregulated merchant generating plants has been created almost instantly out of the existing fleet of regulated generators, and these generators are now the core of wholesale markets in the Northeast and California. Their owners now have high-powered incentives to optimize performance. The effective demand placed in competitive wholesale markets grew dramatically with divestiture of these generators. Without these generation asset divestitures, the competitive merchant plant wholesale market would have grown much more slowly than it has in the last couple of years. More important, merchant plants with state-of-the-art generating technology are being proposed and built, and improvements in the thermal efficiency and costs of new generators are continuing to be made. The economic prospects for very small generating plants that can be located close to demand continues to improve as well.

Several nuclear plants have been retired because they could not cover their going forward costs, and stranded-cost recovery mechanisms have taken sunk costs out of the decision to continue to operate or close these plants. It is especially gratifying to see that investment in generation has largely been depoliticized in most regions; however, one cloud on the horizon is a requirement in restructuring legislation proposed in some states that would force suppliers to adhere to renewable energy portfolio standards.

A significant cloud on the long-term horizon is associated with the institutions that govern expansion of the transmission network, both to support more effective competition among existing generators and to support new entrants to meet growing demand and to replace existing plants, often in new locations. The success of the ongoing restructuring of the nation's electricity sector and its reliance on decentralized, competitive generation service markets depends heavily on the existence of a robust transmission network that operates efficiently. Indeed, the changes in the structure of the industry create the need for a *more robust* transmission network and *enhanced operating capabilities* than was the case during the era of vertically integrated regulated monopolies. The recent historical evidence suggests that resources devoted to maintaining, operating, and expanding the nation's transmission networks are *declining* rather than increasing in relative terms.[98] This should not be surprising. Historically, major transmission enhancements generally accompanied the development of new generating resources by vertically integrated utilities (individually or cooperatively with their neighbors). Similarly, the maintenance and operation of transmission and generation were closely coordinated within individual vertically integrated firms or joint ventures in the form of tight power pools. Restructuring has destroyed the old institutions that supported transmission system maintenance and expansion decisions but has not yet replaced them with new ones that work well. The development of good institutions to govern transmission network congestion management and transmission investment needs much more attention.

References

Borenstein, Severin, James Bushnell, and Frank Wolak. 1999. "Diagnosing Market Power in California's Deregulated Wholesale Electricity Market." University of California Energy Institute Working Paper PWP-064. Berkeley, Calif. July.
Borenstein, Severin, and others. 1999. "Price Convergence in the California Electricity

98. Hirst, Kirby, and Hadley (1999, pp. 4–5).

Markets: Some Preliminary Results." University of California Energy Institute, Berkeley, Calif. July.

Bushnell, James, and Frank Wolak. 1999. "Regulation and the Leverage of Local Market Power in the California Electricity Market." Paper presented at the 1999 Summer Industrial Organization Workshop sponsored by the National Bureau of Economic Research. July.

California Independent System Operator (CAISO). 1999. *Annual Report on Market Issues and Performance.* Folsom, Calif. June.

CAISO Market Surveillance Committee (Frank A. Wolak, chairman). 1999. "Report on Redesign of California Real-Time Energy and Ancillary Services Markets." Folsom, Calif. October.

Cramton, Peter. 1999. "Review of the Reserves and Operable Capability Markets: New England's Experience in the First Four Months." November. University of Maryland, Department of Economics, College Park, Md.

Edison Electric Institute. 1997. *Statistical Yearbook of the Electric Utility Industry.* Washington, D.C.

Energy Information Administration. 1997. *Financial Statistics of Major U.S. Investor-Owned Electric Utilities.* U.S. Department of Energy.

———. Various years. *Electric Sales and Revenue: 1998.* U.S. Department of Energy.

Gilbert, Richard J., and David M. Newbery. 1994. "The Dynamic Efficiency of Regulatory Constitutions." *RAND Journal of Economics* 25 (Winter): 538–54.

Hirst, Eric, Brendan Kirby, and Stan Hadley. 1999. "Generation and Transmission Adequacy in a Restructuring U.S. Electricity Industry." See www.ehirst.com. June.

Hogan, William. 1992. "Contract Networks for Electric Power Transmission." *Journal of Regulatory Economics* 4 (3): 211–42.

———. 1993. "Markets in Real Networks Require Reactive Prices." *Energy Journal* 14 (3): 171–200.

———. 1999. "Designing Market Institutions for Electric Network Systems." Harvard University, Kennedy School of Government, Cambridge, Mass. October.

International Energy Agency. 1997. *Electricity Information.* Paris: Organization for Economic Cooperation and Development.

Joskow, Paul L. 1987. "Productivity Growth and Technical Change in the Generation of Electricity." *Energy Journal* 8 (January): 17–38.

———. 1989. "Regulatory Failure, Regulatory Reform, and Structural Change in the Electric Power Industry." *Brookings Papers on Economic Activity: Microeconomics:* 125–99.

———. 1996a. "Comment on 'Power Struggles: Explaining Deregulatory Reform in Electricity Markets.'" *Brookings Papers on Economic Activity: Microeconomics:* 251–64.

———. 1996b. "Introducing Competition into Regulated Network Industries: From Hierarchies to Markets in Electricity." *Industrial and Corporate Change* 5 (2): 341–82.

———. 1997. "Restructuring, Competition, and Regulatory Reform in the U.S. Electricity Sector." *Journal of Economic Perspectives* 11 (Summer): 119–38.

———. 2000. "Why Do We Need Retailers? Or Can You Get It Cheaper Wholesale?" Massachusetts Institute of Technology, Department of Economics. February.

Joskow, Paul L., and Nancy L. Rose. 1985. "The Effects of Technological Change, Experience, and Environmental Regulation on the Construction Costs of Coal-Burning Generating Units." *RAND Journal of Economics* 16 (1): 1–27.

———. 1989. "The Effects of Economic Regulation." In *Handbook on Industrial Organi-*

zation, edited by Richard Schmalensee and Robert D. Willig. vol. 2. Amsterdam: North-Holland.

Joskow, Paul L., Nancy L. Rose, and Andrea Shepard. 1993. "Regulatory Constraints on CEO Compensation." *Brookings Papers on Economic Activity: Microeconomics,* 1–58.

Joskow, Paul L., and Richard Schmalensee. 1983. *Markets for Power: An Analysis of Electric Utility Deregulation.* MIT Press.

———. 1986. "Incentive Regulation for Electric Utilities." *Yale Journal on Regulation* 4 (December): 1–49.

———. 1987. "The Performance of Coal-Burning Electric Generating Units in the United States: 1960–1980." *Journal of Applied Econometrics* 2 (2): 85–109.

Joskow, Paul L., and Jean Tirole. Forthcoming. "Transmission Rights and Market Power on Electricity Networks." *RAND Journal of Economics.*

Kahn, Edward, P. 1999. "A Folklorist's Guide to the Used Plant Market." *The Electricity Journal* 12 (6): 66–77.

Katz, Lawrence, and Lawrence Summers. 1989. "Industry Rents: Evidence and Implications." *Brookings Papers on Economic Activity: Microeconomics:* 209–75.

Lester, Richard, and Mark J. McCabe. 1993. "The Effects of Industrial Structure on Learning by Doing in Nuclear Plant Operations." *RAND Journal of Economics* 24 (3): 418–38.

Newbery, David, and Michael Pollitt. 1997. "The Restructuring and Privatization of Britain's CEGB—Was It Worth It?" *Journal of Industrial Economics* 45 (3): 269–303.

Office of Gas and Electricity Markets. 1999. "Rises in Pool Prices in July." London. October.

Rose, Nancy L., and Paul L. Joskow. 1990. "The Diffusion of New Technology: Evidence from the Electric Utility Industry." *RAND Journal of Economics* 21 (3): 354–73.

Schmalensee, Richard. 1989. "An Expository Note on Depreciation and Profitability under Rate of Return Regulation." *Journal of Regulatory Economics* 1(3): 293–98.

White, Mathew. 1996. "Power Struggles: Explaining Deregulatory Reforms in Electric Power Markets." *Brookings Papers on Economic Activity: Microeconomics:* 201–50.

Wolfram, Catherine. 1999. "Measuring Duopoly Power in the British Electricity Spot Market." *American Economic Review* 89 (4): 805–26.

SAM PELTZMAN
CLIFFORD WINSTON

5 | *Conclusion*

U ntil policymakers leave deregulated industries
alone and allow partially deregulated industries to
proceed toward full deregulation, academics will continue to have confer-
ences to analyze what "those regulators" are up to. The timing of this
conference was no accident. Regulatory rumblings (and grumblings) have
been getting louder in the airline and railroad industries, regulators have
overstayed their welcome in telecommunications, and the fate of electricity
deregulation may be largely in the hands of California and Massachusetts!

There was a time when many economists were skeptical that U.S.
industries would ever be deregulated because various interest groups, including the regulated industries, benefited greatly from the status quo and
exercised great influence on the regulatory process. After more than twenty
years of regulatory reform, interest groups still exert influence on regulatory agencies and Congress—but which interests? And should we care?

Although the airlines' adjustment to a more competitive environment
has not been smooth, they have become much more efficient, and consumers have benefited as a result. Nonetheless, policymakers and travelers have
been criticizing carrier practices almost since deregulation began, even
though no evidence has been produced to show that these practices are
significantly undermining travelers' welfare. Morrison and Winston show

that the most recent round of complaints—about pricing at hub airports, competitive reactions to low-fare carriers, service quality, and so on—have little empirical basis. At the same time, evidence does suggest that policy-makers could benefit travelers if they took measures to improve air traffic control and carriers' access to airports.

Congress and the Transportation Department may have reacted to matters that have small welfare implications for travelers and ignored issues that have large welfare implications, because they are responding to the interests of organized groups of travelers and competitors. This has been manifested in threats to enact legislation "if things don't improve" and in support for the current allocation of airport gates and slots. Although policymakers have yet to institute new measures that seriously compromise air transportation's efficiency, rent-seeking has certainly not been discouraged. Moreover, the perception that the government can be used to pursue rents has enabled a regulatory mind-set to linger in the airline industry. Carriers are not completely focused on being as efficient as possible and the government is not focused on enhancing public welfare by improving the air transport infrastructure.

Given that the primary objective of rail deregulation was to increase rail's financial viability, it is not surprising that its residual regulatory agency, the Surface Transportation Board, is viewed by many as primarily protecting rail's interests in disputes with captive shippers. Even if this is true, Grimm and Winston find this protection has not led to appreciable efficiency losses. As in the airline industry, however, regulation is still perceived as a vehicle for obtaining or protecting rents. This fosters a lingering regulatory mentality that diverts railroads from focusing on being as efficient as possible.

The 1996 Telecommunications Act can be interpreted as a costly and complicated response to rent-seeking behavior. Crandall and Hausman argue that by trying to micromanage the evolution of competition in local and long-distance services and extending universal service policies to new services and recipients, the 1996 law has seriously impeded the process of deregulation and delayed substantial benefits to consumers from lower prices and new services. The law's main legacy appears to be protracted regulatory disputes and litigation that show little sign of abating. In contrast, competition in deregulated wireless services is flourishing, and rates are falling dramatically. Indeed, these costs are falling so fast that wireless services may soon become effective competitors for many wireline services now provided by regulated monopolies. Accordingly, the traditional rationale for regulation in this industry may disappear well before the regulators do.

Most economists believe that significant benefits will accrue from promoting competition in electricity generation. Will such competition actually occur? Industrial customer groups, independent power plant developers, and electricity marketers in states with relatively large gaps between the cost of electricity and its price have pressed for reform. Incumbent utilities with high costs have obviously been reluctant to cooperate, but some states have shown that it is possible to compensate these utilities for their "stranded costs" and allow reform to move forward. Joskow explains why sound institutions will be needed to address the complex technical problems of facilitating competition in electricity generation. And if experience in other network industries is any guide, organized interest groups will influence the pace and direction of electricity deregulation. Large industrial customers of electricity currently stand to gain the most from reform, while the gains to small commercial and residential customers are uncertain. In addition, the magnitude of gains in low-cost states is unclear. Until these uncertainties are resolved, no one will know which political obstacles will have to be overcome for deregulation in this industry to spread.

The experience to date from deregulating U.S. network industries suggests that "it's *not* over when it's over." Additional steps must be taken to free even a deregulated industry from regulatory bodies that could be used by organized groups to acquire rents and potentially undermine deregulation. The airline and railroad industries should be subject to the antitrust laws like any other industry, but the Transportation Department should not have the authority to intervene in airline competition, and the Surface Transportation Board should be eliminated. The Federal Communications Commission and state regulatory bodies should undo regulatory-created entry barriers and allow full deregulation in telecommunications to proceed. Although it is too early to evaluate the path of deregulation in electricity, Congress and state regulatory bodies would be well advised not to allow political interests to add to the technical challenges of developing competition in this sector.

Contributors

Robert W. Crandall
Brookings Institution

Curtis Grimm
College of Business and
    Management
University of Maryland

Jerry A. Hausman
Department of Economics
Massachusetts Institute of
    Technology

Paul L. Joskow
Department of Economics
Massachusetts Institute of
    Technology

Steven A. Morrison
Department of Economics
Northeastern University

Sam Peltzman
Graduate School of Business
University of Chicago

Clifford Winston
Brookings Institution

Index

J O I N T   C E N T E R

AEI-BROOKINGS JOINT CENTER FOR REGULATORY STUDIES

In response to growing concerns about the impact of regulation on consumers, business, and government, the American Enterprise Institute and the Brookings Institution established the AEI-Brookings Joint Center for Regulatory Studies. The primary purpose of the center is to hold lawmakers and regulators more accountable by providing thoughtful, objective analysis of existing regulatory programs and new regulatory proposals. The Joint Center builds on AEI's and Brookings's impressive body of work over the past three decades that evaluated the economic impact of regulation and offered constructive suggestions for implementing reforms to enhance productivity and consumer welfare. The views in Joint Center publications are those of the authors and do not necessarily reflect the views of the staff, council of academic advisers, or fellows.